More Praise for **The SUPERGIRLS**

"The affection the author holds for these characters is infectious . . . An essential read for pop-culture enthusiasts, feminists, comic-book readers, and social justice warriors."—*Kirkus Reviews*

"Exhaustive in its research, full of interesting lore and little-known details, *The Supergirls* is a high flying trip through comic-book history."
— *Jackson Free Press*

"Entertaining and informative, *Supergirls* is a breezy and thoroughly accessible history of the comic book heroine. A great resource!"
— Marc Andreyko, writer, *Manhunter* and *Torso*

"Mike Madrid's fast-moving, encyclopedic, and often funny *Supergirls* shows the author's lifelong affection for these heroines on every page. He has a great feel for the genre and its history, with evident sensitivity to issues of female power and powerlessness. The section on the She-Hulk is not to be missed!"
— Larry Gonick, author, *Cartoon History of the Universe*

". . . hopefully it will start some new discussions not just about female superheroes, but their cultural significance in American pop culture . . ."— *BITCH Magazine*

"There comes a time in every comic book geek slash fashionista's life when she must ask herself, 'What do costumes and couture have in common?' *The Supergirls* sets out to answer that question...making it informative enough and providing sufficient cultural context for those who may have no prior comic book knowledge."
— *Worn Fashion Journal*

Also by Mike Madrid
from
EXTERMINATING ANGEL PRESS

Divas, Dames & Daredevils:
Lost Heroines of Golden Age Comics

Vixens, Vamps & Vipers:
Lost Villainesses of Golden Age Comics

the SUPERGIRLS

FASHION, FEMINISM, FANTASY, AND THE HISTORY OF COMIC BOOK HEROINES

MIKE MADRID

EXTERMINATING ANGEL
PRESS

EXTERMINATING ANGEL PRESS
"Creative Solutions for Practical Idealists"
Visit **www.exterminatingangel.com** to join the conversation
info@exterminatingangel.com

Title page illustration of Black Cat by Lee Elias
Cover art, interior illustrations, and book design by Mike Madrid
Cover photograph by Alan Disparte

ISBN: 978-1-935259-33-6
eBook ISBN: 978-1-935259-35-0
Library of Congress Control Number: 2016948972

Distributed by
Consortium Book Sales & Distribution
(800) 283-3572   www.cbsd.com

Printed in The United States of America

CONTENTS

Author's Note

Since this book is intended to be a look at the characters in American comic books, and not the industry itself, I have taken a few liberties to streamline some publisher details for easier reference.

First, DC Comics is the present day publisher of Superman, Batman, Wonder Woman, and other well-known superheroes. DC is the amalgamation of two different publishing concerns: National Comics, which produced Superman and Batman, and sister company All-American Comics, which produced Wonder Woman, Flash, and Green Lantern. The two companies merged in 1944 to form National Periodical Publications, whose comic books bore the "Superman-DC" logo. The publisher was known colloquially as "DC," which it later adopted as its official name. Since these business mergers are not integral to the evolution of the characters discussed in this book, I will simply refer to the company as DC throughout.

Second, Marvel Comics, which today publishes Spider-Man, the Fantastic Four, and the X-Men, was known as Timely Publications in the 1940s, when it produced characters like Captain America and the Sub-Mariner. It later changed to Atlas Comics in the 1950s, before taking the name Marvel Comics in the 1960s. For simplicity's sake again, I will refer to this publisher as Marvel Comics only.

Introduction to the new edition

Back when I worked on the original edition of *The Supergirls*, and I would tell people it was a history of female superheroes, the usual response was, "Oh, it's about Wonder Woman." When I explained that Wonder Woman was only one of many superheroines, I would hear, "Like who? There are no other women in comic books besides Wonder Woman!" But I knew better. And I was on a mission to make those other women known to more people.

After *The Supergirls* came out, something interesting happened. I got emails from readers who had no idea that there had been female superheroes in the 1960s, much less in the 1940s. Some said the book introduced them to characters they had never heard of, while others found themselves using it as reference for their own dissertations on the role of women in comic books. One woman who had read Mary Marvel comics in the 1940s thanked me for finally explaining the young heroine's origin to her. Had I completed my mission of sharing the histories of these amazing women of comic books?

Which brings us to this edition of *The Supergirls*. It's been updated to reflect some developments in the world of female superheroes, along with other information I've come across in my continuing research. I've also added new artwork of some of my favorite women from the early days of comic books.

And if anyone thinks this is my final word on the subject of female superheroes, I assure you that's not the case. There are more exciting stories to share with you. Many more.

Goddesses of Tomorrow

The first comic book that I remember owning is *Superman* #195, from 1967. The story was entitled "The Fury of the Kryptonian Killer!" Captivating imagery filled its cover. Mighty Superman was on his knees, succumbing to the effects of deadly Green Kryptonite. In the background was a tiny city in a glass bottle, and a flying dog wearing a cape. But the element that grabbed my attention was the pretty blonde girl wearing a costume that matched Superman's. I learned she was called Super*girl*.

I was about six at the time, and although I didn't really understand what was going on, I had a vague idea who Superman was. Maybe my older sister or some other kids at school had given me the rundown. I was more fascinated, however, by Supergirl. She could fly and was incredibly strong, and I could tell from the way she was drawn that she was brave and noble. I thought she was great. Although I wasn't sure exactly what her relationship to Superman was, I could tell she was somehow considered inferior. And I didn't understand why.

Back in those days, comic books cost twelve cents, and my mother gave me the choice of selecting two single issues from the comic book rack, or one giant annual for a quarter. As I flipped through the titles on the spinning rack to try and make my weighty decisions, unconsciously a pattern developed. When it came to movies, my mother had once said that if there wasn't a woman in the story, nothing could possibly happen, so I guess I thought the same held true for comic books. I skipped the war comics and westerns, and wound up selecting the superhero titles with cool looking women in them. And as my collection slowly grew, I assembled a cast of these amazing females.

Other boys always thought that the women in the comic books were stupid, because they were portrayed as weak. And, of course, because you weren't supposed to like girls. So there was no thought of buying a Supergirl comic, or one of that other lady named Wonder Woman who all of the other guys seemed to really hate. It didn't much matter anyway, because I never saw her comic books for sale on the racks. Male heroes like Captain America, Cyclops and Green Lantern were the powerhouse stars of superhero teams like the Avengers, the X-Men, or the Justice League. But these groups always had a token female member like the Scarlet Witch, Marvel Girl, or Black Canary to capture my interest.

Male superheroes always seemed consumed by meting out justice through violent means. The female superheroes struck me as being more interested in making the world a better place, and not just beating their foes into submission. I suppose I was drawn to their compassionate natures, just as I had been captivated by the Virgin Mary a few years earlier. To me, the superheroines were as beautiful and alluring as movie stars or the models I saw in my sister's *Vogue* magazines, but with a bonus—these women were powerful like men. I just didn't understand why they were never allowed to be *as* powerful as the males.

The superhero is one of those uniquely American concepts. Just as average American children are told they can grow up to become president, superheroes are often ordinary people elevated to levels of benevolent, godlike greatness. Superhero comic books are about maximizing human potential for the betterment of all society. One of the things that I noticed is that female superheroes are often not allowed to reach their potential; they are given powers that are weaker than their male compatriots, and positions of lesser importance. There are a lot of "men" in comic books: Super*man*, Bat*man*, Spider-*Man*. Besides Wonder *Woman*, there are not that many "women," and even fewer "ladies." But there are lots of "girls": Super*girl*, Power *Girl*, Marvel *Girl*, Invisible *Girl*.

Any power these women may have is often overshadowed by their overly sexualized images. But at the same time, those very images that objectify these heroines can be seen as a source of power. Recently I took a female friend to see the movie adaptation of the graphic novel *Watchmen*. When she caught sight of the movie's heroine, Silk Spectre, descending a staircase in slow motion, sheathed in a skintight latex costume and thigh high boots with garters, my friend leaned over and said, "I want to be her." My friend is an educated, successful career woman, so it struck me that she would find this very sexualized female image inspiring and powerful. In this way, as outlandish as comic books may seem, they actually are a reflection of the world that we all live in, which I will refer to in this book as the "real world."

When I mentioned to people that I was working on this book, many asked if it was about Wonder Woman. Most were unable to even name any other comic book heroines that they knew, reflecting on what little exposure these characters get within the industry. Yet the archetype of the powerful and beautiful female is one that has become engrained in the American pop cultural sensibility. Whether it be television heroines like the Bionic Woman or Xena, or movie heroines like Ripley from *Alien*, or The Bride from the *Kill Bill* films, the larger-than-life image of the strong and fearless, yet compassionate, woman on a quest for justice is part of our modern day pantheon of deities.

Decades have passed since I stood at that spinning comic book rack trying to find the perfect comic to transport me to a new world of adventure. The years have introduced me to a multitude of other fascinating female superheroes, and they still remain my primary reason for reading comic books. I still plan my week around Wednesdays, when the week's shipment of new comic books arrives at Amazing Fantasy, my local comic book store. My friend Frank is the owner, and I've known him for over twenty years. In that time, he has come to understand my interests and tastes, and as both a good businessman and friend, he will find things for me that he knows I'll like. "Something new came in that I thought you might want," Frank will say, handing me a comic book that's just hit the stands that week. And there on the cover will be some dazzling lady champion, some heroic angel of mercy, some brave and powerful goddess to inspire and delight me with her beauty and strength.

Just like Supergirl did when I first laid eyes on her, over forty years ago.

1940s : A Secret Life

Sandra Knight steps out of the shadows. The world knows her as a bored society girl: a pampered senator's daughter with a glamorous wardrobe. But, the outfit that Sandra is wearing didn't come from any couturier's salon. The slinky blue costume is as skimpy as a swimsuit, and its fabric is as delicate as the finest French lingerie in Sandra's trousseau. Delicate beaded chains just barely hold the low-cut neckline in place. The long red cape that Sandra fastens around her throat does little to cover her shapely form. What would her high society girlfriends think if they could see Sandra wearing this getup in broad daylight? But this isn't Sandra hanging off of a fire escape in this silky blue costume. Now she is the Phantom Lady, enemy of criminals and evildoers.

Phantom Lady is on the hunt for a racketeer who's targeting an innocent man for death. As the mob boss' thugs drive off, she jumps on a nearby police motorcycle without thinking twice. "It's an SOS, officer! Got to borrow your go-devil for a while, but I'll return it to you!" Phantom Lady says, as she speeds off after the gangster's car. Phantom Lady's filmy costume offers her supple flesh little protection as she races after the getaway car at breakneck speed, dodging a hail of bullets.

"Oh, brother! Some crook is going to get it now!" a secretary gasps, as the nubile form of Phantom Lady bursts into an office across the street from the mobster's lair. The fearless Phantom Lady slips out a window and jumps onto a nearby flagpole. Swinging from the ropes towards the window of the racketeer's den, Phantom Lady thinks, "The faster I get through that glass, the better!" The mob boss is shocked to see the pulchritudinous avenger of evil come crashing through his window. Before he knows it, Phantom Lady has blinded the gangster into submission with her secret weapon—the black light ray.

Later that day, Sandra's perplexed fiancé Don, tennis rackets tucked under his arm, shows up at the office of her father, Senator Knight. He hasn't been able to find Sandra all day for fun and frolicking. What had she been up to? Senator Knight tells Don about the bang up job Phantom Lady had done at forcing the mob boss into signing a full confession. "What a gal that Phantom Lady is!" exclaims Don. "Sometimes I wonder ...but no ...it couldn't be ...Sandra isn't that clever ..."

Once more fully dressed and curled up in her father's armchair, Sandra is back to playing the well-behaved daughter. "What are you talking about, Don?" she coyly asks, in her best, unassuming voice. Phantom Lady had her fun for the afternoon. The senator and Don would never need to know about Sandra's secret life.

It's 1947. American women had been granted the right to vote less than thirty years earlier. In twenty years, they would be talking about liberating themselves. But for now, women would have to be content to put on scanty costumes and assume a disguise in order to act like themselves.

When America was in the throes of the Great Depression, people looking for an escape from tough times found refuge in the newspaper comic section, which literally became a passport to other worlds. There was the tough as nails crime drama of Dick Tracy, the plucky optimism of Little Orphan Annie, the exotic eastern locales of Terry and the Pirates, the cinematic sci-fi grandeur of Flash Gordon, or the medieval romance of Prince Valiant to enthrall readers and transport them away, temporarily, from the grim realities of bread lines and unemployment. The first comic books were collections of much beloved newspaper comic strips, appearing as early as 1934. As this cheap new form of entertainment became more popular, a handful of companies began publishing original material. The stars of the first comic books of the 1930s were hard-boiled detectives, aviators, soldiers of fortune, magicians, or gun-toting vigilantes. But it wasn't until two young men named Jerry Siegel and Joe Shuster created Superman, in 1938, that the fledgling comic book medium found its unique voice, offering the public something it didn't see in newspaper comics—the superhero.

In those early days there were few rules. It seemed as though in no time flat, scores of caped heroes sprang up in Superman's wake, like the offspring of Deucalion of Greek myth. Like Superman, some were the last scions of lost races, others were monarchs of mythical lands, scientists who had stumbled on some transformative formula, adventurers who happened on a magical artifact, or ordinary tough guys who didn't like seeing honest people getting pushed around. No matter what their origin was, these magnificent modern day gods, gladiators, and giants roamed the empty concrete canyons of the 20th

century like mighty saviors, embodying the answer to a cry for heavenly intervention. The early superheroes were rugged individuals who took the law into their own hands, dishing out a tough brand of "frontier justice."

Although the prevalent image of the female comic book crime fighter is that of a sexy nymph in a revealing costume, this was not always the case. The Woman in Red, thought to be the first female crime fighter of comics, wore a sweeping scarlet cloak with matching mask and skullcap. Fantomah, described as "the most remarkable woman ever known," was a beautiful blonde protectress of the jungle. When evil struck, she transformed into a terrifying, skull-faced goddess who judged the guilty with lethal force. Then there was 1940's Madam Fatal, who wasn't even a woman at all. Well, biological woman anyway. In "her" alter ego, Madam Fatal was retired stage actor Richard Stanton. He adopts the guise of an old lady to stamp out evil, becoming the first transvestite crime fighter. Red Tornado appeared a few months later, and was the yin to Madam Fatal's drag heroine yang. Red Tornado is actually Ma Hunkel, a burly, working class mother who dresses in long johns and a cape, and disguises herself by wearing a cooking pot over her head. Passing herself off as a man, Ma Hunkel stamps out crime in her New York neighborhood, becoming one of the first female superheroes, and certainly the first "drag king" heroine.

Whatever road led these men and women to superheroism, the one plot device that almost all had in common was the secret identity. They were, after all, vigilantes, and were taking the law into their own hands. Heroes like Superman and Wonder Woman created a disguise to fit into society. They were godly creatures that had been transplanted into our world, and in order to live side by side with mortals, they dumbed themselves down. They wore glasses to make themselves more homely. As Clark Kent, Superman assumes the persona of a meek mouse, while Wonder Woman's Diana Prince is a Plain Jane with a biting wit. These identities were the opposites of their heroic personas, which, the reader had to assume, were their "real" natures. Superheroes like The Flash or Green Lantern were normal men who gained powers that elevated them to demigod status. They remained the same men they had always been, but assumed a larger than life persona to fight injustice. The

LEFT: Fantomah was the first woman in comic books with superhuman powers. Here she transforms from lovely blonde to fearsome avenging angel, *Jungle Comics* #14, 1941

costumed identity was the fictional invention, while the man who lived behind the mask was the reality.

Batman was another case altogether. Millionaire Bruce Wayne invented the dark avenger Batman to rid the world of the evil that had killed his beloved parents. In a sense, the identity of Batman is a reflection of who Bruce Wayne truly is. He then crafts the image of Bruce Wayne as a frivolous, sybaritic playboy to throw any suspicious minds off of the track. He sacrifices the integrity of the man that the world sees every day in order to give himself the freedom to don a mask and be the person he truly is. This was also the case of many of the heroines of the early comic books. They had been forced into the roles of well-mannered daughters or girlfriends, and a secret life gave these women a chance to be themselves. Putting on a cape and mask liberated these women to live the kind of life that they dreamed of— one where they could help make their world a better place.

THE DEBUTANTES

The secret identity was vitally important for superheroes to maintain, and provided much of the tension for their adventures. If a crime fighter's identity was exposed, it would mean the end to his or her nocturnal activities. But there was also an added complication. Like the Shadow and his alter ego Lamont Cranston, many of the early heroes like Batman, Sandman, and Hawkman were wealthy, prominent figures in society. These aristocratic gents who put on masks to help protect their fellow citizens were not unlike President Franklin Delano Roosevelt, the wealthy, privileged leader who was stepping in to save the luckless downtrodden of his nation. Their family fortunes

Phantom Lady, *Police Comics* #17, 1943

afforded these heroes tricky gadgets and fancy vehicles with which to fight crime, and lavish mansions and swanky townhouses that made the ideal headquarters and lairs. But exposure of their secret crime fighting lives could be scandalous for this millionaire boys club.

There was also a sorority of rich girls who fought crime. We'll call them the *Debutantes*. They were the daughters of affluent families, and led lives filled with dances, parties, and fittings for custom made wardrobes. Like the madcap heiresses of '30s and '40s movies played by the likes of Carole Lombard and Katherine Hepburn, these daughters of privilege craved a different kind of excitement than one might encounter at a nightclub. In 1941, Washington D.C. "society girl" Sandra Knight fashions a costume for herself consisting of a revealing yellow swimsuit and a green cape. Brandishing a blinding black light ray that renders her foes helpless, Sandra dubs herself the Phantom Lady, the "mysterious woman of wonders" and declares war on spies and criminals. Sandra never wears a mask as Phantom Lady, but neither her senator father nor her fiancé Don ever make the connection. Maybe they were too busy looking at her legs. "What a gal!" Don bellows, as the mysterious Phantom Lady slinks off into the shadows after solving yet another crime.

Sandra's secret identity freed her from her life of entitled boredom. But she wasn't the only one. Beautiful and athletic debutante Dianne

Spider Widow, *Feature Comics #59*, 1942

Grayton leads a tedious life of leisure, but finds herself frustrated by the rampant activities of criminals and enemy agents. In 1942 she dons a hideous green witch mask, long black dress and floppy hat to wage war on the forces of evil as Spider Widow, Grandmother of Terror. With her frightful looks and an arsenal of deadly black widow spiders at her disposal, Spider Widow literally scares her foes into submission. "Popular social butterfly" Diana Adams put on a mask and red fedora, packed a pistol, and joined this secret sisterhood as Miss Masque. These girls were thrill seekers with time and money at their disposal, and they were able to enjoy a double life of danger and excitement, while also doing good.

But not all of the Debutante heroines enjoyed their double lives. Miss Fury was one of the most resourceful and fearless of the founding mothers of superhero comic books, but unlike her Debutante sisters who fought injustice, she had no real desire to be a vigilante or lead a secret life. Intrigue just seemed to cross her path, like a black cat. She debuted, in 1941, in Sunday newspaper comics as the Black Fury. By the time her adventures were reprinted in comic book form the following year, she went by the more feminine title of Miss Fury. Marla Drake is a beautiful and wealthy New York society girl who lives a life of luxury in her penthouse apartment. When Marla learns that another woman is wearing the same costume as hers to a swanky masquerade ball, her maid Francine suggests the debutante wear the black panther skin bequeathed to her by her uncle. "What? Why, that was worn by a witch doctor in Africa—as a ceremonial robe! Ugh!" gasps Marla. But with no other options, Marla dons the panther pelt, which fits her like a second skin made of black satin. But it was indeed made from a black panther's skin, and had razor sharp claws and a tail to prove it. The panther's head forms a mask that gives Marla a mysterious, menacing appearance. "At least no one else will be wearing the *same* thing!" Marla says, as she departs for the masquerade party, evening bag clutched in her clawed hand.

On the way to the party, a series of misadventures results in Marla becoming the inadvertent, and somewhat unwilling heroine Miss Fury. The witch doctor's ceremonial robe gives its wearer powers to "accomplish whatever mission he or she set out upon." In Marla's case, it increases her acrobatic and fighting skills. Marla is ready to go back to her comfortable life as one of the idle rich, but she soon finds herself tangling with treacherous Nazi spies like the ruthless Baroness Erica Von Kampf, and getting pulled deeper

Marla Drake dons her slinky Miss Fury attire, 1942

and deeper into a life of deception and danger. Marla seems to hate her secret identity, feeling that it brought her nothing but misfortune. "As for this costume, I *never* want to see it again." she says at one point, when she recklessly abandons the panther skin. But circumstances always arise that force Miss Fury to once more don her black catsuit, and prowl the night righting wrongs.

Like Batman, who had debuted in 1939, Miss Fury was a mysterious creature of the night. She was similar to Batman in that both were rich and privileged. But there was a significant difference between them. Batman was more his true self when he hid behind a mask, while Miss Fury used a disguise as a last resort. The catlike indifference that Marla displayed toward a secret life of crime fighting stemmed perhaps from the fact that her creator was a woman. June Tarpé Mills was one of a handful of female cartoonists working in the 1940s. Like fellow female and Brenda Starr creator Dale Messick, Mills worked under the sexually ambiguous name Tarpé Mills to give the impression that a man may have been penning the adventures of Miss Fury. Mills modeled Marla Drake's looks after her own, and gave the character a unique attitude towards her secret identity.

Female superheroines whose adventures were written by men were similar to their male compatriots, in that they single-mindedly and willingly lived lives of duality in order to fight injustice. Mills' approach to the secret identity seemed more realistic, injected with a feminine practicality. Marla didn't play the wilting flower in order to cover up her secret identity of Miss Fury. She was a strong, determined woman who lived her life the way she wanted. Her Miss Fury persona was a means to an end rather than the answer to her dreams, and one that she didn't particularly enjoy. If anything, Marla was less like herself when events forced her to assume the disguise of Miss Fury. "Somehow, I've had nothing but misfortune since my uncle left me the black leopard skin! If the things that happened to me are blessings, they *certainly* have been well disguised!"

The Debutante who had the best time leading a secret life was Lady Luck. First appearing in 1940 in a comic book supplement to the Sunday papers, Lady Luck was referred to as a "modern lady Robin Hood." She is Brenda Banks, the "debutante who traded diamonds for danger." Dressed in a green dress and cape, and disguised with a wide-brimmed hat and diaphanous veil that obscures her face, Brenda uses her jiu-jitsu skills and crack marksmanship as Lady Luck to assist the police in battling crime. Her trademark is a little note marked with a shamrock that she leaves at the scene where she's mopped up some mobsters. Despite her refined appearance and sobriquet, Lady Luck was as tough as any of the male vigilantes who roamed the comic book pages. When her father tells Brenda that she could learn a lot from an "admirable girl" like Lady Luck, her uncle pipes in, "She might inspire you to do more than just run around to

Lady Luck takes charge, 1943

parties!!"

Like Batman's alter ego Bruce Wayne, Lady Luck's indolent, shallow Brenda Banks persona is a façade that protects her secret identity. But unlike Bruce Wayne or even Marla Drake, Brenda Banks lacks a certain freedom and independence that would enable her to more easily live out her secret life. Brenda, like the Phantom Lady's Sandra Knight, still lives in the family home, always under the watchful eyes of parents and beaus. The burden of maintaining the Brenda Banks persona seems to be a weight around Lady Luck's neck. In one story, the death of an Axis spy impersonating Brenda Banks becomes an unexpected boon for Lady Luck. The story's last panel shows a newspaper headline announcing Brenda Banks' death, and a beaming and self-satisfied Lady Luck thinking, "Hmm...*this* has definite possibilities!!" Now, Lady Luck could be herself *all* the time.

THE PARTNERS

While the secret identity was a precious commodity for most male heroes, some were confident enough to share theirs with a special someone. Heroes like Dr. Fate, The Flash, and Sandman revealed their heroic identities to their girlfriends, who then became their assistants, or "helpmates." Hawkman and his girlfriend Shiera were the reincarnations of an ancient Egyptian prince and princess. Shiera's eagerness to help her winged boyfriend often got her into trouble. "I hope this will teach you to stay out of affairs that aren't your concern," Hawkman snaps after he has rescued his sweetheart from yet another scrape. But by 1941, Hawkman needs help, and Shiera is a prime candidate. Hawkman's costume consisted of tights, mask, and wings that were attached to his bare chest by crisscrossing straps. After quickly making some modifications that would not violate any obscenity laws, Hawkman presents Shiera with a feminized version of his costume, now complete with discreet bikini top. "...you mean I'm going to pose as you...oboy! This is going to be fun..." gushes Shiera, as she slips on the green and red costume. Thus was Hawkgirl born, joining another club for 1940s heroines: the *Partners*.

Hawkman was a member of the Justice Society of America, an assemblage of most of DC Comics' crime fighters, and the first superhero team. Wonder Woman was the only female member. In one 1943 story, she finds all of her Justice Society comrades missing, and races off to round up their girlfriends. "This is the opportunity of a lifetime for us girls!" Wonder Woman says, as she tells the women of her plan to create a distaff version of the Justice Society to find her missing teammates, and show up the men in the process. "Yeah, man! I've been waiting for a chance like this all my life!" exclaims Doris Lee, the sweetheart of Starman. Dressed in female versions of the men's costumes, the women rush into the night to fight for their men, and their own independence. In the end, the well-intentioned females get themselves captured by the villainous Brainwave, and the men of the Justice Society must save their sweethearts. This story reinforced the notion that women were better as assistants to male heroes, rather than working on their own—an idea that comic books held onto for many years.

Despite often being portrayed as ineffectual heroines, the Partners would become an important force in superhero comic books throughout the 1940s. Bulletman and Bulletgirl soared through the skies in matching antigravity helmets. The Owl had Owl Girl, Rocketman had Rocketgirl, and even the diminutive Doll Man had Doll Girl. These ladies were all inducted into the world of crime fighting by the men in their lives, who played a fatherly role by sanctioning a secret life for their girlfriends. It may have been taboo by society's standards to be a vigilante, but these heroines didn't have to deceive their loved ones, and vice versa. But also, the message here was that these women didn't have any inherent desire to do good; they were merely fighting crime to prove their love for their boyfriends. As a result, these heroines were not highly regarded by male readers, who considered them simply as weak appendages to the men. Often, they were portrayed as liabilities, as the heroes often had to routinely rescue their screaming female partners from one fiend or another. The Partners were always referred to as "girls," never "women," and their names were never featured in a comic's title. But while these women were always a reflection of their men and never got top billing, they assured that female superheroes maintained a presence in comic books, and established one of the longest lasting lineages of heroines in the medium.

The exception to the Partner rule was also the most famous member of the group—Mary Marvel. She was different for a number of reasons. First off, she was the sister, not the girlfriend of Captain Marvel. While other Partner heroines may have been referred to as "girl," Mary truly was one, and was the first of the young superheroines. And despite being a reflection of a more famous male hero, Mary Marvel was also a heroine who enjoyed a great degree of success on her own, out from the shadow of her more famous brother.

In his day, Captain Marvel was the most popular superhero on the newsstands. He debuted in 1939, just a year after Superman took to the skies of Metropolis. His origin told how an old wizard entrusted a poor orphaned newspaper boy named Billy Batson with the magic word "Shazam." With a clap of thunder, Billy was transformed into Captain Marvel, the world's mightiest mortal. Clad in a brilliant red costume with a big gold lightning bolt cutting across his mighty chest, Billy the young boy could use the magic word to become an adult man. This was perhaps the ultimate in childhood wish fulfillment, more so than Peter Pan's desire to remain forever youthful. Billy drew on the powers of the ancients, represented in the letters of "Shazam," those being Solomon, Hercules, Atlas, Zeus, Achilles, and Mercury. He flew, he bent steel girders, and he was bulletproof. The jovial powerhouse eclipsed Superman in popularity, and was the first superhero to come to life in movie serials. Realizing that they had struck gold with the good captain, Fawcett Publications went back to the mine in 1941 for more. First Captain Marvel bestowed a portion of his powers on yet another orphaned newsboy in order to save the lad's life. This newsboy, named Freddie, was transformed into a pretty spit curled teen boy in a blue body stocking named Captain Marvel, Jr. Later that year, the good Captain created the Three Lieutenant Marvels—a trio of lads magically made into adult men.

Now, it seemed like Fawcett Publications was handing out military honors to these boys left and right. But as the nation was heading to war with the Axis powers, Captain Marvel's Squadron of Justice was strictly a men's club. That is, until 1942, when Billy learns

A jubilant Mary Marvel embarks on her new magical life of wonder and adventure, *Wow Comics* #9, 1943

that he has a long lost twin sister named Mary. Once reunited with his sibling, Billy reveals his secret identity to her, although he is sure that the old wizard would *never* give powers to a girl. However, when Mary utters the magic word "Shazam," she turns into a preteen girl in a red miniskirt with a lightning bolt across her flat chest. Billy becomes a grown man, but his sister just turns into a stronger version of herself, not a woman. The old wizard tells Billy that Mary has all of the same powers as Captain Marvel, "though she is a girl."

Mary draws her powers from female deities—Selena, Hippolyta, Ariadne, Zephyrus, Aurora, and Minerva. Billy gets strength, speed, wisdom, stamina, and power from his male celestials, while the ladies give Mary strength, wisdom, fleetness, and skill, along with grace and beauty. Who needs power and stamina when you could be pretty, right? Mary may have the "wisdom of Minerva," but she doesn't even get to pick her own *nom de guerre*. Captain Marvel dubs his new partner Mary Marvel, because...well, that's her name. And even in wartime, there was no military rank for her. No Sergeant Marvel, or Corporal Marvel. Not even Cadet. She is too young to be called Lady Marvel. So, she's just plain Mary. But she needn't have felt like she was singled out. Hoppy, the Marvel Bunny, a funny animal rabbit who also had powers like the Captain, also worked on a strictly first name basis, free of unnecessary military rank.

Had she been created as a young girl who could transform herself into an adult woman, Mary Marvel could have had the ultimate secret life. Here would have been not only the perfect secret identity, but also an appealing fantasy for young female readers as well. But Mary Marvel was modeled after Hollywood good girl Judy Garland, which is why she was merely the "world's mightiest girl" instead of a full-grown buxom woman. Fawcett apparently preferred the image of a nice kid sister to attract girl readers, rather than that of a voluptuous virago. And since Mary Marvel was merely a partner to Captain Marvel, her younger age put her on an appropriately lower level than her more celebrated male sibling. Despite these obstacles, Mary Marvel became one of the most popular heroines of the 1940s, headlining solo adventures in *Wow Comics* and her own *Mary Marvel* title, as well as appearing as a member of the Marvel Family along with her big brother and Captain Marvel, Jr. Her stories involved doing good deeds and helping others, and were devoid of romantic overtones. Too busy helping Captain Marvel to have thoughts of boyfriends, it seemed. She was, as intended, a virtuous helpmate—a flying, bulletproof Judy Garland, minus the diet pills.

THE VICTORY GIRLS

Comic books told readers that crime was rampant in the great cities of the nation, but a bigger threat was facing America, and the world, in the 1940s. As early as 1940, foreign spies and fifth columnists were threatening the nation's shores, according to the comic books. The Shield, a superhero dressed in red, white and blue made his debut in 1940. The following year came Captain America, the product of America's experiments to make a super soldier, clad in chain mail and bearing a star spangled shield. Before the Japanese had attacked Pearl Harbor in December of 1941, comics already had a battalion of patriotic heroes like Captain Victory, Yankee Eagle, Fighting Yank, Captain Flag, Minute Man and Flag Man, all battling the Nazis. Once the United States actually entered the war, comic books became a huge propaganda machine, as superheroes battled evil dungeon-dwelling Nazis ready to brand beautiful American maidens with swastikas, or inhuman, fanged yellow-skinned Japanese offering blood sacrifices to pagan idols.

The Amazon princess Wonder Woman made her debut in 1941,and was the most famous female to defend American democracy. The Axis powers were anathema to the values of peace and love that Wonder Woman stood for, so she fought them with unstoppable fury. But World War II was a big fight, and everyone needed to pitch in. In the real world, women came out of the kitchen to take up blowtorches in American war plants, making planes and bombs to ensure that their country would remain free. In comic books, women had a chance to help out as well. A group of patriotic, freedom-loving ladies put on costumes to fight the good fight. They were the *Victory Girls*. Part patriot, part pinup, these ladies proved that everyone had a part to play in this war.

Unlike the Debutantes, the Victory Girls came from all walks of life. Joan Dale was an ordinary reporter until the Statue of Liberty itself granted her magical powers, transforming her into Miss America. Another Joan, this one with the last name Wayne, was a timid Washington, DC stenographer. But when trouble erupts, Joan puts her glasses and her inhibitions aside to become the "dreaded bundle of female dynamite" known as Miss Victory. With the heroic persona of Miss Victory to steel her, Joan no longer has to act like a mousy secretary, "Heil your grandmother! You murdering maniac-how do you like *that*?" Miss Victory cries, as she plants her bright red boot in a Nazi agent's posterior. Like their fellow proud Americans Liberty Belle and Yankee Girl, the Victory Girls all carry on their wartime activities in secret. Mysteriously, few wear masks, yet no one ever guesses their secret identities.

The most glamorous of the Victory Girls was the Black Cat, who made her debut in 1941, as America was entering World War II. She wasn't a wealthy debutante, but instead was Hollywood starlet Linda Turner. Linda was referred to as "America's sweetheart," and apparently she was also a patriotic daughter of Uncle Sam. She suspects that a foreign movie director is a Nazi spy, and so decides to do a little snooping around. Inspired by her pet kitty, the pretty, redheaded star fashions a sexy little costume and calls herself the Black Cat. After cracking the Nazi spy ring, Linda, who is "bored with her ultra-sophisticated life of make believe," decides to continue slinking around Hollywood as the Black Cat to crack down on more enemies of America. Since Linda is a famous Tinseltown actress, it's vital that she keeps her Black Cat persona a secret.

Black Cat's allure was steeped in healthy, American athleticism. She wore a black backless swimsuit that showed off her ample cleavage, gloves, and buccaneer boots. Claws

Black Cat shows her claws, *Pocket Comics* #1, 1941

and tails and other kitty gimmicks were not Black Cat's forte. If she owed anything to her feline namesake, it was that she was a ferocious fighter. No weapons, just her fists, judo skills and unswerving love of democracy to propel her forward. Black Cat was like the hardworking kitty that rids her home of pesky vermin. In her case, her home was the free world, and the vermin were the Nazis and Japanese.

Black Cat usually battled scheming spies and fifth columnists working in the Hollywood movie industry. But because Linda Turner was a movie star, she also traveled the world entertaining the troops in USO shows, giving her alter ego Black Cat a chance to strike at the enemies of freedom beyond the United States' borders. After defeating a regiment of Japanese who had infiltrated Afghanistan, Black Cat rushes off, thinking, "Now to skip out of here to change back to the beautiful-but-dumb Linda Turner!" She displays the kind of disdain that many heroines felt for the tedious identities that they had to create to mask their true natures.

War Nurse, *Speed Comics* #19, 1942

Perhaps the most ironic of the Victory Girls was Pat Parker, whose day job took her overseas into the thick of the war. You see, Pat was a nurse. However, when a good bedside manner wasn't enough to save the day, Pat put on a mask and became War Nurse. Dressed in a scanty outfit with a bare midriff, red high heel boots, and a mask with a red cross on the forehead, War Nurse looked more like she should be entertaining the troops rather than fighting beside them. "Who's that fugitive from the chorus?" a wisecracking officer remarks when the sultry War Nurse enters a top-secret military meeting. Despite her chorus girl attire, War Nurse dispenses the Allies' values with a no nonsense attitude. For someone trained to save lives, she is quick to pull a gun, and use her fighting skills to dole out a violent response to conflict. Like all mysterious heroines, War Nurse disappeared when her job was done, content to go back and roll bandages until she was needed again.

The Victory Girl who benefited the most from leading a secret life was the ruthless aviatrix Black Angel. Sylvia Manners is a frail young woman with a sensitive nature, who lives with her elderly aunt in a gloomy castle in the English countryside. Sylvia's aunt worries that the horrors of war will take their toll on her young niece's nervous disposition. Sylvia's delicate condition causes her to take to her room and hide in bed for fear that the Nazis are on the castle's doorstep. Or so she would have her aunt believe. As soon as auntie's back is turned, Sylvia slips into her skintight black costume and hotfoots it to her secret airplane hangar. "C'mon baby! We're going to show these Nazi night raiders a new landing field...a British graveyard!" she says, as she climbs behind the controls of her fighter plane. The other wartime heroines seemed to be fighting the enemy because it was a noble cause that preserved the dream of democracy. But Black Angel enjoyed it just a little too much to be completely altruistic. She was every bit as lethal and deadly as the rabid male superheroes who were beating the pants off the Nazis and Japanese.

Black Angel takes aim at her foes,
Air Fighters Comics v.1 #7, 1943

BlackAngel'sMephistophelian skullcap emphasized her cruelly beautiful face, dramatically lit by searchlights as she piloted her plane on missions of death. "From scrap you came, and back to scrap you go!" she says, as she pitilessly sends another Nazi fighter pilot to his doom. Black Angel's secret life liberated her from the role of a conventional female relegated to staying on the sidelines while men fought for honor and glory. But it also absolved her of any need to show traditionally feminine emotions of compassion and mercy. When the brilliantly diabolical Japanese agent Madame Claw chooses suicide over surrender after being defeated by Black Angel, the aviatrix's response is typically heartless. "Her kind always pick the wrong side. Well, can't stay here wasting sympathy on her!" Black Angel's meek Sylvia Manners persona was so vastly different from the slinky and lethal being that rained death and destruction on her enemies from the skies, that it seemed as though the war had been a blessing to her. It allowed her to release all of that pent up aggression. How would she ever go back to a normal life?

This would be a question for many heroines. The end of World War II also brought an end to much of the freedom and lives of derring-do that these women had enjoyed. Like the brave soldiers returning home from the war who now faced an uncertain future, the patriotic men and women who had donned red, white and blue costumes to fight the Hun now had no role in the comic book world. But it wasn't just the patriots who were suffering in the postwar years. Superheroes in general were losing their popularity with readers, and slowly were starting to fade away. Soldiers fighting overseas had been a huge audience for comic books, but as they retired to peaceful postwar lives, sales of superhero titles dropped like bombs. If comic book heroines were going to hang on, they'd need a few new tricks up their sleeves.

THE GLAMOUR GIRLS

With World War II over America focussed its attention back on its own shores, and on the evil that lurked in the shadows of its own cities. The movie style eventually known as 'Film Noir' served up hard-bitten crime stories featuring morally bankrupt men and mysterious femme fatales, blending violence and sexual desire into bleak tales of modern life, without clear messages of morality. The comic book industry offered younger readers its own version of the Film Noir mood with a wave of crime comics that began sweeping the newsstands around 1947. Along with graphic violence, crime comics upped the sexual ante with images of curvaceous, scantily clad women.

By 1947, Phantom Lady had left her original publisher, Quality Comics, to move to Fox Publications, which had a reputation of serving up more sensational fare. Sandra Knight was still keeping up the pretense of being a pampered socialite, while maintaining her secret life of adventure as Phantom Lady. But the heat was about to be turned up. At Fox, Sandra underwent a makeover, which over the next sixty years would become a surefire way to renew interest in a heroine. Artist Matt Baker, known for his provocative drawings of women, changed the Phantom Lady's original yellow and green costume to a slinky blue number that draped her shapely body like lingerie, and showed off the heroine's increased bust size. Sandra Knight was now often shown changing from mufti into her Phantom Lady togs, giving a glimpse of lace edged undergarments or flashing a shapely gam in a seamed stocking. Like the sensational crime comics of the day, Phantom Lady's stories were now filled with a bevy of seductive female victims shown lounging about in lingerie or filmy nightgowns, moments before falling prey to a murderer's touch. In her one-woman crusade against crime, Phantom Lady threw herself into action, as Baker filled the pages with dynamic depictions of her sexy half-dressed body, thrusting cleavage and long, flying legs. And, most notoriously, sex and violence blended, as Phantom Lady's secret escapades often resulted in the heroine in bondage. Phantom Lady had graduated

Phantom Lady in her sultry postwar costume, *Phantom Lady* #17, 1948

to a new sisterhood, the last of the heroines of comics' Golden Age. They were gorgeous pinups whose job it was to fight crime and also keep male readers visually entertained. They were the *Glamour Girls*.

The Glamour Girls were different from the Debutantes that had preceded them. Many were working class females rather than society darlings. Their world was a little harder and grittier than the rarified world from which the Debutante heroines had sprung, although only a few years separated them. They weren't wealthy young women with fabulous wardrobes, but were depicted as wallflowers that kept their charisma bottled up. When they let their hair down, they became ravishing creatures that made men drool. Just as their everyday backgrounds denoted a certain sobriety that was pervasive in the postwar America, their reasons for adopting secret lives were different from their predecessors as well. They shared a thirst for justice with the Debutantes, but their different motivations were more than just thrills. Like the Partner heroines, the Glamour Girls often donned mask or wig to help a man, although these lookers did it in secret.

Making her debut in 1947, Black Canary was the archetype of the new Film Noir era heroine. Originally, Black Canary was a mysterious female vigilante, who played the role of criminal in order to infiltrate the underworld and bring its gangsters to justice. A gorgeous blonde in a low cut black swimsuit, bolero jacket and fishnet tights, Black Canary was actually Dinah Drake, a florist who wore her black hair tied in a bun, and sensible, high-necked blouses. When trouble brewed, Dinah slipped into her fishnets and pinned on a blonde wig to become the gutsy, karate chopping Black Canary. But Dinah had another incentive to lead a secret life. A roguishly handsome private detective named Larry Lance became a frequent customer in Dinah's florist shop. He had a knack for getting into trouble, and Dinah would usually end up switching into her Black Canary guise to rescue him. Larry couldn't have been that great a detective, since a simple blonde wig tricked him into thinking that Dinah and Black Canary were two different women. Larry became Black Canary's *de facto* partner in her adventures, often winding up as the helpless male hostage while fancying himself the brave hero.

Naturally Larry was smitten by the glamorous blonde Black Canary, often overlooking Dinah, who played the droll, brainy career female who must hide her emotions and feelings from the detective. In this updated version of the secret life, Dinah's alter ego offered her a different kind of thrill than the Debutantes, who went out fighting crime on a lark, got from theirs. The Black Canary gave prim Dinah a dynamic persona through which she could express her sexuality, and charm the man she loved. Larry, in turn, fell in love with the vivacious image she had created, rather than Dinah herself. The Black Canary's adventures would usually end with an exchange of snappy banter between Larry and Dinah which allowed the heroine to share a wink with the reader, while also reinforcing the loneliness that her duplicity had caused. "When the police came, Black Canary disappeared!" Larry says at the conclusion of a 1948 story. A deadpan Dinah doesn't even look up from the flower arrangement she is fashioning as she retorts, "What...again? I bet you made her up!" Dinah had created her own rival in the Black Canary that would bedevil her chances for happiness. As a result, she has to pretend to resent her alter ego.

Black Canary's battles with the underworld show the influence of postwar crime comics. But the emphasis on unrequited love in these stories resulted from another new popular comic book genre of the late 1940s: the romance comic. Romance comics first appeared in 1947, and targeted a female audience with tales of lovelorn females, tragic marriages, and salacious "true" stories patterned after confession magazines. With the comic book industry struggling to maintain sales after World War II, publishers tried to appeal to girls with a double-barreled blend of adventure and romance in the exploits of the Glamour Girl.

Like the Black Canary, the Blonde Phantom also fought crime to keep her man safe. In real life, she was Louise Grant, the bespectacled secretary to private detective Mark Mason. Whenever Mark needed help, Louise would excuse herself. Taking her long blonde hair out of the ubiquitous bun and letting it cascade around her shoulders, putting on a mask and a long red bespangled evening gown, the Blonde Phantom was ready to thwart evil. Mark is infatuated with the Blonde Phantom, but it would never occur to the detective that his dowdy Girl Friday is the object of his affections. "I sure wish I could get a date with the Blonde Phantom!" the clueless Mark laments to Louise, all the while oblivious to the fact that his heart's desire is sitting right in front of him. Once again, a capable woman hid behind a meek persona and only let her hair down, literally, to come to the aid of a man who completely ignored her unless she assumed a disguise. In a 1947 story entitled "I Hate Me!" Louise even dreams that Mark finally confesses his love for her, only to have the Blonde Phantom persona appear and steal him away.

The most glamorous of the Glamour Girls, appropriately enough, was Venus. Debuting in 1948, Venus was introduced as the ancient goddess of love and ruler of the world that bore her name, a "planet of pleasure and song." Venus was shown as a platinum haired, Hollywood style siren, clad in a flowing white gown and spike heeled sandals. She was the mistress of an empty citadel patrolled by swarthy, turbaned guards: "For centuries I have lived the life of a goddess-adored, admired, and envied! But, alas, unloved!"

Venus' desire to be loved transports her to Earth. When Venus meets Whitney Hammond, the publisher of *Beauty Magazine*, he dismisses her outlandish claims to be a goddess. But, he is so dazzled by Venus' looks that she is made editor of the magazine. In order to be near Whitney, Venus plays down her divinity, only working her goddess magic when no one is looking. Here was the ultimate in slumming. Venus hides her godhood and lives her life as a normal human woman in order to win the love of a mortal man. The gods of Olympus try to thwart Venus' romance with Whitney and force her to resume her godly duties, but she refuses. This was certainly sending young female readers a clear message about how important it was to make sacrifices to keep a man.

The romance angle plays heavily in Venus' adventures. Since she is the goddess of love, Venus uses sex as a weapon, as it were. Venus is shown solving the world's problems with love in stories like 1950's "The End of the World." Scientist Michael Templar hopes to win himself fame, fortune, and the love of a heartless beauty. But tragically, his experiments go awry, and leave the earth hurtling towards the sun. Venus implores Templar to save the world, pointing out that he already has won the love of his faithful but dreary assistant Maria. Since Maria predictably wears glasses and her hair in a bun, Venus summons forth a divine beauty task force that includes Cleopatra, Salome, and Helen of Troy-"Women whose beauty shaped the destiny of the world!" The all-star lovelies share their beauty and grace with Maria, who is transformed into a stunner with perfect vision and movie star looks. Templar is enraptured by Maria's newfound beauty, and reverses the process that would doom the world. Venus rushes back to the arms of Whitney, who is unconcerned with the details of exactly how the apocalypse was just avoided: "Oh, sweetheart, never mind explaining! Just give me a kiss!" After all of her efforts, Venus is basically told to shut her trap and pucker up.

The idea that a beautiful face could save the world was an indication where comic books, and American women, were heading. The focus was now on looks over abilities. The days of fearless women like Lady Luck or the Black Angel, who maintained a secret life in order to live with the same freedom that men enjoyed, were drawing to a close. The war had been won, and women who had done their part to help the war were now expected go back to being wives and mothers. Christian Dior's "New Look" of 1947 changed the face of fashion by making garments frivolous and feminine again with its yards of flowing fabric. But it also put women back into restrictive corsets that distorted their shapes into idealized forms that men would appreciate.

As the 1950s dawned, most of the daring women who had donned costumes to lead thrilling secret lives had vanished from the comic book pages. But they weren't alone. Comic book superheroes in general faced their own *Götterdämmerung* after the war. New comic book genres like westerns, horror, crime, science fiction, and romance flooded the market and stole the thunder from the supergods. The age of gods and heroes had passed.

By the mid-'50s, Wonder Woman was on her own. Most of the marvelous women who had fought beside her during the war years had faded into memory. By 1954, the Comics Code Authority was instituted to clean up the excesses of the industry, ensuring that children would only read stories with wholesome depictions of women. The code specified:

> Nudity in any form is prohibited, as is indecent or undue exposure. Suggestive and salacious illustration or suggestive posture is unacceptable. Females shall be drawn realistically without exaggeration of any physical qualities.

Phantom Lady still lingered about the newsstands in the mid-'50s. Her racy costume and hourglass figure had been toned down to comply with the Comics Code. But now it was her daredevil persona that was also out of style. Sandra Knight may have been called Phantom *Lady*, but apparently she wasn't ladylike enough for more conservative times. By 1955, she was gone.

A new day had dawned. America was wracked with suspicion, censorship, and conservative values. If women had any aspirations to be more than what they were, they would have to keep them a secret.

The Queen
and the Princess

One was a beautiful blonde, the other a striking brunette. One was a savage fighter, who could deal death with her bare hands. The other had been trained since childhood in the art of war, but preferred to think that love was the true solution to conflict. One had only the strength of her body and her dagger to protect her. The other was blessed by the gods with amazing powers, and was girded with fantastic weapons. They were both comic book royalty—one a queen, the other merely a princess. The queen was the first of her kind, but the princess outlived her in life, and in legend. The queen was named Sheena, and the princess was called Wonder Woman. As different as they were from one another, these two sovereigns ruled the early days of comic books as the medium's two most popular heroines, and the archetypes that would define the female superhero. Sheena was a passionate, savage beauty who embodied the erotic fantasies of men, while Wonder Woman was a powerful female who served as a role model for young girls.

The early comic books were often a case of throwing something against the wall to see what stuck. Many were crudely drawn, and amateurishly written, yet had an intrinsically "American" feel about them. Fledgling publishers drew inspiration for their daring new heroes from the newspaper strips, but also from pulp magazines. Pulps were cheap fiction magazines that had evolved from the dime novels of the Victorian era, and were hugely popular in the '20s and '30s. The sensational quality of the pulps is often credited as influencing the often lurid quality of the early comic books. While the pulps did have a certain trashy nature, a number of well-respected authors like H.G. Wells, H.P. Lovecraft, H. Rider Haggard and Edgar Rice Burroughs had their work published in these magazines. Many legendary characters like Tarzan, Buck Rogers, and The Shadow first appeared in the pulps, and were the forerunners for the early superheroes and comic book crime fighters.

Technically, Sheena predates even Superman, having first appeared in the primordial dawn of comic books in 1937. But her true origins are older than that. Sheena is often described as the female version of Edgar Rice Burroughs' 1912 creation, Tarzan. The majority of Burroughs' popular works revolves around a tension between the savage and the civilized, also seen in Sheena's adventures. Burroughs' work, like that of fellow adventure writer H. Rider Haggard, came out of the colonial era, and was written for men and boys who yearned for an escape from stifling modern life, through tales of dangerous worlds and exotic women. The common theme of these stories is that a man from the civilized world finds his way to a fantastic, often barbaric, world of adventure, where he falls in love with an intoxicating savage princess. While most of Burroughs' heroines, like Dejah Thoris or Dian the Beautiful, were in need of rescuing, Haggard's 1886 novel *She* introduced a stronger heroine. The novel's English protagonist encounters the beautiful queen Ayesha, the ruler of a lost city in Africa. Ayesha is referred to as "she who must be obeyed," and is a creature that provokes both fear and lust. Ayesha was the ultimate fantasy of civilized man: the beautiful, savage white queen, ruling a kingdom unhindered by the laws of modern morality. This brand of men's fiction produced the swirling foam of exotic and erotic fantasy from which rose the jungle Venus known as Sheena.

Wonder Woman's origins went further back than Sheena's, some 2000 years to be exact. Wonder Woman was one of the race of women called the Amazons, the fierce female warriors of ancient Greek myths. The male-focused Greeks didn't exactly paint the most flattering picture of these women. The Amazons were said to be descended from the war god Ares, savage man-haters who cut off one breast to better enable them to handle a bow and arrow. Men were forbidden in the land of the Amazons, and the women warriors only mated once a year in order to continue their line, killing their male offspring and raising only girl children as ruthless fighters.

Now that we have some historical context on these female monarchs, let's talk about their specific origins. In the 1930s, there were several studios that produced art and stories for the various publishers who were getting into the new field of comic books. One of the most successful and prolific was the Universal Phoenix Studio, operated by two young artists named Will Eisner and Jerry Iger. In 1937, they created a female Tarzan-type character named Sheena for the British tabloid *Wags*. The strip was credited to the pseudonym W. Morgan Thomas, and the heroine's name was meant to remind readers of H. Rider Haggard's *She*. Demand for new comic book material was growing in the United States, and American pulp magazine publisher Fiction House was looking for material for a new comic book. Sheena made her American debut in 1938's *Jumbo Comics* #1, just three months after Superman's now legendary first appearance. She was the first female adventure character in comic books. This would be just one of her claims to fame.

Wonder Woman's genesis was a loftier one. By the time she was conceived, in 1941, the comic book industry was in full swing. Superman was the genie released from a bottle, and in his wake, the newsstands were literally flooded with superheroes. Batman, The Flash, Green Lantern, The Human Torch, Sub-Mariner, Blue Beetle, and Captain Marvel had all come to life by 1941, along with scores of now largely forgotten heroes like the Green Mask, Samson, Neon the Unknown, The Arrow, and Captain Triumph. A handful of ladies like the Woman in Red, the Magician from Mars, and Phantom Lady had joined the pack as well, but the female representation was too meager for a psychologist named William Moulton Marston. In a 1940 interview in *Family Circle* magazine, Dr. Marston had spoken of his belief that comic books might have educational potential. The article brought Marston to the attention of comic book publisher Max Gaines, who hired the psychologist as an educational consultant. Marston wanted to create a hero who would triumph using love rather than fisticuffs, and his wife Elizabeth suggested that he make the character a woman. Marston felt that women were superior to men, and his goal was to create a female role model to inspire young girl readers to stand up for themselves and achieve their true potential. And so, Wonder Woman, who Marston described as "a feminine character with all the strength of Superman plus all the allure of a good and beautiful woman," was born.

The 1938 concept of Africa from which Sheena arose was still a forbidding place of mystery and menace, born of the men's dime novels that spawned her. Her origin story is simple: a widowed explorer named Cardwell Rivington and his young daughter come to Africa in search of lost treasure. Rivington is befriended by a witch doctor named Koba, and the two men teach each other their native languages. Koba unwittingly causes his friend Rivington to perish, and, filled with remorse, he raises his late friend's young daughter and makes the white girl the queen of the natives. As she grows, she develops great strength, hunting prowess, and knowledge of the jungle and its beasts. Koba also teaches the girl her deceased father's language, so she is remarkably fluent in both English and the languages of the jungle folk. And thus is Sheena, Queen of the Jungle, born. Like Haggard's Ayesha, blonde Sheena is a beautiful, white-skinned female ruler of fierce savages, and a creature to spark male fantasies.

The young Sheena is crowned queen, *Jumbo Comics* #2, 1938

Wonder Woman's origin is set in the world of the ancient Greek gods, albeit with a more female friendly twist. The story begins with a divine difference of opinions. The war god Ares declares that "might makes right," and that men will rule the world with a sword. The love goddess Aphrodite objects, and maintains that women will succeed using gentler tactics. While Ares' soldiers wage war and enslave women, Aphrodite magically creates the Amazon race to spread her message of love. The Amazons are shown as pretty women in chitons and sandals, with nary a helmet or breastplate in sight. The goddess gives the Amazon queen Hippolyta a magic girdle that will make all of her women warriors unconquerable.

What follows is a variation of the Ninth Labor of Hercules, told less as a Greek myth, and more as a cautionary tale to warn young girls about the devious ways of men. In the comic book version, Ares sends the burly demigod Hercules to capture the magic girdle of Hipployta, with the goal being to conquer the Amazons. Hercules allows himself to be beaten by Hippolyta, and then seduces the Amazon queen with his bestial charms. Once Hercules seizes the magic girdle, the powerless Amazons are placed in chains and enslaved. A mournful Hippolyta beseeches Aphrodite for aid. The goddess frees the Amazons, but at a price. The women rise up and defeat their Greek captors, and then escape on the men's ships. Aphrodite leads the Amazons to an island where they will live in peace forever, but with conditions. First off, no man can ever set foot on their new home, Paradise Island, lest all of the Amazons lose their youth and power. Second, the Amazons must forever wear the shackles with which they were enslaved to remind them "the folly of submitting to men's domination." These are called the Bracelets of

Submission.

Once the Amazons are ensconced in their new home, the goddess Athena shows Hippolyta how to fashion a child out of clay, into which Aphrodite then breathes life. Hippolyta calls her "little wonder child" Diana. As the princess grows up, the other Amazons marvel at the godlike strength and speed that Diana exhibits. Diana drinks from the Amazon fountain of youth, which keeps her vibrant and beautiful as long as she remains on Paradise Island. The fairy tale elements of the story of Wonder Woman's birth show the effort made to appeal to young female readers with a taste for magical, escapist fantasies, while also creating a world where women could live unhampered by the brutish, small-minded ways of men.

At this point, in keeping with the adventure novel formula, a man enters the picture. In Sheena's case, handsome young engineer Bob Reynolds comes to Africa to work on a big oil project. Bob contracts a deadly plague, and as he writhes in a fever delirium, a beautiful angel of mercy arrives, bringing the rare jungle herbs needed to save his life. Once recovered, Bob becomes obsessed with finding the ravishing creature who has saved his life, and searches the jungle for her. One day, he and his party are ambushed by a group of natives. Bob is reunited with his savior when Sheena swings

Bob and Sheena meet for the first time, *Jumbo Comics* #1, 1938

down from a tree, announcing that all the outsiders are her prisoners. Eventually Sheena realizes that Bob is not the enemy, and the two fall in love. Like Jane Porter in the Tarzan novels, Bob decides to remain in the jungle with his savage sweetheart.

For Wonder Woman, a man literally falls out of the sky. The plane piloted by Captain Steve Trevor of American Army Intelligence is shot down near Paradise Island. Princess Diana rescues the dying airman, lifting him in her arms lest his foot touch the ground of the Amazon's homeland and destroy its immortal enchantment. Steve is the first man Diana has ever laid eyes on, and she is instantly smitten. Apparently the Amazons hadn't been sitting around just polishing their shields for the last thousand years, because they have a wealth of futuristic technology at their disposal. Steve dies, but Diana revives him using the miraculous purple ray machine that she has invented. Aphrodite and Athena instruct Hippolyta to select the strongest and wisest Amazon to take Steve Trevor back to America, described as "the last citadel of democracy, and of equal rights for women." Hippolyta answers the goddesses' command, saying that her greatest Amazon will save the world, "She shall go forth to fight for liberty and freedom and all womankind."

The queen holds a tournament to select the strongest Amazon, and Diana defies her mother's wishes and dons a mask to enter the competition. The final test is called Bullets and Bracelets, and it tests an Amazon's ability to deflect bullets with her Bracelets of Submission. (As peaceful and loving as the Amazons were, it is a bit ironic that they invented firearms on their own.) As expected, Diana wins the competition, and a proud Hippolyta must relent and let her little sparrow leave the nest, even though she knows her daughter will forfeit her immortality. Diana uses yet another fabulous Amazon creation, the invisible jet, to whisk Steve back to Washington, DC, where the press dubs the princess Wonder Woman.

Now, with both of these heroines, clothes were firmly part of their legends. Sheena wore a nondescript short dress in her first adventures, which followed the standard "exotic lost girl in the wild" formula of pulp magazines. In *Jumbo Comics* #10, Sheena exerts her authority over her kingdom, and shows readers why she bore the title of queen of the jungle. Sheena and Bob come to a village that had been ravaged by a killer lion, known in jungle lingo as Namu. The sovereign calmly announces, "Sheena will kill Namu." She then confronts the lion with only her dagger and fighting skills to protect her. Then, as the text describes, "eyes narrowed, nostrils twitching, Sheena slowly advances." After a fierce fight, Sheena is the victor. "He has killed the last of my jungle people," proclaims Sheena, her dress in tatters from the lion's raking claws. This was 1939, and there had never been a heroine in a comic book that fought either man or beast, much less with the same ferocity as a male. Minutes later, a leopard attacks the twosome, which Bob quickly dispatches with a bullet from his pistol. The dead leopard's pelt is put to good use when Sheena emerges with a surprise. "There! How do you like my new dress, Bob?" Well, to call it a dress would be exaggerating, more a skimpy leopard skin swimsuit with a plunging neckline. But it signified that a star was born. Sheena's new costume not only confirmed her title of savage jungle queen, but the first sex symbol of

Sheena, *Jumbo Comics* #20, 1940

comics as well. Taking in the sight of Sheena in her new costume, Bob sums up the jungle queen's combination of strength and sensuality, "Just proves that though you're a fierce fighter and have the courage of ten men, you're still a woman."

Wonder Woman's look was a bit more modest, but equally symbolic. Queen Hippolyta designed a costume to show that the Amazons supported the American cause of democracy. With her strapless bodice emblazoned with the American eagle and star-spangled culottes, Wonder Woman was like an allegorical figure of victory, charging across the battlefield to preserve freedom for womankind. (Oddly, the Amazons lived in complete isolation for thousands of years, yet they invented not only guns, but also high heels.) When Wonder Woman was introduced in *All Star Comics* #8, in December of 1941, the United States had not officially entered World War II. But by the time she began her starring spot in *Sensation Comics* #1, in January 1942, the war had gone global, and the Amazon princess joined other patriotic heroes like Mr. America, The Shield, and Captain America in smashing Axis spies. Wonder Woman's star spangled regalia showed young girls that females could also play a part in this war. Within six months, Hippolyta gives her daughter the perfect accessory for her new outfit, her magic lasso. The lasso compels anyone held in its clutches to tell the truth, and was no doubt inspired by creator Marston's involvement in developing the polygraph, or lie detector test.

Outfitted for comic book stardom, the two crowned heads embarked on their respective missions. But, though they were only born four years apart, Sheena and Wonder Woman represented two different visions of America, which showed how much the nation had changed in that brief time.

As a ruler, Sheena embodied the pre-Pearl Harbor isolationist stance that the United States had in relation to the rest of the world. Sheena ruled her jungle kingdom, but she did it all from within the borders of her verdant realm. It was all about maintaining the status quo: "Once more the jungle sings of Peace, Bob. Let us hope the melody does not change." Sheena encounters unscrupulous ivory hunters, ruthless treasure hunters, maniacal witch doctors, evil rulers of lost races, and all manner of wild beasts that threaten to knock the monarch off her throne. But she rules with an iron will and a flashing knife. "Know you not that I rule this jungle? You must die!" Sheena proclaims, as she plunges her dagger into the throat of a killer beast. But despite her savage nature, Sheena's goal is to rule a peaceful kingdom where all jungle people can live in freedom. She is a protectress of the black natives of her land, usually represented as a simple, superstitious lot sporting bones through their noses, always on the verge of reverting to their cannibalistic ways. Though she is

LEFT: Sheena cracks down on a Nazi sympathizer in her jungle kingdom, *Jumbo Comics* #42, 1942

no more than an uneducated savage herself, Sheena embodied the colonial concept of the naturally intelligent and rational Caucasian, looking after her gullible black underlings. As the 1940s progressed and the war escalated, Sheena even cracked a few Nazi skulls when they dared to enter her kingdom. But she did it all from her seat of power deep in the mysterious jungle. The isolationistic Sheena never left her stronghold; she just dug in and fought to preserve the way of life of her subjects, human and animal alike.

Wonder Woman represented modern America as leader of the free world, and champion of the downtrodden. She forsook her kingdom and immortality to make the whole world a better place and, most of all, to fight for the rights of females. Just as America emerged as a global peacekeeper, Wonder Woman's adventures took her wherever women were in peril and their freedom was threatened, like the planet Venus with its butterfly-winged women, or the subterranean paradise Eveland. The "loving ways of the Amazons" that she was sent to teach the world were presumably the wisdom of the matrilineal society that predated the Greeks. "I can make bad men good and weak woman strong!" she says, as she spreads her message of empowerment across "man's world." Wonder Woman took on the strangest assortment of adversaries—Olympian gods, sadistic criminals, evil queens, and cruel conquerors from the stars—anyone who stood in the way of justice and freedom. Her greatest foes were the cruel and oppressive Axis powers. With rabid comments like "Oh, now I feel strong enough to beat the whole Jap army single-handed," Wonder Woman proved she was just as serious a fighter for democracy as her other jingoistic patriotic compatriots. Writing under the pen name Charles Mouton, Marston peppered all of his Wonder Woman stories with a feminist sensibility that was revolutionary in its day. It wasn't enough for Wonder Woman to rescue her fellow women; she wanted to teach them to stand up for themselves. "Earth girls can stop evil when they refuse to be dominated by evil men."

When it came to romance, it was clear that Sheena was targeted to a male audience. Bob is referred to as Sheena's mate. Not her boyfriend or fiancé, but the animalistic term "mate." This refers to Tarzan and his mate Jane, but the term had different connotations when used in this way. Unlike the white princesses of Burroughs novels, Sheena was not an inviolate virgin goddess living in the wild, but a passionate creature willingly engaging in what could be presumed to be animal sex. Sheena and Bob were lovers, and lived together in a tree house. The implication was also that along with the sex, the traditional female/male roles were reversed here. Sheena was the strong half of the relationship. She was the take charge, quick to action, not much for words leader. Bob was the traditional damsel in distress in need of rescuing, and always ready with a clever quip to lighten the mood. The freewheeling sexual part of the formula seemed to cancel out any of the emasculating aspects of Sheena's personality male readers may have been uncomfortable with.

Wonder Woman's creator Marston enjoyed a unique, polyamorous relationship with his wife and his secretary. He also felt that submission to the superior ways of women was the answer to the woes of the world. Ironically, Wonder Woman's own love life was very conventional, and sent a mixed message about male/female relations to young female readers. In the beginning, Wonder Woman's main reason for leaving Paradise Island is not to save "man's world," but because she's fallen in love with the virile, khaki-clad American, Steve. For his part, Steve is a military man, conquest is his number one goal. As impressed as Steve is by the Amazon's strength, he is determined to have her settle down and be his wife. Rushing off to meet Wonder Woman on a dangerous mission, Steve fumes, "Blistering Blazes! Why will that beautiful gal always invite trouble? If she'd only married me, she'd be home cooking my dinner right now!"

Although Wonder Woman preaches female empowerment, she represses her own powerful self by hiding behind the secret identity of bespectacled Navy Lieutenant Diana Prince, so that she never has to leave Steve's side. To Steve, Diana Prince is just a drab busybody who is perpetually fawning over him, and completely beneath his notice. Wonder Woman, meanwhile, vexes Steve by acting charmingly aloof towards him. She behaves as though her

Sheena races to save her helpless mate Bob from certain death,
Jumbo Comics #108, 1948

mission to end tyranny is more important than romance, all the while fretting to herself that Steve might lose interest. Wonder Woman extolled the merits of truth, sisterhood, and freedom from the suppression of men. Yet she gave young girls a strange picture of romance as a battle of wills, with submission as the ultimate outcome. Steve's desire to wed Wonder Woman makes her feel she would have to play the submissive wife, which brings up all of her Amazon fears of being dominated by a man. "Some girls love to have a man stronger than they are make them do things. Do I like it? I don't know—it's sort of thrilling. But isn't it more fun to make the man obey?"

This brings us to the subject of sex appeal. Sheena's, publisher Fiction House, was one of the great purveyors of what is known as "Good Girl Art," which translated to cheesecake with a little kink thrown in for good measure. Publishers incorporated half-dressed, leggy females in pinup poses into comics during World War II to entertain the troops fighting overseas. Good Girl Art had its heyday in the postwar years, when publishers began making comics more racy to combat dwindling sales. Sheena was drawn in provocative poses that best showed off her ample breasts carefully concealed by strategically placed leopard skin. Long shapely legs broke out of the panel borders in High Baroque style to arch across the page. Sheena swung from vines or leapt across the page, prominently showing off a spotted rump or widely spread legs. Her long blonde hair was wild and free flowing. Stories mixed shades of Eros and Thanatos by showing the erotically drawn Sheena locked in combat with a wild snarling beast, or writhing in the tentacles of a giant squid. Sheena was the

Sheena, *Jumbo Comics* #105, 1947

untamed fantasy, the wild sensual creature that was not confined by polite society's idea of how a woman should dress or act. Besides racy pinup art, a trademark of Fiction House's comic books was bondage. Fiction House featured a number of sexy underdressed heroines like Sheena, and they all spent a good amount of time getting tied up and tortured. Sheena was no exception, although another crowned head was the undisputed queen of bondage.

Wonder Woman was drawn in an unconventional comic book style. Artist Harry G. Peter was sixty-one when he began drawing Wonder Woman, and his unique, often bizarre drawing style has been likened to woodcuts. He drew Wonder Woman with a shapely, athletic figure, but not an exceptionally sexy one. She wasn't especially busty, and her face had the round shape and bee-stung lips of a 1920s flapper. All of this made sense for a comic book heroine who was meant to appeal to young girls, not to titillate men. Wonder Woman was radiant, confident, and inspiring, but not as luscious as a Hollywood starlet or Vargas Girl pinup. However, the mystifying erotic element that Marston added to almost every adventure was a healthy, or unhealthy, dose of bondage. Wonder Woman's bizarre, kinky rogue's gallery of villains was constantly finding new and elaborate ways to restrain the Amazon, which she always overcame with great resolve. She was tied up, chained up, buried underground, sealed in tanks of water, and tied to railroad tracks. She lost her powers when a man forged chains onto her Bracelets of Submission, so naturally this happened quite frequently. Conversely, Wonder Woman exhorted the virtues of "loving submission," an Amazon version of dominance. "If girls want to be slaves, there's no harm in that . . . A good mistress could do wonders with them." How this was meant to inspire young girls is not exactly clear.

Many male superheroes of the 1940s had a supporting cast consisting of a love interest and a humorous sidekick for comedy relief. Bob filled the former role in Sheena's world, while her mischievous pet monkey Chim filled the latter. Although Sheena was clearly fond of her mate Bob, she displayed a somewhat stoic, masculine affection toward him. It was only with Chim that Sheena softens, and displays traditional female, even maternal, behavior. "Now, will you be naughty again, and tease Sheena?" the jungle monarch cooes to her little primate pal, after rescuing him from certain doom once more. There was a cast of interchangeable, busty native girls who looked just like Sheena, but were colored brown. Otherwise, Sheena was essentially a one-woman act. There wasn't much of a female presence in this queen's world, owing, no doubt, to the fact that she was created to entertain men.

Wonder Woman's world, on the other hand, was brimming with females. Her pal was the sugar addicted Etta Candy, a boisterous and bulky college coed from nearby Holliday College. With a rousing "Woo woo" and her ever present box of candy in hand, the redheaded Etta was Wonder Woman's enthusiastic partner in peril. Etta was joined by her sorority sisters, the Holliday Girls, an athletic group of young women in school track uniforms. Whenever Wonder Woman was in really deep trouble, she sent a message to Etta via the Amazon mental radio. The girls came running to Wonder Woman's aid, eager to smack some fascists in the name of freedom. While this abundance of frolicking females made some critics feel there was too much of a Sapphic atmosphere in Wonder Woman's comic, Marston did inject a good message of sisterhood that was missing from other comics of the day. Here were women helping other women to beat oppression through self-reliance and strength, certainly a positive message for young girls who would be coming out of wartime to help build a new modern world. A regular feature in Wonder Woman's comics recounted the stories of famous women in history. There wasn't much of a message for males here, which is why young male readers may have felt threatened by Wonder Woman's powerful ways.

While often dismissed as a mere pinup in a leopard print bikini, Sheena holds a very important place in comic book history. Besides being the first female adventure character, Sheena is also the first woman to star in her own comic book. Buoyed by the success of the jungle queen in *Jumbo Comics*, Sheena starred in her own eponymous title beginning in 1942, beating Wonder Woman to this particular honor. Sheena proved that a female comic book character could be beautiful and strong, and while she may not have had much to say, she showed through her actions that a woman could be every bit as tough as a man. There wasn't a lot to Sheena's persona behind the image of savage sensuality, and she shared precious few words of wisdom with her readers. Sheena was perhaps the perfect male fantasy, exhibiting all of the traditional characteristics of a man like bravery and nobility, while looking like the ultimate, sexy woman. She was the mother goddess of jungle girls, and her daughters filled the pages of comics for years to come. Her success gave birth to an entire genre, and the jungle was literally packed with gorgeous white women like Tiger Girl, Jann of the Jungle, Princess Pantha, Judy of the Jungle, Tygra, Rulah the Jungle Goddess, and Lorna the Jungle Girl, all swinging their way into the hearts of male comic book readers well into the 1950s. As appealing as they may have been, none of these other exotic flowers ever matched the appeal of the original queen of the jungle.

Wonder Woman was not the first, but she is considered by most to be the most recognized and iconic female superhero. She rode a wave of popularity throughout the 1940s, and fans revere her adventures from the war years as the first truly feminist comics in America. Wonder Woman was strong and confident, trouncing her foes with ease and humor. "You're a strong boy . . . it's fun to defeat you!" Wonder Woman tells a big bruiser gangster, as she easily disarms him. She knew she was superior to everyone else, so she never doubted that she would win, and she inspired her girl readers to feel the same way about themselves. Wonder Woman continued to star in *Sensation Comics* throughout the '40s, while also starring in her own quarterly self-titled comic beginning in 1942, and a regular feature in 1943's *Comic Cavalcade*. Wonder Woman may have espoused messages of liberation and freedom in her own comic books, but she became the inadvertent victim of sexism. In 1942, DC Comics decided to induct Wonder Woman as the first female member of the Justice Society of America. But Marston didn't much care for the idea of someone else joining the team in the writing of Wonder Woman's adventures, and demanded total control of the character. Unfortunately, he wasn't able to meet the deadlines to write Wonder Woman's stories for three other comics and her Justice Society tales as well. A compromise was reached, and Wonder Woman was relegated to being the mere secretary of the Justice Society, even though she outclassed most of the men of the group in power. "Good luck, boys! I wish that I could join you!" the mighty Amazon would say, as the men raced off to fight evil and she dutifully stayed behind at the group's headquarters to record their adventures. Within the comic book industry, Wonder Woman was not emulated as much as her jungle bred rival Sheena. There were a number of patriotic heroines like Miss America, Pat Patriot and Liberty Belle, but few had the gusto and feminist sensibility of Wonder Woman. Perhaps her message was a bit too strong for other publishers, who may have thought a Wonder Woman copy would be too threatening to their male readers.

Sheena's conservative costume, *Sheena, Queen of the Jungle* #12, 1951

In the end, it was the very sex appeal that made Sheena a star that proved to be her undoing. As the 1940s drew to a close, tastes were changing. By 1954, Dr. Frederick Wertham's book *Seduction of the Innocent* had alarmed America with the idea that comic books might be corrupting the youth of the nation. Drawing particular fire was the violence and highly sexualized imagery featured in many of the more lurid comic books. By 1949 Fiction House had already begun to draw Sheena in a less revealing costume in an attempt to stave off the wave of criticism. But, in 1954, faced with angry parents and increasingly poor sales, Fiction House eventually cut its losses and got out of the comic book business entirely. Sheena disappeared from the newsstands in 1953, only to reappear two years later in living rooms across the nation, when the queen of the jungle came to television. The statuesque Irish McCalla portrayed Sheena, albeit in a more modest leopard skin outfit. The female who was a pioneer in comics was now at the forefront of a new entertainment medium. When the show ended in 1956, Sheena herself drifted into the realm of fantasy and myth. She resurfaced from time to time in a movie or television adaptation, and still inspires latter day jungle queens in the comic book pages. But for the most part, the queen of the jungle shunned the spotlight. Sheena helped launch an industry; she deserved her rest.

As for Wonder Woman, she was in it for the long haul. After the war, Wonder Woman's future became cloudier. Rosie the Riveter was done working in the war plant, and was going back to making pies for her menfolk. The Axis had been beaten, so what would Wonder Woman's next mission be? After creator Marston died in 1947, Wonder Woman was finally allowed to become a full-fledged member of the Justice Society. But with the popularity of superheroes dwindling, the Justice Society was gone by 1951. In her own comics, the Amazon princess' fortunes took a turn for the worse. Artist Peter continued working with different writers, but the quality and energy of his art began to fade. Without Marston's feminist guiding vision, Wonder Woman became less interested in the welfare of her fellow women, and more in keeping Steve happy. Her pro-female persona retreated in the 1950s, as questions about Wonder Woman's sexuality made a feminist stance too controversial, and drew unwanted suspicion about her character. Wertham characterized the mighty Amazon this way in *Seduction of the Innocent*:

> For boys, Wonder Woman is a frightening image. For girls she is a morbid ideal . . . Wonder Woman has her own female following . . . Her followers are the "Holliday girls," i.e. the holiday girls, the gay party girls, the gay girls. Wonder Woman refers to them as "my girls." Their attitude about death and murder is a mixture of the callousness of crime comics with the coyness of sweet little girls.

Wonder Woman may have dressed like a symbol of America, but how American was she really? After all, she wasn't even Christian. The Amazon had met her Olympian gods, so she had no doubts as to who created her. America, the "last citadel of democracy, and of equal rights for women" that Wonder Woman had sacrificed her immortality for, was beginning to feel a little less friendly than it had just a few years earlier. The freedom loving Amazon princess kept a low profile throughout the next two decades, until the times caught up with her, and it was OK to act like herself again.

1950s : The Girlfriends

Batwoman never left her lair without her handbag. After all, a girl has to be prepared for any situation. Take that night when a pair of thieves robbed the new terminal at Gotham City airport, for example. When Batwoman arrived to thwart the ne'er-do-wells, one of the oafish robbers guffawed, "It's a Bat-Woman! Ha, ha! What can she do?" He'd soon find out, as Batwoman's lightning fast moves knocked him flat. Pulling a large powder puff from her purse, she used it to blind the other robber. "My charm bracelets are really disguised steel handcuffs that'll hold you two like a charm until police come!" Batwoman said as she secured the thieves with her judicial jewelry. Batman and Robin arrived at the crime scene just in time to see the masked beauty speed off into the night on her motorcycle.

The following night, Batman and Robin searched the dark streets of Gotham City for the mysterious Batwoman. Batman was so intent on finding the female vigilante that he didn't notice the car full of criminals sneaking up behind him and Robin as they entered a blind alley. But someone else was watching. From a rooftop, Batwoman was surveying the scene. Opening her handbag, she pulled out a bottle of perfume. "—It's Tear Gas No. 51!" she yelled, tossing the vial into the criminals' car, which erupted in a cloud of smoke.

Robin was peeved when the morning paper's headlines announced that Batwoman had saved Batman. "Batman, she's making you look bad!" the Boy Wonder gasped. Batman claimed to not be concerned with his own public image, but for Batwoman's safety. Fighting crime was too dangerous a job for a woman, especially one as reckless and inexperienced as Batwoman.

A few nights later, they cross paths again. A scuffle with a thug leaves Batman knocked out cold. As the goon tries to make a break for it, Batwoman once more reaches into her handbag of tricks. "Lots of woman carry a hairnet, but the one I carry—is a big one—and super-strong! It'll hold you!" Batwoman says, as she ensnares the crook before he can escape. As Batwoman tends to the unconscious Batman, his trusty sidekick enters the room. "Batman, I—oh! Maybe I'm intruding!" the shocked Robin exclaims at the sight of his mentor reclining in the arms of the slinky Batwoman.

"Don't be foolish!" snaps the startled Caped Crusader.

It's 1956. *My Fair Lady*, the story of a woman transformed by a brilliant man, is the huge hit play on Broadway. Hollywood star Grace Kelly's marriage to Prince Rainier of Monaco is like a fairy tale come to life. And there's a new girl in Gotham City. Let Wonder Woman keep her Herculean strength, her bulletproof armbands, and her unbreakable lasso. Batwoman has all she needs to clean up crime in Gotham City right in her little red handbag. With her lipstick, powder, perfume, and hairnet, Batwoman would show the Dynamic Duo a thing or two about how a lady fights crime.

Of all of the condemnations that Dr. Frederic Wertham made against comic books in his 1954 book *Seduction of the Innocent*, perhaps the most scathing were his views on the relationship of Batman and Robin:

> *Only someone ignorant of the fundamentals of psychiatry and of the psychopathology of sex can fail to realize a subtle atmosphere of homoerotism which pervades the adventures of the mature "Batman" and his young friend "Robin"...They are Bruce Wayne and "Dick" Gray-son [sic]. Bruce is described as a "socialite" and the official relationship is that Dick is Bruce's ward. They live in sumptuous quarters, with beautiful flowers in large vases and have a butler, Alfred. Batman is sometimes shown in a dressing gown. It is like a wish dream of two homosexuals living together...Robin is a handsome ephebic boy, usually shown in his uniform with bare legs. He is buoyant with energy and devoted to nothing on earth or in interplanetary space as much as to Bruce Wayne. He often stands with legs spread, the genital region discreetly evident.*

It was one thing for Bruce Wayne, AKA Batman to be considered a homosexual. But the idea that he was perhaps having an improper relationship with his underage partner Robin was shocking. There certainly had been plenty of other strapping male heroes with young boy sidekicks. Why was Batman the one to be "outed"?

Perhaps the suspicions stemmed from the distinct lack of women in Batman's world. True, he crafted his Bruce Wayne alter ego to be an idle playboy, which meant there were a lot of beautiful women in his life. But, the most important female figure in his world seemed only to be his sainted, slain mother, to whose memory, along with that of his late father, Bruce swore to uphold justice and thwart evil. Bruce and Batman might have had romances with girls like debutante Julie Madison or reporter Vicki Vale, but showed neither any true affection. The one female who generated the most heat with Batman was the seductive, whip-wielding jewel thief Catwoman. Of course, since she was on the wrong side of the law, any chance of a romance with Batman was immediately crushed.

In the world of comic book superheroes, romance has always been an ever present and troublesome story element. At least from the male point of view. Like the dwarf Alberich in Wagner's *Ring of the Nibelungen*, male superheroes forfeit love for a loftier treasure: in this case justice. They hide behind masks and secret identities that prevent healthy relationships from ever blossoming. Even if they do find love, many male heroes will let their heart's desire slip through their gloved fingers, because they have dedicated their lives to a cause that's more important than their personal happiness. In the case of Batman, the hero is the real persona, while Bruce Wayne is just the convenient deception that serves a purpose. His fortune funds Batman's war on crime, while his ne'er do well persona erases any suspicion that he is, in fact, the Caped Crusader. Since Bruce Wayne is a front, any of his romances will likewise just be hollow, and put on purely for show.

Female superheroes are another story. Comic book writers often suggest that women don't have that same dedication to the noble cause, because their need for love is often of equal or greater importance than their quest for justice. Superheroines want to fight crime, but want to to settle down as well. If Mr. Right popped the question, a heroine could easily retire that mask and cape and settle down to a life as wife and mother. The implication is that no matter how powerful a woman is, she needs the love of a man to complete her.

Male heroes were given female partners for two reasons: they provided sex appeal for male readers, and romantic storylines to attract girls. But this romance angle also proved that these superheroes were all-American, heterosexual men, who just happened to be gadding about in colorful tights. But no lady crime fighting partners dwelled in Batman's night-dark, all-male world. There was only loyal Robin, who served as helper, confidant, and best pal. This formula worked for years, and Batman's comic was a steady seller. He didn't need a gorgeous girl to parade through his pages in order to sell copies, the way other suffering postwar superheroes did. Batman sailed into the '50s with his popularity intact, but his reputation under attack.

Wertham's book and the Senate Subcommittee on Juvenile Delinquency hearings that followed cast a pall over comic books. In order to avoid government regulation, the comic book publishers created the Comics Code Authority, a ratings code by which the industry would police itself, and produce sanitized fare for impressionable youngsters. The Code's rules about subject matter, violence, and sexuality were the nails in the coffin for sensational and prurient crime and horror comics. Sexy, half-clad women had starred in titles like *Crimes by Women*, *Reform School Girl*, and *Women Outlaws*, and had been heavily featured on the covers of superhero, crime and horror comics. But with the Code's clean up, women had to be drawn "realistically," and as a result, many simply disappeared from comic books. Batman's sexy foe Catwoman was deemed too racy for the new world of the Comics Code. She was gone by 1954.

With their comics still being published but their relationship in question, Batman and Robin needed to clean up their act. And what could be more wholesome than a dog? In 1955, readers met the first member of what would be called the Batman Family—Ace, the Bat-Hound. Ace was a German shepherd that Batman and Robin rescued from a river. When he jumped in the Batmobile and insisted on accompanying the Dynamic Duo on their missions, they slapped a mask on him and made the pooch a member of the team. But as cute as Ace may have been, he was just another boy lifting his leg in the Batcave.

The following year would bring bigger changes to Batman's male-centric world. 1956 saw the debut of the Batwoman. Kathy Kane was a circus aerialist and motorcycle stunt rider who inherited a vast fortune from her uncle. Kathy idolizes Batman, and so she decides to use her newfound wealth to finance a career as a crime fighter. She moves to Gotham City, where much like Bruce Wayne, she creates the persona of a bored heiress. Her new society friends have no idea that the new girl in town had once been a circus daredevil. Meanwhile, Kathy secretly builds a Batcave of her own under her mansion, complete with a laboratory for solving crimes. Filling her shoulder bag with a variety of "feminized" weapons like a lipstick, compact, and perfume, Batwoman roars off on her red motorcycle to fight crime.

With her flowing black hair and red lips, Batwoman and her alter ego Kathy Kane had a certain movie star allure. But while Batwoman may have modeled herself after Batman, she obviously didn't take any cues from him in the costume department. Bruce Wayne created Batman as a dark creature of the night that would strike fear into the hearts of evildoers. Batwoman's look was not frightening at all—a satiny yellow leotard with a long red cape that was neither sexy nor intimidating. Unlike alluring heroines like Phantom Lady and Black Cat who had fought crime in comics a decade before, Batwoman's fashion sense was very modest, and complied with the Comics Code. No cleavage or bare midriff for this girl. Her costume featured a prim collar and little buttons down the front, along with a large pointed mask that looked like the ears of a bat. To complete the ladylike look, there was the shoulder bag, which held Batwoman's arsenal of cosmetic weapons. The whole effect was matronly rather than menacing.

Batwoman would learn that her greatest obstacle to bringing justice to Gotham City would not be the nefarious criminals of its underworld, but her idol, Batman. She was not exactly welcomed into the Batcave with open arms. When the caped twosome meet, Batman tells Batwoman that crime fighting is too dangerous for a woman. The pompous Batman assumes that there was no way a woman could possibly succeed at fighting crime the way he has. Explaining to his little crony Robin why Batwoman needs to hang up her cape, Batman spouts off, "She doesn't realize that she's been successful thus far because of *good luck*! And she's so reckless that some criminal is bound to find out her secret identity. Then, when that happens, she'll be in bad danger!" The plucky Batwoman proves Batman wrong time after time, even saving him from danger a number of times. But Batman has to have the final word. He uses his keen detective skills to figure out that Batwoman is actually socialite Kathy Kane. Confronting Batwoman in her secret lair, Batman and Robin demand that she call it quits. "Listen Kathy— if I found out, crooks could do it too, eventually!" Batman tells the would-be heroine. Batman has been ingenious in protecting his own secret identity over the years, but the implication is that a woman would not be as clever to safeguard her own. Batman gets his way, and Batwoman throws in the towel.

For a while, at least. Situations kept arising that called for Kathy to get the old Batwoman cape and mask out of her hope chest. But even when she was back in action, Batwoman was not ever really part of the Batman and Robin team. They never took her into their confidence, and she was used merely as a pawn in one or another of Batman's schemes to catch a crook. ". . . It was fun while it lasted . . . but it looks like the Batwoman is going back into retirement again!" Kathy would say with a deep sigh, folding up her costume to stick away in a drawer, along with her dreams. Batwoman was the product of an era that discouraged women from pursuing careers in favor of staying home and acting like a lady. With his patronizing attitude, this was an era that Batman was apparently well suited for.

The irony is that Batwoman had been introduced to be a love interest for Batman, in order to make him look more heterosexual. But it took quite a while for the romance to get off the ground. Apparently, Batman shared that same "girls are icky" opinion of most of his young male readers. It seemed that having Robin and the revered memory of his murdered parents in his life left little room for love. In their daytime alter egos of Bruce Wayne and Kathy Kane, Batman and Batwoman shared a tepid attraction. Kathy is unaware that her country club beau Bruce is in actuality her idol, Batman, and chides the playboy for not being more like the Caped Crusader. "*Sigh* I wish you could be more like him, Bruce!" Kathy remarks, as Bruce shares a knowing smirk with the reader. Batman has orchestrated a situation where he is always in charge, and he can manipulate everyone in his circle to perpetuate his falsehoods.

The turning point came in 1957's "The Super Batwoman." The heroine inadvertently ingests a capsule that gives her incredible powers like Superman for twenty-four hours. When Batman tells Batwoman to go home and wait for the powers to wear off, she turns on him. "Batman, I'm tired of your bossing me! Just because you found out my identity, you think you're superior and keep lecturing me!" Batwoman declares that she will use her new powers to learn the secret identities of not only Batman and Robin, but their buddy Superman as well. Exposure was always the trump card that women held to bend these heroes to their wills. The men of this era lived in fear that the women in their lives would learn their secret identities, bringing an end to their fun. The implication was that with this knowledge, the women would be in control, and force the heroes to settle down and get married. In Batwoman's case, it was an act of desperation to regain her own freedom. "I'm going to find out your secret identities! I won't tell anyone, but that'll keep you from bossing me!"

In the course of trying to expose the three heroes, Batwoman uses her new fantastic powers to avert a number of disasters. "It's wonderful to have super-strength!" an airborne and liberated Batwoman gushes as she saves a small town from an avalanche. The now invincible Batwoman fearlessly follows Superman through raging thunderstorms, and even over Niagara Falls in order to learn his secret identity. But the wily Superman foils Batwoman's schemes by leading her to an old, abandoned house. Naturally, she is shown as a squeamish female, despite the fact that she is now indestructible. "There are *mice* in this old house—I can't go in here!" Batwoman shrieks, recoiling in horror. In the end, the men outwit Batwoman, whose powers fade away before she can learn their secrets. But, Batman and Superman throw Batwoman a bone. "You showed such cleverness and courage that I can't ask you to drop your career completely. Just be careful!" A grateful Batwoman is relieved that Big Daddy Batman has finally allowed her to play with the boys.

But life as a heroine still is no walk in the park for Batwoman. Even though Batman sanctions Batwoman's crime fighting activities, he continues to lord it over her, treating her more as an annoyance than a valued partner. Batman certainly wasn't teaching Robin about a woman's value, and a young male reader following their adventures during the late 1950s would also come away with the impression that women were completely inept creatures. The staunchly sexist Batman constantly bullies Batwoman with his insistence that woman are not cut out to fight crime. Batman shows more faith in Ace, the Bat-Hound than in Batwoman. To her credit, Batwoman displays an unflappable spirit that refuses to be squelched by Batman's nonstop belittling. Like an abused wife, Batwoman takes the verbal battering and defamation, and still keeps coming back for more. Batwoman's role in life is to help her idol Batman, no matter how much he puts her down.

While Batwoman was far from becoming Mrs. Batman, it seemed as though her mere presence was all that was needed to dispel any gay speculation. There certainly wasn't much of a romance going on, and the skewed relationship that Batman and Batwoman had surely was not a foundation for a great love affair. But by the late 1950s, Batwoman's admiration for the domineering Batman inexplicably turns from admiration to love. Batwoman's feelings are shown to be just one more of her weaknesses, and one more hindrance to her ability to fight crime. Batman, as expected, is impervious to any emotional attachment, except, perhaps, to Robin. The underlying message was that men were strong enough to be in control of their emotions, but even a powerful woman still needed love. Things change when the Bat-duo take off their masks. The romantic situation is reversed in their alter ego lives, where

Kathy Kane continues to see Bruce Wayne socially, but feels that he is not her type. Bruce Wayne, meanwhile, is so proud of himself for constructing a multitude of complex ruses and falsehoods that he can't see past it. "Kathy doesn't know that I'm Batman, and that I know she's Batwoman." Presumably that self-congratulation kept him warm at night.

The romantic stalemate is broken in 1962's "Prisoners of Three Worlds," one of the weird science fiction adventures that Batman was regularly featured in. In this story, Batman and Batwoman are transported to a hostile alien planet. As they face imminent death, Batwoman breaks down, "Hold me close! If I must die, I want it to be in your arms! Oh, Batman, you know I love you—dying wouldn't be so bad, if I knew you loved me too . . ." The icily stoic Batman finally thaws as he admits, "I—I *do* love you! I never wanted to admit it before . . ." The couple finally shares a passionate kiss. Once the twosome is safely back on Earth, though, Batman freaks out. "*Whew* I've always managed to escape death traps . . . all kinds of danger! But how do I get out of this?" Love was seemingly a fate worse than death. Batman quickly tells Batwoman that he only confessed his love to make her "last moments happy ones."

"Hmm . . . I wonder . . ." thinks a skeptical Batwoman, not certain whether she has just been dumped.

Batman kept his romance with Batwoman in perpetual limbo, to retain his freedom, while also looking more heterosexual. His best buddy Superman didn't have the same image problems.

After all, Lois Lane was part of the Superman dynamic from the very start. The intrepid star newspaper reporter had made her first appearance in 1938's *Action Comics* #1, the same issue where Superman made his debut. She was infatuated with the powerful, godlike Superman, while repulsed by his meek pantywaist alter ego, her rival reporter Clark Kent. Lois' 1940s persona of tough crusading reporter was in the mold of Hollywood dames like Rosalind Russell. Lois' tireless effort to get her next headline, along with her impulsive personality, often put her in danger, from which Superman would have to rescue her. But the 40s Lois was no pushover. She was a modern career woman, and her dream was to get her greatest scoop: Superman's secret identity.

The Superman/Lois Lane relationship had many complicated factors that would prevent a romance from ever reaching fruition, while still providing the right tension to sustain the relationship for decades. First off, they were literally from different worlds. Superman was the last survivor of the doomed planet Krypton, and was raised by simple midwestern farm folk. Lois Lane was very much a woman of 20th century America: emancipated, headstrong, and unwilling to take "no" for an answer. Superman's timid farm boy Clark Kent persona crumbled before Lois' ferocious, emasculating temperament, while his heroic Man of Steel found himself constantly confounded by her impetuous nature.

Meanwhile, the very issue of Superman's secret identity always threw a wrench into his romance with Lois. Besides the basic duplicity, Superman becomes his own rival, squelching any chance for a healthy relationship. Superman loves Lois Lane, but tries to win her heart as meek Clark Kent, with the rationale that he wants to be sure Lois really loves him for himself, not for his glamorous superhuman persona. But since he's created a wallflower persona that Lois will never find attractive, he sabotages any chance for love. Lois, for her part, is enamored with Superman, yet has a burning desire to discover his secret identity. Lois never considers that she risks losing Superman's love if she learns his secret identity, or that the world may lose its champion and protector.

In the postwar years, the popular image of the American female was one of a woman devoted to her home and family, and not a career. Movies portrayed the successful career woman as lonely and bitter, compensating for the emptiness in her life with driving ambition. In the 1950 film *All About Eve*, Bette Davis' acid-tongued Margo Channing, a stage actress in her forties, reflected that all of the fame, success, and accolades that a successful career woman can garner merely amounted to nothing without a man to love her. "It's one career all females have in common whether we like it or not—being a woman. Sooner or later we've got to work at it, no matter how many other careers we've had or wanted." And so in the '50s, Lois Lane's career ambitions cooled off as well. She is still a feisty reporter, but her thirst for a scoop seems more driven by her desire to upstage the nebbish Clark Kent at every turn. Now Lois' true ambition is to become Mrs. Superman. No longer a longhaired beauty in daring hats and shoulder pads, the '50s Lois wears a pert beauty shop hairstyle, prim suits or shirtwaist dresses, always complete with white gloves.

If the Lois Lane of the '40s owed much to the tough talking

heroines of that decade's screwball comedies, the Lois of the '50s was defined by the medium of the new era—television. Superman had made the transition from movie serial to the small screen in 1953, which kept his legend alive during the years that superhero comics were on the wane. The TV Lois Lane was played as an adoring damsel in distress, often trussed up in a chair or tied to railroad tracks. But if the Lois Lane of the comic books resembled anyone from the early days of television, it would be Lucille Ball, queen of the new medium. Ball played the crafty, yet often misdirected Lucy Ricardo on the popular series *I Love Lucy*, the first TV show with a woman as its star. Lucy was wily and ambitious, often getting herself into outrageous situations in an effort to finagle her way into her husband Ricky's nightclub act. Played by Ball's real life husband Desi Arnaz, Ricky acted as mate and parent figure, often laying down the law to a misbehaving Lucy to ensure that she didn't get involved in any shenanigans.

Just as Lucy dreamed of breaking into show business, the 1950s Lois was single-minded in her quest to become Mrs. Superman. Her efforts to bag the Man of Steel were chronicled in *Superman's Girl Friend, Lois Lane*, her regular comic book series that began in 1957. The Lois Lane comic was a blend of romance and superhero adventure, no doubt intended to win over the much-coveted female comic book reader. Much like the companion series *Superman's Pal, Jimmy Olsen*, Lois' comic injected more humor into its stories than Superman's own title did. The Lois Lane comic was a twist on the Superman legend, seen from a woman's perspective.

Just as Lucille Ball used physical humor and self-humiliation to get laughs, the writers of Lois' comic embroiled the girl reporter in one harebrained scheme after another in her quest both for a scoop, and to win Superman's love. Over the years, Lois' plotting resulted in a series of fantastic transformations. She becomes a machine gun toting criminal, the leader of a pack of leopards in the jungle, and a water breathing mermaid. She gains x-ray vision, elastic powers, and invisibility. Lois goes to great lengths to keep Superman from learning that her beauty has been defaced when she is accidentally turned into an old woman, an obese woman, or a super-intellect with a bald, lightbulb-shaped cranium. Lois becomes a spy, a convict, a queen, a dictator, and a witch doctor. Just as Lucy's schemes often blow up in her face, the joke is often at Lois' expense. But, like Lucy, Lois is the star of her comic, and she always comes out on top at the end of an adventure. As preposterous as the stories may have been, *Superman's Girl Friend Lois Lane* was a wildly entertaining, cleverly written and beautifully illustrated comic, and its heroine, while often portrayed as irritating, had a genuinely endearing quality.

Lois Lane's comic brought up some interesting questions about the actual romance between the girl reporter and Superman. First off, are they really in love with each other? Lois is clearly obsessed with Superman, but it isn't clear whether she is in love with the man himself, or his legend. Obviously, there is a cachet to being seen with the most famous man in the universe, and, as the title of her comic implied, Lois is known to the world as "Superman's girlfriend." So confident is Lois in her hold on Superman, that she throws herself out of the skyscraper windows of the Daily Planet offices when she wants to talk to him, knowing he will drop whatever he is doing anywhere in the universe to fly to her rescue. Part of the thrill of the relationship, for Lois, seems to be controlling the unbeatable Superman. If she learns his secret identity, she will have him in her power, like Delilah cutting the locks of Samson.

Superman is the last survivor of his race, and perhaps the loneliest man on earth. He craves the companionship of a woman and can have his pick of any of the world's great beauties. When he travels through time, famous sirens like Cleopatra, Helen of Troy and Marie Antoinette all swoon for him. Yet, Superman can't commit to anyone. His excuse for not getting married is that any woman he takes as a wife will be a target for reprisals by his enemies. Duty comes before wedlock, and Superman says that perhaps one day when he retires, he will marry. The only women Superman truly falls in love with and proposes marriage to are those with whom he can have no future, like Lori Lemaris, the lovely mermaid from Atlantis. Since Lori can't survive out of water, there isn't much hope for wedded bliss there. Like Lori, the women that Superman woos—Lyla Lerrol, Luma Lynai—all bear the initials "L.L.", and the romances are always star-crossed.

And then there is Lois Lane. Superman claims to be fond of Lois, yet never truly reveals his feelings. Perhaps it is Lois' tenacious campaign to win his love that ultimately drives Superman away from her. Unlike the docile Batwoman, the 1950s Lois embodied an archetype that was distinct to postwar America: the adult female brat. These were spoiled, willful women who were used to getting whatever they wanted in an age of prosperity, regardless of the consequences. In a 1960 story, Superman gives Lois one of his coveted signal watches for a birthday present. The watch is to be used only in case of dire emergency, but Lois uses it to call Superman when the zipper on her purse gets stuck or when one of the heels on her shoes comes loose.

As flighty as she may have appeared, Lois always attempts to make a good impression on Superman, all the while revealing her worst face to his alter ego, Clark Kent. Clark, who she refers to as a "meek mouse," disgusts Lois and becomes the beleaguered recipient of her contempt. Lois does nothing to disguise her disdain for the timid reporter, while at the same time harboring a strong suspicion that he may secretly be her beloved Superman. Once again, the secret identity destroys any chance that Superman will ever marry Lois after the endless petty humiliations that he has experienced at her hands as Clark.

Perhaps it is seeing this ugly side of Lois' personality that brings out the worst in Superman himself. In his own comic, Superman is a staunch hero who is even-tempered and just. In Lois Lane's comic, Superman is shown as a man at his wit's end, driven at times to cruelty by her machinations. Lois' insatiable inquisitiveness transforms Superman into a controlling father figure who must concoct elaborate ruses to teach the reporter to mind her own business. Like Pandora of myth, snoopy Lois can't resist handling the mysterious objects from space that Superman warns her not to touch. When exposure to the objects gives Lois deadly Green Kryptonite vision, Superman lashes out, "You little idiot! I warned you to keep hands off! Now, you're a menace to my life! Go far away! Get lost!!" Lois isn't always aware of Superman's tricks meant to teach her a lesson, but when she does learn the truth, she becomes a tigress. In a 1963 story, Superman tricks Lois into thinking she has sold her soul to Satan himself in order to get married. When the wedding day arrives, and the wily Lois reveals that she has seen through Superman's deception, she tosses her bouquet in his face, shouting "Marry a cad who would play a shabby trick like that? Not on your life..." Later, however, Lois dreamily gazes at a photo of the Man of Steel and thinks, "The lovable idiot meant it for my own good!"

Because Lois is so intent on marrying Superman, any woman who catches his eye becomes her rival. Even Superman's young cousin Supergirl is a threat to Lois. In one imaginary story from 1960, Lois and Superman marry, and adopt Supergirl. On the cover, Lois is cast aside like an old shoe, as the super cousins are shown happily entwined in what looks to be more than just a familial embrace. "Superman and Supergirl are so excited, they've practically forgotten about *me*!" thinks Lois, once a glamorous reporter, now a housewife knitting in an armchair. "But I don't mind . . . *choke* . . . I love them *both*!" The idea that a man would grow tired of his wife and push her aside for a more sparkling younger woman played into a married woman's most basic fears.

By far Lois' greatest threat is Lana Lang, a gorgeous redhead who was the Man of Steel's high school sweetheart, when he was known as Superboy. Lana hosts a TV show called *I Remember Superboy*, and is equally obsessed with becoming Mrs. Superman.

Lois and Lana are both rivals and best friends. The two women stop at nothing to undermine each other's attempts to charm Superman into a proposal. Although both claim to adore Superman, he doubts whether either Lois or Lana really loves him for himself. In 1963's "The Girl Who Refused to Marry Superman," the Man of Steel loses his powers after exposure to Red Kryptonite. As an injured and partially blind Superman lies in his hospital bed, Lois and Lana discuss the future. One girl swears she would love Superman "even if he were deaf, dumb, and blind," while the other declares that she was "always in love with the super-hero, not the man beneath the costume." Since he can't see clearly, Superman never knows which woman truly loves him. In the end, it all turns out to be a hallucination caused by the effects of Red Kryptonite, but the story shows how Superman, invincible as he might be, was still susceptible to the angst that was gripping the world of the 1960s, as it grappled with the uncertainty of the Cold War. Here is a man who can withstand an atomic explosion or fly into the heart of the sun, but is plagued with doubt about the two women who claim to love him the most.

Occasionally, Lois and Lana are able to ascend to Superman's level, when some twist of fate gave them superpowers. While the girls use their new abilities to do good deeds, they also take their rivalry to a whole new level. Super-Lois and Super-Lana know that if they are invincible, Superman might marry one of them, so they set out to prove which would make a better super-wife. Super-Lana bakes a giant pizza for Superman with her x-ray vision, while Super-Lois squeezes maple syrup out of trees with her bare hands to accompany the ton of flapjacks that she whips up to impress him. Even when gifted with godly powers, Lois and Lana don't attempt to transcend the traditional female homemaker roles that society has placed them in.

Lois is said to be in her twenties, but there is a real sense that the clock is ticking. As much as she wants to marry Superman, she doesn't want to put all her eggs in one basket. Millionaires and sultans all throw themselves at Lois' feet. She travels through time and is courted by Samson, Hercules, and Robin Hood. In the end, she turns down the all of these offers of love, because none of these swains can make her forget Superman. But Lois' need to feel desired is strong. And the thing that is stronger than her love for Superman is her pride. In 1960, when the handsome silver haired superhero Astounding Man meets Lois and lavishes her with affection, she can't help but give in. "I've come to my senses! Superman doesn't want me! But you do, and you're just as handsome, and super, as he is! I want you!" When Lois meets the love struck alien X-Plam, he has hideous blue features and antennae, but exposure to Earth's atmosphere transforms him into a dreamboat. More horrified at the prospect of winding up an old maid than married to an alien male, Lois consoles herself with bitter thoughts, "I've turned down every proposal of marriage, hoping Superman would marry me some day! Once and for all, I'll show Superman I won't die of a bleeding heart because he never returned my love." All of Lois' courtships end unhappily, and she always winds up back in the arms of Superman, who is more than happy to pawn her off on some other unfortunate hero. Lois' actions suggest she is nothing more than a superhero groupie, so it should be no surprise that Superman doubts her love.

With both Batman and Superman's romances, the presumably young comic book reader got a strange and skewed message about male/female relationships. These men were the hunters in their "professional" lives, but were prey in their personal lives. Both Batman and Superman seem perfectly happy with their lives as bachelors, while Batwoman and Lois Lane each want to force their respective heroes into roles that the men are uncomfortable with. Batwoman's goals are modest: she wants Batman to respect her and admit his love for her. Lois is more ambitious: she wants to tame a god, and have him home for dinner every night.

The most telling visions of marital bliss are the "imaginary stories" which offered readers a glimpse into future events that may or may not happen. In a 1959 story, Robin dreams that Batman's alter ego Bruce Wayne marries Batwoman Kathy Kane. The bride refuses to give up fighting crime, and when hoodlums expose her secret identity, she is seen as the cause of her husband Batman's downfall. "You've wrecked Batman's career! And it's all your fault because you wouldn't listen!" cries a distraught Robin.

Lois Lane fares no better, as her imaginary stories of wedlock end miserably. When Lois becomes Mrs. Superman, she faces a lonely existence trapped within her husband's Fortress of Solitude, or as a bedraggled mother of mischievous super-offspring. When she must masquerade as Mrs. Clark Kent, she seethes with jealousy, because the world at large still thinks Superman is the world's ultimate bachelor. Her rival Lana Lang faces an equally bleak fate. In a 1961 imaginary story, Superman marries Lana and gives her a serum that grants her superpowers. Since Lana is not from the planet Krypton, she is not harmed by Kryptonite, and essentially is stronger than Superman! Because of this, Lana is a threat to her husband's reputation, and in the end, she leaves him lest her superior powers belittle his legend. "I won't have people saying that Mrs. Superman has to protect her husband!" Lana says, as she flies off to another galaxy, suitcase in hand. A shattered Superman obeys Lana's plea not to follow her, thinking, "In time, our love would have been destroyed by her pity for me! How can I be her hero when she's mightier than I am? . . . *choke!* . . ." How, indeed? The real future would hold more interesting twists of fate than these imaginary stories.

When the sales of Batman's comics dropped in 1964, DC Comics editor Julius Schwartz decided that the Caped Crusader needed to move away from outlandish science fiction adventures and get back to his detective roots. Despite the fact that many readers liked her, Batwoman was unceremoniously eliminated, as though she had never existed. 1964 brought readers the "New Look" Batman, with a move away from the signature, archaic art style, an updated costume, and a return to earthbound crime stories.

As for Lois Lane, she continued to display her survivor's instincts. After all, she had been around since 1938. Thirty years after she made her debut, readers saw a change in Lois' temperament, and perhaps a return to her original personality. A 1968 issue showed a mod Lois in miniskirt and boots tearing the "Girl Friend" off of the cover of the comic, and telling a shocked

Superman that they are through. In the years that follow, Lois, tired of waiting for Superman to marry her, embraces women's liberation and becomes more independent. Along with her new sexy wardrobe of hot pants and fishnet stockings, Lois displayed a new "take it or leave it" attitude towards Superman. It seemed to do the trick, because as the '60s waned, Superman actually started acting affectionately towards Lois, even going so far as calling her "honey."

As comic books made an effort to become more relevant in the '70s, Lois once more became a crusading journalist, and underwent perhaps her most amazing transformation. In a 1970 story provocatively entitled "I Am Curious (Black)," Lois attempts to infiltrate "Little Africa," the black ghetto of Metropolis, in order to write a hard-hitting exposé. When she encounters resistance from the community, Lois asks Superman for help, and he uses a Kryptonian device to transform the reporter into a black woman for twenty-four hours. After experiencing firsthand the struggles of being black and underprivileged, Lois, clad in an African blouse and sporting an Afro, tests Superman's love with a tough question. "Suppose I couldn't change back? Would you marry me? Even if I'm black? An outsider in a white man's world?" Superman never has to reveal whether he was racist or not, because the effects of the machine wear off at that moment, and Lois goes back to being Caucasian.

Superman's Girl Friend, Lois Lane came to an end in 1974, after a seventeen-year print run. This was an amazing accomplishment for an industry that historically does not support a comic book starring a woman. Only Wonder Woman had headlined her own comic book for a longer time. A scan of the letters pages in Lois Lane's comics show that her readers were a balance of males and females. Lois continued to play a featured part in Superman's comic books, and got a starring role in 1979 when the Man of Steel flew onto the big screen. That same year Batwoman was tragically killed off, having been brought out of the mothballs two years earlier for a few guest appearances.

Batwoman and Lois Lane may not have been feminist firebrands in the '50s, but they did keep the fires alive for heroines throughout that era. At the time, DC Comics' official Editorial Policy Code addressed the presentation of women in this way—

> *The inclusion of females in stories is specifically discouraged. Women, when used in plot structure, should be secondary in importance ...*

At a time when the only strong female seen in comic books was Wonder Woman, Batwoman and Lois Lane gave young readers another glimpse of gutsy, oftentimes independent women. They may have both bowed to the whims of the men in their lives, but these "girlfriends" persevered through the '50s until Supergirl's arrival in 1959 ushered in a new era of heroines.

In 2006, a new Batwoman made her debut. Like her predecessor, she is a beautiful heiress who dresses up in a skintight costume, high-heeled boots, and a pointed mask to battle crime in Gotham City. But while she may prove to be a valued ally for Batman, he never needs to worry that the new Batwoman will want to become his wife. The new Batwoman is a lesbian.

Supergirl and the Ballad of American Youth

Lesley Gore was a good girl. Or that's what her record company wanted young America to think. A pretty white girl from New Jersey with a good voice, she became the most successful solo singer during the girl group era of the early 1960s. She was the ideal pop star that parents would approve of. Her songs evoked images of a world of well-behaved sons and daughters, who attended good high schools, lived on streets with freshly mown lawns, and attended dances where young ladies wore wrist corsages.

In the pantheon of the comic book heroes, Supergirl was a good girl too, perhaps the best girl in the universe. In the early 1960s, Supergirl was DC Comics' pop princess. She was the ideal teenager of her day: pretty, perky, courageous, and obedient. The freshly scrubbed pop stars who belted out their hits on *American Bandstand* represented the best of American youth, and Supergirl embodied the perfect American *Überteen*. Her comics were light and frothy as a parfait to appeal to girl readers, while also filled with enough superheroics to keep boys interested. With her good manners and selfless heroism, Supergirl was also a role model for the kind of teenager that girls were supposed to grow up to be.

Lesley Gore passed away in 2015, bringing to a close a singing career that spanned more than forty years. Though in later years she was a songwriter and activist, Gore will always be remembered as the ideal American teen singer of the early 1960s.

Five decades after her debut, Supergirl is *still* a teenage girl, and meant to represent the perfect adolescent heroine. Pop stars like Lesley Gore are meant to epitomize their era. But has Supergirl truly personified the typical American teenager of her time?

When Superman proved to be a hit in the early days of comic books, DC Comics looked for new ways to cash in on his popularity. By 1944, DC began publishing the adventures of Superboy: Superman when he was a teenager. Several stories throughout the 1940s and 1950s featured Superman's reporter girlfriend Lois Lane gaining great powers and donning the costume of Superwoman. Lois always wound up losing her powers, settling back down behind her typewriter to focus on her next scoop. But DC Comics had trademarked the name Supergirl with the idea of someday doing a female version of the Man of Steel.

By the late 1950s, superhero comics had begun to rebound with newfound popularity after a post World War II slump. Superman and Superboy were still selling issues, and effort was underway to expand the Superman franchise further. Superboy already had Krypto the Superdog, so a female was the logical choice.

DC decided to give readers a taste of female power in 1958. Superman's pal, freckle-faced cub reporter Jimmy Olsen, finds a magical Indian totem that holds the power to grant wishes. Jimmy wishes that his best friend and idol Superman had a super helper, and a gorgeous blonde appears in a puff of smoke, wearing a duplicate of Superman's costume, but with a short flaring skirt. Super-Girl is pretty, powerful, and virtuous, but, because she is a magical manifestation, has no real personality to speak of. Super-Girl's primary goal is to be of aid to the Man of Steel, but lacking life experience or, presumably, common sense, she impulsively flies into danger, causing more damage than good. In the end, Super-Girl sacrifices her life to save Superman from deadly Green Kryptonite. As her life forces ebb, she begs Jimmy to wish her back to the magical ether from whence she came. Super-Girl fades away, as did the prospect of a super mate for Superman.

Although her name may not have implied it, the first Super-Girl was an adult woman, much to the chagrin of perpetually jealous Lois Lane. "What chance have I anymore with Super-Girl around? They'll fall in love and get married . . . *choke*!" thinks the crestfallen reporter. A Superwoman would have seemed the logical mate for the Man of Steel, and would have destroyed the ongoing tension of the Superman/Lois Lane/Clark Kent love triangle. At the time, Wonder Woman's comic book was not exactly flying off the stands, as DC struggled to retool their strong Amazon princess' image for more conservative times. The Super-Girl story was meant to test readers' reaction to a female joining the Kryptonian clan. The response was favorable. An adult Superwoman may have been too threatening to young readers, and perhaps to Superman himself. So, a teenage girl with a demure persona became a better choice.

So, in 1959, Superman met the hyphen-less "Supergirl from Krypton." Superman investigates a mysterious rocket ship that has crashed to Earth, only to encounter a pretty blonde teen flying out from the wrecked spacecraft. Mysteriously, she wears a matching version of his costume, although hers features an ice skating skirt. Her name is Kara, and like Superman and Krypto the Superdog, she is yet another survivor of the doomed planet Krypton. She recounts how, when Krypton exploded, a large chunk of the planet remained intact. On this planetoid was Argo City, where Kara was later born. The residents of Argo City erected a huge dome to protect their home from the ravages of outer space. When a shower of deadly Kryptonite meteors threatened to destroy the domed city, Kara's father built a small rocket to carry his now teenaged daughter to Earth. Having observed Superman on the family's space telescope and deducing that he was a fellow Kryptonian, Kara's mother made a feminine version of his costume for her daughter. After comparing family histories, the super duo realizes that they are actually cousins! They happily fall into one another's arms. "We may be orphans, but we have each other now." says Superman, as his little tearful cousin clutches his mighty chest, "I'll take care of you like a big brother, Cousin Kara!"

While most of Lesley Gore's hits were songs of teenage heartbreak and longing, the anomaly in her discography is 1964's "You Don't Own Me," now considered to be an early feminist anthem. The song is the voice of an independent girl who doesn't want to be held back by her boyfriend, or to have him tell her what to do. She wants to be free to speak her mind, go out with other guys, and to not be treated like a possession.

"You Don't Own Me" was not Supergirl's theme song. A parental status quo is set up as soon as she arrives on Earth. Superman establishes the rules, and Supergirl has to abide by them. When a tearful Supergirl asks, "You mean I'll come live with you?" her dreams of a happy new home are dashed by her big cousin's response. Superman is concerned a little girl cousin will jeopardize his secret identity, so he has other plans. Rather than offer her the kind of loving home he found when arriving on Earth, Superman creates the alter ego of Linda Lee for his cousin, and deposits her in an orphanage while she learns how to use her powers.

Sporting a mousy brown wig with braids and drab plaid jumpers, Linda becomes the female equivalent of Superman's Clark Kent persona—shy, smart, and unloved. Supergirl becomes Superman's secret weapon, her existence hidden from the world until he decides otherwise. Like some heroine from a Victorian novel, Supergirl's fate is in the hands of her adult guardian. She is the obedient and dutiful daughter who does what she is told and stays out of sight. Beginning in 1959, her solo adventures became a regular feature in *Action Comics*, the title that had introduced her cousin to the world in 1938.

1963 was a big year for both Lesley Gore and Supergirl. Sixteen year-old Lesley had her first #1 hit with "It's My Party"—and Supergirl had her own Sweet Sixteen party. Feeling his young cousin isn't an impetuous kid any longer, Superman decides that it is time for the world to meet Supergirl. The cover of *Action Comics# 285* shows the Kryptonian cousins flying through the skies of Metropolis amidst a shower of streamers and confetti as throngs below cheer. Supergirl, now the ultimate homecoming queen, clutches a bouquet of flowers as she greets her new adoring public. She is presented to the United Nations, but that can't compare to the thrill of meeting

Jackie Kennedy. "The president's wife is gorgeous," Supergirl thinks, as she meets the First Family on the White House lawn. By the following year, President John F. Kennedy would be killed in the real world, and this seemingly innocent era in which Supergirl and Lesley Gore reigned as princesses would begin to wane.

Despite her newcomer status, Supergirl is now hailed as the "world's greatest heroine," pushing Wonder Woman further into a dark corner. Cute and perky Supergirl becomes the sweetheart of the world, the idol of millions, and the luckiest girl in the universe. She is the cuter blonde version of Superman, able to do almost all of his same incredible feats, but in a skirt. She travels through time and space and plunges into the heart of the sun. She is the Girl of Steel, the Maid of Might, the Teen of Steel. Supergirl is invited to join the Legion of Superheroes, the ultra-exclusive 30th century honor society for super teenagers from across the galaxy. She even has super pets—a kooky orange Supercat named Streaky, and every teenage girl's dream, a snow-white telepathic super horse named Comet.

All the while, Supergirl maintains the same unpretentious persona that everyone loves. She is a girl, not a woman, and therein lies the secret of her appeal. Supergirl isn't a threatening Superwoman who might develop ideas of her own. She is the sweet kid sister who can withstand an atomic explosion, appropriately decorous in form and nature to meet the standards of the Comics Code Authority. Supergirl uses her powers for good, and never for selfish purposes as a normal teenager might have. It should come as no surprise that Supergirl was the brainchild of Otto Binder, who seventeen years earlier had created Mary Marvel, the original virgin princess superheroine.

Superman was sent to Earth as a baby, and so all he ever knew was growing up in American, Christian society. Supergirl lived in futuristic Argo City until she was a teenager, and should have had a harder time fitting into a world that she would have found foreign and primitive. But if this was the case, Supergirl buried her true feelings like the good girl she was. When a nice suburban couple adopts Supergirl's alter ego Linda, she settles into the ideal life of a Camelot era suburban teenager. Now sporting a more stylish pageboy wig and a smart coed wardrobe, Linda's new life becomes a swirl of high school dances and beach parties. While she is less of a wallflower now, the earthbound brunette Linda still lives in the shadow of her alter ego, the stunning blonde Supergirl. Linda is the girl readers could relate to; Supergirl is the girl they could aspire to be.

"Sometimes I Wish I Were a Boy," sang Lesley Gore in 1964, frustrated by the rules which a proper young lady had to follow in polite society. While the character of Supergirl, the standard bearer of the good daughter archetype, seemed beyond reproach, writers seemed to love the chance to show that she was a wild, rebellious female at heart. Superman is often shown as a harsh authoritarian parent whose disappointment with surrogate daughter Supergirl results in more than just revoking TV watching privileges. Apparently, Supergirl held a grudge, because in several stories, Superman finds out firsthand how much sharper than a serpent's tooth it is to have a thankless child. Supergirl is a super "kitten with a whip," turning on her cousin, exposing his secret identity to the world, or even kicking him out of his Fortress of Solitude. In 1965's bizarre "The Black Magic of Supergirl," the Girl of Steel falls under the sway of a demonic "Satan ring." Before she knows it, Supergirl has sprouted horns and is stirring a bubbling cauldron with a pitchfork. "I can't help myself! Even though I'm fighting it, I must obey the compulsion to do fiendish deeds," she laments. In the end, all of these betrayals conveniently turn out to be the result of amnesia, magic, or an imposter. Supergirl is never consciously liable for her bad-girl actions, but gets to enjoy the temporary thrills of being a fallen teen angel—the safest form of rebellion.

In her day, Supergirl was the most powerful female in the comic books, outclassing even Wonder Woman in sheer power. But since these were stories written to appeal to young girls, adventures often focused less on adventure, and more on a quest to find love. While the wartime Mary Marvel tirelessly helped those in need, the Camelot era Supergirl of the early 1960s balanced performing super feats with an ongoing quest for a dream date. But, romance was something that was handled in an interesting manner with Supergirl. Superman tries to win over Lois Lane as meek Clark Kent, while rejecting her as Superman. Supergirl is different. Supergirl and Linda are essentially treated as two separate personalities, both looking for love independently. As Linda, she dates Dick Malverne, a nice human boy with a flattop and a cardigan sweater, while Supergirl dates more exotic fellows like the Atlantean teenager Jerro the Merboy or Brainiac 5, the green-skinned super intellect of the Legion of Superheroes. Naturally, the duality of Supergirl and Linda's identities foils any chance of these relationships developing into real romances.

Supergirl's strangest romance is with Bronco Bill, a handsome singing cowboy who she meets while vacationing at a dude ranch as

Linda. The two fall in love, but Bronco Bill is keeping a secret from Supergirl: he is in reality Comet, her Superhorse! Comet was actually a centaur from ancient times that had been inadvertently transformed into a horse by the legendary sorceress Circe. To make up for her blunder, Circe made the white stallion immortal, indestructible, and telepathic. A comet passing through the solar system can temporarily change the steed into a human. This makes it very convenient for Comet, as Bronco Bill, to woo his mistress, with whom he has secretly fallen in love. Eventually the celestial enchantment wears off, and Bronco Bill reverts back to his equine form. Supergirl is crushed that her cowboy beau has seemingly vanished without a word of goodbye, and cries on the shoulder of her faithful pet, Comet. Comet gives Supergirl some telepathic words of comfort, never revealing the bizarre love tryst that the two briefly shared. For as wholesome as DC Comics were at the time, there was something disturbing about this entire scenario.

With Supergirl, there was a distinct emphasis on marriage and settling down, even though she was only a teenage girl. This made sense, since pop music of the '60s always had young girls dreaming of taking a walk down the aisle, and romance comics were rife with stories of high school age girls getting engaged after the first date with a new beau. In a bizarre 1969 story, Supergirl uses a computer to find her ideal mate, decades before Internet dating services. The computer sends Supergirl to the distant planet Torma to meet its local superhero, a cute teen named Volar. While he is indifferent to her, Supergirl is attracted to Volar, although something about his mannerisms makes her suspicious. Things go sour when Supergirl finds out that Volar is actually a girl in disguise. Sexism is rampant on the planet Torma, so "Volar" adopted man drag in order to be a superhero. "I'm heading back to Earth—where I belong! I found out Volar was no hit—but a real miss!" thinks a teary-eyed Supergirl as she flies home, not ready to test the waters of Sapphic love.

A strange schizophrenia emerges from this manhunt for a mate. Girl-next-door Linda longs for love but is usually overlooked, and her life becomes the stuff of pop songs: loneliness, tear stained pillows, and sad diary entries. Meanwhile, her stunning alter ego Supergirl also searches for her true love, and can potentially have her pick of any guy in the galaxy. However, the heroine ultimately forsakes any real potential romance because of her devotion to the most important man in her life—Superman. Supergirl's first responsibility is to support Superman in his good works. Should anything ever happen to Superman, Supergirl will be the one to take his place. Imaginary stories showed a future where an adult Superwoman would replace a geriatric Superman, but in the meantime, the Maid of Might was in no hurry to spread her wings. The middle-aged writers and artists who created Supergirl's stories portrayed her as the ideal submissive daughter, apparently the image of the ideal teenage girl of her day.

While the relationship between Superman and Supergirl usually stayed within the boundaries of big brother/little sister, there were times when the family lines got blurred. They were the last two survivors of their race, so why not consider mating and perpetuate their mighty Kryptonian lineage?

Curious feelings are revealed in 1962's "Superman's Super-Courtship!" when Supergirl decides to play matchmaker for her cousin. After her trips to the ancient past and the distant future yield no mates for Superman, he confesses to Supergirl, "If I ever did marry . . . it would be to someone super and lovable like . . . you!" He goes on to say that under Kryptonian law cousins are not allowed to marry, which seems to be the only thing stopping him from becoming the Jerry Lee Lewis of the superhero world.

But perhaps more revealing is *Superman's Girl Friend, Lois Lane* #55, in which Supergirl guest stars. Lois suspects that Superman may secretly be married, and confronts him in his Fortress of Solitude. There, Superman introduces Lois to his family—a pair of flying tots, and his wife, Supergirl! "I needed a super-wife...you're too ordinary, Lois...and you have no super-brains...you're not very pretty...frankly, you're the last girl I would want to marry!" an amused Superman confesses to a shattered Lois. A cruel Supergirl captures Lois, intent on placing her into suspended animation for a thousand years. Superman comes to his senses and saves the day, and readers learn that Supergirl had succumbed to the always-unpredictable effects of Red Kryptonite three days earlier. Mistakenly thinking that she and Superman were married, Supergirl then hypnotized her cousin into believing the delusion as well, building robotic children to complete the sordid scenario. Everything is put to rights, and there is no mention of what had gone on in those three days when the cousins lived as man and wife, the hateful feelings that Superman apparently harbors in his subconscious for his supposed "girlfriend," or Supergirl's subconscious sexual desires.

"You Don't Own Me" was Lesley Gore's last top 10 hit, released as the American suburban ideal faced a turning point in the face of the British Invasion, when shaggy-haired bands brought miniskirts, decadent European sexuality, and irony to the shores of the United States. While staid pop singers like Lesley Gore fell out of style as the 1960s progressed, the idyllic American world into which Supergirl's rocket crashed remained frozen in time. She still buzzes around the globe and the galaxy doing good deeds, while her alter ego Linda Danvers graduates high school in 1964, becomes a freshman at Stanhope College, and enjoys a college life that is remarkably free of antiwar rallies or racial tensions.

Supergirl could have been a potent force to bring change to a world that was on the brink of social upheaval. It's not like she was going to fly off to Viet Nam and end the war or anything, but she could have been a voice of youth as opposed to the more conservative Superman. By the dawn of the '70s, comic books began a "relevant" period, where they tackled tough, real world problems like drug addiction and organized crime. Supergirl's fellow adolescents, the Teen Titans, gave up their costumes and powers to become a youth group dedicated to improving the world. So, what did Supergirl do to keep up with the times? She put on a pair of hot pants and a choker.

Like an indestructible Tricia Nixon, Supergirl went into the 1970s unfazed, remaining the good girl she was, steering clear of any controversy, and remaining the ideal American girl of a bygone era. Couldn't besmirch the family name, after all. Linda graduates from college in 1971, and gets a job at TV station in San Francisco, the ultimate cool, single career-girl destination of the day. Supergirl's trips to the 30th century to fight alongside the Legion of Superheroes become less frequent. In 1974, the now 21-year-old heroine resigns from the Legion, telling her boyfriend Brainiac 5, "I'm not even sure if I want to be a Supergirl anymore!" In the spirit of the early '70s, Supergirl was trying to "find herself."

But the bloom was apparently off the rose for Supergirl. She got her own self-titled comic book in 1972, which lasted only one year. After that, Supergirl starred in the quarterly *Superman Family*, or made the occasional guest appearance in someone else's comic. By 1976, Linda was working as a college guidance counselor, before trying her hand at being a soap opera actress. In terms of the pop stars of the day, Supergirl was in a league with Australian songbird Olivia Newton-John, Mormon priestess Marie Osmond, or Christian hit maker Debby Boone—pretty, safe, and well behaved. Supergirl may have stayed the same, but time was marching on. In the post Watergate years, the American dream of marriage, family, and a life of suburban splendor had lost some of its luster. Women's liberation and the sexual revolution were merging in ways that would create a new persona for young women, who felt that Mr. Right might not be the answer to all of their problems. Young women had to rely on themselves to make it in a world that was becoming more cynical, and less idyllic than the era in which suburban princess Supergirl had reigned. By the end of the '70s, Supergirl was still wearing those hot pants. The costume now looked as tired as Supergirl must have felt. Always the "girl," she was never allowed to grow up into Superwoman. By the decade's end, twenty years after her introduction, she had been drawn back into Superman's mighty caped shadow.

The 1980s weren't a great time for Supergirl. In fact, they couldn't have been worse. Twenty years after her debut, she was still adrift in the comic book universe, and still didn't show any signs of ever growing up to be a Superwoman. A whole new group of pop stars had emerged to dominate the music charts with a harder sound and attitude. Deborah Harry, Chrissie Hynde, and Pat Benatar were the new role models for young women, and they projected an outspoken, independent, and sexually confident image. But these women's brand of independence passed Supergirl by. In 1982, DC Comics tried to re-launch the Girl of Steel in a new comic, *The Daring New Adventures of Supergirl*. Despite the fact that Linda had graduated college and was a career woman, she once again reverted to being a nineteen-year-old university student. Apparently a younger girl had more story potential than a woman. "I've been Supergirl for such a long time. It seems I've forgotten what it feels like to be just a person . . . instead of a symbol!" thinks Linda Danvers, as she prepares to begin a new academic life in Chicago.

Around this time, a certain Madonna Louise Veronica Ciccone first appeared on the pop music charts, bent on world domination. She was overtly sexy, smart, and manipulative, and wasn't afraid of being a symbol. She gave young girls a new, worldlier role model. Madonna exploited the medium of music videos played twenty-four hours a day on the new youth focused network MTV. DC tried to make Supergirl look more *au courant* with an MTV style costume that made her look more like a Valley Girl—flounced skirt, headband, and big permed hair. It didn't save her comic from being cancelled after two years.

In 1984, Supergirl was poised for that evolution that should have made her a pop culture icon—movie star. The big screen feature

Supergirl was intended to extend the Christopher Reeve Superman movie franchise launched in the late '70s. Pretty blonde actress Helen Slater looked absolutely perfect for the part of Supergirl. But lovely looks weren't enough to save this bomb of a movie, or Supergirl for that matter. By 1985 her head was on the chopping block. If the *Supergirl* movie had been a hit, the Supergirl of the comic books would have been spared. But now the powers that be decided that she was redundant, and took away from Superman's own iconic status. Superman wasn't that unique if there was someone else who could do everything that he could do. So that year, Supergirl valiantly gave her life in battle to save the universe and her beloved cousin Superman. Even as she lies bleeding in Superman's arms, her devotion to her cousin never wanes. "You taught me to be brave . . . and I was . . . I . . . I love you so much for who you are . . . for how good you are." And with that, Supergirl was dead.

After her demise, Superman finds out that an amnesiac Supergirl had briefly been married to a young man on a distant alien world. The story implies that Superman is able to lay his beloved cousin to rest knowing that she'd known true fulfillment and happiness as a woman before death. Supergirl was gone, and the books were officially closed on the innocent days of comics. Eventually, time in the DC Universe was altered, and the deceased Supergirl was erased from existence and continuity. No one, including Superman, remembered that she ever existed.

The original Supergirl was deemed redundant, but a new one was introduced three years after the first bit the dust. Apparently, the appeal of a blonde girl flying around in a short skirt is undeniable.

This one wasn't even a real girl; she was something that had been grown in a laboratory. She was followed by another new one in 1996, who turned out to be a fiery angel of God. Then there was another who turned up in 2003. She came from the future, and for once, wasn't a blonde. But readers hated her, so she didn't stick around very long. The original Supergirl battled evil for over twenty-five years, and none of the young women who bore that name in their brief careers could ever match her legend, or popularity.

This brings us to 2004. By this time, the image of the American teenage girl had moved well beyond the proper daughter of the original Supergirl's era. In 1999, 17-year-old former Mouseketeer Britney Spears flashed the world a taut and tanned stomach above her schoolgirl kilt, becoming America's new pop princess and changing the image of the teenage girl. Spears is credited with kicking off a revival of the teen pop star, updated with a sexually mature image. By 2002, Spears' fellow Mouseketeer Christina Aguilera was gyrating in a bikini and leather chaps, singing that she wanted to get "dirrty," while 2004 saw the release of heiress Paris Hilton's amateur porn video. The media became obsessed with these new celebrity Lolitas who entertained the nation with tales of drunken revels, emotional meltdowns, and general rude behavior. This was the world into which a new Supergirl would arrive.

Debuting in 2004, the new Supergirl's introduction was an updated retelling of the original Girl of Steel's origin. The Supergirl of 2004 is a pretty blonde named Kara who is sent to earth from Argo

City, which has survived the destruction of the planet Krypton. She is Superman's cousin, is as strong as him (maybe even stronger), can fly, and is indestructible. She wears a costume with a big red "S" on the chest, and a short skirt. Sounds a lot like the original Supergirl of 1959, right? Well, that's where the similarities end.

First off, rather than arrive in a cute little Supergirl costume, this version of Kara emerges from her crashed rocket ship nude. "This is Kara Zor-El . . . my cousin from Krypton," Superman says, as he introduces the exposed blonde teenager to his ally Batman. She modestly drapes her naked form in Superman's famous red cape. When Kara decides to become a superhero, it's Supergirl reimagined as a 21st century "hot girl." Her body is drawn to look borderline anorexic, with a skirt that is now much shorter and flutters to give readers an occasional glimpse of her panties. The costume now has a bare midriff that showed off Supergirl's tight abs. She laments to her fellow teenage superheroine Stargirl that she can't get her navel pierced because ". . . the whole 'Girl of Steel' thing makes piercing kinda impossible."

There is no lengthy probationary period with the 2004 Supergirl. Like Britney Spears and the other manufactured pop singers of the 21st century, this new Supergirl leaps right into heroic superstardom. While the original Supergirl was sweet and obedient, the new one has anger issues, and doesn't take well to adult supervision. She especially resents Superman trying to tell her how to run her life. "And next time, let me fight my own battles . . . I swear, you treat me like a four-year-old," Supergirl tells the Man of Steel. Once Supergirl sells Batman some futuristic Kryptonian technology from her ship to pay for her own apartment, she begins a life free of parental supervision, much like the mega rich young stars of Hollywood.

"I'm not a girl, not yet a woman," Britney Spears sang in a syrupy 2001 ballad. So it was with the new Supergirl. Like the original Supergirl, she was a teenage girl, but she lived her life with the freedom of a woman. The new Supergirl pursues men much older than she is, arguing that through the technicality of "suspended animation," she's not actually underage. Sulky, feeling adrift and misunderstood, Supergirl spends the night drinking beer, smoking, and flying around the world to party. "I'm getting my head together," she says, as she stubs a cigarette out in the palm of her indestructible hand.

As unflattering as this portrayal may seem, the 2004 Supergirl was more like a real life teenager. She wasn't as perfect and beyond reproach as the original, and better suited for more cynical 21st century readers. While this new Supergirl may have looked like a male fantasy, DC Comics claimed she was meant to appeal to young women. So from time to time Supergirl showed she actually had a good head on her shoulders by sharing wisdom with readers. "Do yourselves and each other a favor . . . be yourself. It makes life a hell of a lot easier," Supergirl tells a group of high school students, after she attempts to adopt a drab alter ego in order to fit in. And when her romance with the buff Power Boy turns physically abusive, Supergirl offers him, and her female readers, a bit of advice. "No one who says he loves you should hit you. Ever," Supergirl says, as she prepares to drop an airplane hangar on the startled Power Boy and mar his boy band looks.

Over time, Supergirl toned down her wild behavior. She started wearing longer skirts, and was drawn to look like she ate regular meals. Artist Jamal Igle even drew a pair of bike shorts under her skirt to make flying more discreet. Now Supergirl actually acted heroic, and stopped picking fights with her fellow superheroes. And she became more like a kid sister to Superman again, albeit an independent one. "I want to be a family with you ... but I don't need your ... validation! I can get by on my own terms, and I'm doing just fine ... ," she tells Superman, as she tries to make amends for past lapses of judgment. Supergirl was indeed doing just fine. Until the universe ended.

In 2011, DC Comics announced that all of its comic books would be canceled and relaunched with new titles that would offer readers more modern and accessible interpretations of famous characters like Superman, Batman, and Wonder Woman. Dubbed "the New 52," this new line included a fresh take on Supergirl. We all are familiar with her origin story by now, so let's cut straight to the details. Young Kara emerges from her Kryptonian ship, which has crashed in Siberia. This time she's clad in futuristic body armor, the chest emblazoned with a large 'S'. The skirt is gone, replaced by a high cut swimsuit with a red area shaped like the Superman emblem placed strategically over the crotch. Confused by where she has landed, Kara becomes angry. When Superman arrives to greet her, Kara attacks him, resulting in a fight that almost destroys the Great Wall of China. Not off to such a good start...

Perplexed by her newfound powers, Kara flies off in a rage (she does this a lot). What follows is a series of events where Kara becomes embroiled in one fight after another, leaving a path of destruction in her wake. The public dubs her Supergirl because of her costume and fantastic abilities. But the 2011 model Supergirl doesn't actually want to use those powers to help others. She's too busy acting petulant and self-absorbed, lamenting how she'll never fit in on earth. "No offense," Supergirl tells the one friend she is able to make, "but your planet—to use your expression—has been nothing but a big bucket of suck since I got here." DC Comics' vision of a Millenial Supergirl was less than charming.

At the same time that the New 52 Supergirl was trying to find her place in the world, pop singer Miley Cyrus was also undergoing an evolution. The former star of Disney's *Hannah Montana*, whose toothsome grin had adorned millions of children's backpacks, was transforming herself from brunette girl-next-door to platinum-haired provocateur. With a newfound penchant for displaying her nude, tattooed body to the world, Cyrus scored a hit in 2014 with her song "We Can't Stop," a battle cry for youth to party, take recreational drugs, and do whatever they pleased. This could have been the New 52 Supergirl's theme song as well, for by this time she's finally feeling like she has found where she belongs. She's become a member of the Red Lanterns, a violent group of interstellar antiheroes fueled by anger—something that Supergirl has in abundance. "We seek out injustice and kick it in the teeth," she muses. "It feels good."

But as it turned out, readers preferred a heroic Supergirl to a bad-tempered one. Comic book buyers never warmed up to the New 52 Supergirl, and in 2015 her series was cancelled due to poor sales. Apparently America still liked a nice girl, as evidenced by the chart topping success pop star Taylor Swift had in 2015. The pretty blonde singer who grew up on a Christmas tree farm wrote her own music, had a "squad" of famous celebrity girlfriends, and was the youngest entry on Forbes' list of 100 Most Powerful Women in 2015. She even visited sick fans when she wasn't performing to stadium audiences. It would seem Taylor Swift could do no wrong. No wonder she had once been rumored to be in consideration to play Supergirl in a movie.

And there was yet another new Supergirl in 2015. This one was blonde, wore a skirt, and possessed mighty abilities. Heroic and selfless, she dedicated herself to protecting the world. She was much like the original Supergirl, with one major difference— she was on television, not in comic books. The *Supergirl* TV series made its debut in 2015, and was to give audiences a version of the heroine that stayed true to the original while still updating her for modern times. A new generation of young girls could now see a powerful young woman performing amazing feats every week on their TV. Actress Melissa Benoist's Supergirl is noble and smart, yet human and adorably goofy. And for the first time, Supergirl has an older sister figure to mentor her, rather than a brother. The result is a Supergirl that is utterly likable, much like a Taylor Swift song. Sadly, a "likable" Supergirl is something comic books have struggled to produce for the past three decades.

Styles constantly change. There will be new pop stars in the years to come, and no doubt a new Supergirl as well. The one certainty is that America prefers a princess to a queen. A princess is young and pretty, and less threatening than a queen who actually wields authority. That is why Supergirl will never grow up to be a Superwoman.

1960s: The Modern World

Elasti-Girl looked to the heavens. The attack had begun. A squadron of deadly missiles descended upon the globe, bent on raining death and destruction. But mankind had one hope. The Doom Patrol had arrived. As the trio of misfit superheroes surveyed the scene, the team's female member, Elasti-Girl, said what was on all of their minds. "If *we* don't stop them, there'll be a *thousand* more close behind!" A look of concern crossed her screen goddess face.

Bracing herself and planting her high heeled violet boots firmly in the ground beneath her, Elasti-Girl grows to a height of fifty feet. The tinny voice of her teammate Robotman roars up to the gorgeous giantess. "Atta girl, 'Stretch Sox!' Show them how it was when you were the tallest girl basketball player at Amazon High!" Coolly confident, the gargantuan beauty lifts a white-gloved hand to easily catch one of the speeding missiles. Without batting an eye, Elasti-Girl responds to her robotic compatriot. "You got it wrong, Cliff! It wasn't basketball I played—it was right field on an all-girl's softball team!" Elasti-Girl flashes a cover girl smile as she grasps the rocket in two hands like baseball bat, and takes a swing. "And here's how I used to hit my favorite—a high fast ball!" Elasti-Girl crashes the missile in her hands against one of the oncoming rockets, shattering it in two. Robotman races to avoid the rain of destruction that his titanic companion has wrought across the landscape. Amidst the wreckage towers a triumphant Elasti-Girl, as a breeze slightly lifts the miniskirt of her red and white uniform.

Despite her name, Elasti-Girl is so much more than just a girl. To the world, she is a hero. Although her Doom Patrol companions never doubt Elasti-Girl's power or bravery, they are still sometimes perplexed by her gutsy nature. Once, Elasti-Girl has to brave shark-infested waters in order to salvage medical supplies from a sunken ship. The serum is located in a locked trunk, so the heroine shrinks to miniscule size, enters the lock through its keyhole and acts as a human key to open it. When asked why she hadn't simply used an explosive device to open the lock, Elasti-Girl responds that she "got a kick out of" doing it the more difficult way.

It's 1965. The British Invasion of America is in full swing. Artist Andy Warhol's paintings of Campbell's soup cans hang on the walls of New York art galleries. And former movie star Rita Farr reigns as Elasti-Girl of the Doom Patrol. She is an emancipated superheroine, with strength and power to put her on par with her male counterparts. She's intelligent, and takes her role as a superhero seriously. She fights evil because it is the right thing to do, but also because she loves the thrills.

Was Rita Farr, Elasti-Girl of the Doom Patrol, the quintessential superheroine of the 1960s?

Unfortunately, not.

By the mid-'50s, comic books had become pretty tame stuff indeed. 1954's Comic Code Authority scoured the industry, banishing the bloody horror and crime titles, and leaving nothing but a lot of good, clean fun on the comic book racks. But by 1956, DC Comics decided it was time to try selling superheroes to a new generation of kids. Rather than revive its old 1940s heroes, DC tried a new take on a new hero with an old name. And so, the October 1956 issue of *Showcase Comics* featured a new Flash, the Fastest Man Alive. The new Flash wore a sleek red costume that looked modern and streamlined. The Flash was a hit with readers who may have been too young to remember the superheroes of just a few years before. And so a new superhero era began.

Over the next few years, DC introduced updated versions of heroes like Green Lantern, Hawkman, and the Atom who were slim, athletically muscled, and wore costumes with modern, geometric designs. Unlike their 1940s predecessors, these new heroes were not playboys or wealthy aristocrats, but solid American white-collar workers. The stories for these Atomic Age heroes focused on science, space, and time travel. Magic was a mysterious enemy, meant to be defeated. In the idyllic, pastel-colored world of these new heroes, justice always prevailed, good and evil were well defined, and everything met the requirements of the Comics Code. The artwork wasn't dark and brooding like 1940s comics, but clean and slick as commercial advertising. Overall, these new heroes projected a sense of optimism for a new America that had shaken off the specter of World War II, and was looking towards the future. This was the beginning of what would later be called the Silver Age of Comics.

While a new generation of comic book readers embraced this

bright new incarnation of superheroes, it was essentially a stag party. That's not to say that there were no women around. The new heroes were almost always involved in chaste and proper romances with pretty sweethearts who, in keeping with the times, were smart career girls: lawyers, reporters, and lady executives. And, there was the new Hawkgirl, the partner of Hawkman, and half of one of the only husband and wife teams in comics. But most of the heroes like Batman and Green Arrow were bedeviled by the bothersome likes of Batwoman or Queen Arrow—portrayed as impulsive women who wanted to insinuate their way into a life of danger better suited for a man. The overzealous Lady Blackhawk even infiltrated the Blackhawks, the exclusive squadron of all-male fighter pilots. The new breed of scientific adventure teams like the Sea Devils and the Atomic Knights always had a token female member to provide a love interest for the group's leader. But these women were all merely supporting characters, and usually considered trivial. It wasn't until Supergirl was introduced in 1959 that a new heroine headlined in her own comic, joining that relic from a bygone age, Wonder Woman.

As the 1960s dawned, Wonder Woman was approaching her 20th anniversary. In keeping with the ultra modern times, much of the magic and fantasy in Wonder Woman's own comic was downplayed. This is a tough thing, since Wonder Woman was a clay statue that had been magically brought to life by the gods of Olympus. But no longer. Now she is the daughter of the ageless Amazon queen Hippolyta and a father lost at war. Her Amazon race is depicted less as immortal female warriors and more as pretty women in short Grecian robes who possess a wealth of futuristic knowledge. In an era when First Lady Jacqueline Kennedy was setting a standard for demure femininity and poise, Wonder Woman had to leave most of her Amazon roots and pro-female thinking behind to fit in with the times.

By 1960, DC decided that it was time to unite their hottest new heroes into an update of the old Justice Society of America. Editor Julius Schwartz thought that a "society" felt a little snooty, and, inspired by the all-American pastime of baseball, opted instead for a Justice *League* of America. The Justice League took on foes that were too big for just one hero to handle. It consisted of newcomers Green Lantern, Flash, Aquaman, and Martian Manhunter, along with Wonder Woman. Superman and Batman were also members, but did not appear in adventures as much, lest their well-established star power overshadow the appeal of the neophytes.

Interestingly enough, Wonder Woman is not considered to be in the same "league" as Superman and Batman, and is lumped in with the new kids, despite the fact that she has been fighting crime almost as long as the two men. Luckily, as a member of the Justice League, Wonder Woman gets treatment that befits her status as one of the few original female heroes left in comics. To make her more of an equal to her male counterparts, the emphasis is put on the dazzling feats she performs with her lasso and invisible jet, and less on her prodigious strength. Wonder Woman fights side by side with the men and never has to be rescued or protected by them. In keeping with the somewhat sexless image that Wonder Woman is given in the early 1960s, none of her male comrades ever vie for her attention. She is essentially one of the guys, albeit in a strapless swimsuit and spike heeled Roman sandals.

Wonder Woman may have enjoyed a form of sexual equality in the Justice League, but her sisters in the real world were not as lucky. The inauguration of John F. Kennedy, in 1961, marked the beginning of a new era in American culture. The newly elected Democratic president ushered in what is generally regarded as a period of optimism for America, moving the country away from the paranoia of the 1950s to focus on quality of life, civil rights, culture, and the exploration of space. But things were changing more slowly for women. While the future occupation of choice for good women was still wife and mother, the concept of the career girl was becoming more prevalent in popular culture. But even in careers, women were still portrayed in gender appropriate roles as supporting characters to men: teacher, nurse, secretary, stewardess. 1961 saw the premiere of *Apartment 3-G*, a newspaper comic strip about three Manhattan career women. But in the comic book world, few females were written as wanting to transcend their roles in society.

Third tier publisher Marvel Comics had limped along through the postwar era following the demise of its star heroes Captain America, Human Torch, and the Sub-Mariner. While Marvel had tried throughout the 1950s to revive its heroes, it hadn't had any raging successes. Its main focuses, circa 1960, were giant monster comics and romance books. When publisher Martin Goodman got wind of DC's plans to launch *The Justice League of America*, he suggested to writer Stan Lee that Marvel should try its own superhero team comic. Rather than resurrect some of Marvel's old 1940s superheroes, Lee decided to start fresh. Partnered with artist Jack Kirby, Lee took a new approach that shook up the comic book industry, starting the superhero revolution of the 1960s.

In November, 1961, Lee and Kirby's new creation, The Fantastic Four, hit the stands. The creative duo wanted this new superhero comic to be different from what readers had seen in years past. The Fantastic Four didn't have secret identities; they were known as much by their real names as their heroic sobriquets. Unlike the jovial and perfect Justice League, the Fantastic Four bickered and argued like real people, and one of their members was a horribly disfigured monster. The cover of the first issue looked cruder and less slick than the graceful images featured on DC titles. Three bizarre looking characters—a flaming youth, a grotesque rocky creature, and a slim rubbery-limbed male—are about to take on a giant monster erupting out of the streets of Manhattan. A caption announces the names of the members of this new team: The Thing, Mr. Fantastic, and the Human Torch. The last member listed is the Invisible Girl. On the cover, she is shown as the helpless, vanishing girl in the monster's clutches, being rescued by the three men. It looked like *everything* wouldn't be different in this comic.

The Fantastic Four proved to be a hit, kicking off what writer, and later editor, Lee would immodestly dub The Marvel Age of Comics. The self-proclaimed comic book revolution of the early 1960s took place at a pivotal time in American culture. The 1962 death of Hollywood sex goddess Marilyn Monroe in many ways closed the books on the conservative 1950s, as the world of petticoats,

Elvis, and sock hops would give way to miniskirts, the Beatles, and discotheques. Marvel's flawed superheroes were plagued with real-life problems, and reflected the angst that Americans were feeling in an imperfect world fraught with intangible enemies, the world of the Cold War. The "Marvel Comics" style reached its pinnacle with the publisher's most successful creation—the Everyman hero Spider-Man. He was a wisecracking superhero who fought crime by night, a nerdy high school student leading a life of loneliness, rejection, and heartache by day. It felt like anything could and would happen in Marvel's comic books. These were comics for the cool kids who were looking for more sophisticated fare.

The world that Marvel Comics created in the 1960s was an exciting one. But if you asked if the world of the Marvel superheroes was a reflection of the great social changes that would sweep America in the 1960s, the answer would be no. James Brown summed it up best in his 1965 hit—"It's a Man's Man's World." Marvel Comics was a man's world, inhabited by a pantheon of male superheroes that starred in their own comics. There were no women who headlined their own titles at Marvel, with the exception of the romance book *Millie the Model*. Not an equivalent to Wonder Woman or Supergirl in the lot. Women were the co-stars, not the leads, and this would be the status quo in Marvel comic books for the next three decades.

Heroines Invisible Girl, Wasp, and Marvel Girl formed a female trinity in the early days of Marvel Comics. All three have similar backgrounds and are around the same age, probably late teens or early twenties. They are all nice, upper-middle class suburban girls who have left their homes to move to the big city or go away to school, and wind up becoming heroines. They are not like the madcap debutante heroines of the 1940s who became costumed vigilantes to fight crime and seek thrills. Each is a girl transformed into a heroine as a result of the work and machinations of the older men in their lives. Marvel Girl wears a mask, but the other two heroines have no secret identities, and all three have no personal lives or careers outside of their full-time superhero activities. The career girls of *Apartment 3-G* were building lives for themselves in the big city. The three young women of Marvel's superhero world can be seen as accepting their fates, or at least biding their time until the men in their lives popped the question.

As heroines, these women are the token female members of teams, where the males are shown to be substantially more powerful. Their weaker powers usually force them to act only as a distraction or decoy when their team battles a foe. Despite the fact that a teenager like Spider-*Man* was referred to as an adult, these heroines still go by the more adolescent appellation "girl." Additionally, they take on traditional female roles within the group as mothers and handmaidens: sewing uniforms, making coffee, and doing secretarial work. All the while, they conceal their femininity beneath unisex costumes that match those of their male counterparts. When they aren't fighting crime, the heroines enjoy stereotypic feminine pastimes like going to tea, shopping, or reading fashion magazines.

Marvel's premier team, the Fantastic Four, was formed when a daring quartet of adventurers launched themselves in an experimental rocket in order to beat "the commies" into space. Disaster strikes when the ship is belted with cosmic rays. After the foursome crash to Earth, they find themselves drastically altered. Brilliant scientist and team leader Reed Richards gains the power to stretch his body into any shape, and renames himself Mr. Fantastic. Reed's girlfriend, Sue Storm, can turn invisible, hence her rather lackluster title Invisible Girl. Sue's teenaged brother Johnny calls himself the Human Torch because he can burst into flame and fly. The final member is Reed's best friend Ben Grimm, who is transformed into a powerful, rocky-hided orange monster called The Thing. They make a solemn vow to use their newfound powers to help mankind, and the Fantastic Four is born.

The Fantastic Four were first and foremost a family, and they often behaved like one, constantly battling each other. Ben blames Reed for his horrible deformity. Johnny teases Ben endlessly about how ugly he is. Sue feels slighted and peeved when Reed spends more time with his experiments than with her. Reed sees the other three members as squabbling children that he must constantly look after.

If the Fantastic Four was more like a bickering family than a superhero team, Sue Storm, the Invisible Girl, played the dual role of mother and daughter. Sue designs the team's matching, unisex space age jumpsuits, and makes a semblance of a traditional home for them in their futuristic skyscraper headquarters. Like Wendy Darling looking after Peter Pan's "Lost Boys," Sue takes care of the three male members in very maternal ways. She consoles the tragic and strangely lovable Ben, reprimands rebellious, impetuous

Johnny, and acts as confidante and cheerleader for brilliant team leader Reed. On TV, Samantha Stevens of *Bewitched* downplayed her black magic powers in order to look like a normal suburban housewife, and the mystical and subservient Jeannie used her seemingly limitless powers to serve her "master." Wielding great power was shown as being less important for a woman than keeping her man happy. Like them, Sue is always there with a fresh pot of coffee and words of encouragement when Reed locks himself away in his laboratory trying to invent some new savior machine to fend off a world shattering menace.

But it is Sue's romantic relationship with the much older, grey-templed Reed that also puts her into the submissive role of daughter. Sue truly is the "invisible girl"—the woman in the shadow of her older, more important fiancé, who takes the back seat to his brilliance. Paternal Reed often gets impatient with Sue's apparent immaturity, and chastises her when her unpredictable feminine nature confounds his rational, scientist's mind. "Just like a woman!! Everything I do is for your own good, but you're too scatter-brained and emotional to *realize* it!" While harsh words like these might hurt Sue, Reed can always appease his trophy girlfriend by letting her go shopping. While Sue may enjoy a trip to the boutiques on Fifth Avenue, she seems to live in her unfeminine costume, even pouring coffee for her teammates with her gloves on. The only outlet for her frivolous femininity seems to be her hairstyles. Throughout the '60s, Sue models virtually every hairdo in fashion: bouffant, pageboy, chignon, bubble, flip, you name it. While Reed may be able to control what is going on inside of Sue's head, she at least gets to pick how it looks on the outside.

While each of the men have a distinct power that can be used to fight a foe, Sue just turns invisible. She can spy on an enemy, or sneak up on them, but that is about the extent of it. Or at least, that's how she was written. Issue #12 featured a story called "A Visit with the Fantastic Four," in which a tearful Sue confesses to her teammates that several readers had written letters demanding that she be kicked off the team for not contributing enough. The male members give Sue a pep talk, and then present her with a birthday cake that quickly distracts her from her feelings of inadequacy. By the following year, Reed has figured out a way to boost Sue's powers, giving her the ability to create invisible force fields. But even this power wasn't used to its true offensive potential for decades, and merely allowed the already maternal Sue to find new ways to protect her male compatriots from the sidelines, while they did most of the heavy lifting in battles with Doctor Doom and The Mole Man.

Despite being portrayed as the weakest member, it is the fact that Sue is a woman that casts her in the role of world savior. In issue *Fantastic Four* #4, Lee and Kirby revived the amphibian antihero Sub-Mariner. The Sub-Mariner had been a star of Marvel Comics of the '40s and '50s, when he vacillated between being enemy of the surface world and scourge of the Axis powers. By 1962, he discovers that his submerged kingdom of Atlantis had been destroyed by underwater atomic tests. His campaign against the surface dwellers brings him into conflict with the Fantastic Four. But he quickly falls in love with Sue, declaring, "You're the loveliest human I've ever seen! If you will be my bride, I might show mercy to the rest of your pitiful race." The fate of humanity lies in Sue's hands, and presumably between her legs. In the end, the Sub-Mariner is defeated, but the pretty blonde Invisible Girl continually finds herself drawn to the fierce undersea king in his skimpy, scaly trunks. This love triangle went on for several years and often split Sue's loyalties between her family and the team's enemy. But it was this very infatuation that kept the Sub-Mariner from annihilating the surface world.

Ant-Man was one of Marvel's less stellar creations. Hank Pym was a scientist who discovered a serum that could shrink him down to the size of ants. Donning a boldly graphic costume, he set out to fight crime as The Ant-Man in 1962. He followed DC Comic's Atom, who shrunk and also sported a cool costume, who had debuted the year before. So what was the difference between these two runts? Well, Ant-Man did wear a distinctive bulbous chrome helmet that allowed him to command ants to do his bidding, which clearly was a huge asset in stopping a bank robbery. Astride a pair of flying ants, Ant Man charged into battle like a tiny crime fighting charioteer. Maybe not the sexiest hero on the market. But help was buzzing his way.

In 1963, Ant Man's image got a little boost in the form of a female partner. Janet Van Dyne is introduced as the young daughter of a scientist who was killed by an evil alien creature. Janet is desperate to help bring her father's killer to justice, and goes to her late father's colleague, Hank Pym, for help. Hank reveals his Ant Man identity to Janet, and tells her he can give her the means to exact her revenge. Thus begins a fantastic process that culminates in Janet's transformation into Ant Man's new partner, the Wasp.

Stan Lee and Jack Kirby, both Jewish, must have had a chuckle when they created this character. Even before shrinking to insect size and sprouting wings and antennae, Janet truly was a W.A.S.P.—a wealthy and privileged Gentile girl from the posh suburbs whose greatest aspiration seemed to be landing a husband. By the end of her first appearance, the Wasp has already fallen for Ant-Man, and soon has designs on him. Widower Ant Man is not eager to fall in love again. But like a nagging insect, the Wasp is relentless.

By 1963, Lee and Kirby decided to create Marvel's own superstar team, à la The Justice League. *The Avengers* united the biggest stars in their roster, minus superhero outsider Spider-Man. There was the tragic Jekyll and Hyde monster called the Incredible Hulk, the dashing millionaire Iron Man, the Norse thunder god Thor, and the tiny Ant Man. The Wasp was not generally listed as a real member of the team, but as more of a diminutive hanger-on to Ant Man, who by issue #2 had stopped shrinking and started growing to massive proportions, now going by the name Giant-Man.

With the Wasp and Ant-Man/Giant-Man, Lee and Kirby continued the younger girl/older scientist formula that they had started with Mr. Fantastic and Invisible Girl. As Marvel's version of the Partner archetype, Wasp seems to join Ant-Man in his crime fighting exploits in the Avengers more as a way to bag him as a husband than to rid the world of evil. The Wasp's contribution to the Avengers' epic battles is generally the annoyance factor. She is like the Tinkerbell of the team, buzzing around villains' faces and shooting them with her irritating but essentially ineffective Wasp's sting. This usually distracts the villain so that one of the male Avengers can finish off the baddie.

Off the battlefield, Wasp continues to the play the annoying card. She is usually shown as a lovable ditz, who often flirts with the other Avengers in order to make Giant-Man jealous. When Wasp drools over the longhaired, hunky Thor, Giant-Man intervenes by picking up the heroine by the seat of her costume and reprimanding her. "Aren't you ever gonna grow up, Wasp? Haven't you anything else on your mind??" Over time, Wasp begins to take her heroine role more seriously. But she is always the weakest member of the team, and is portrayed as a flighty female. The Wasp spends more time on her costumes than she does on trying to be a good champion of justice. Every few issues, she debuts a new ensemble. This becomes her trademark for the next fifty years. In *Avengers* #68, a menace threatens to attack the United Nations, and the Wasp's first concern is that she has nothing new to wear into battle. The inheritance from her father's estate leaves Wasp incredibly rich, and she seems just as interested in shopping for a new fur coat as she is in stopping an invasion from space.

Now, up until this point, all of Marvel's heroes had been normal individuals, transformed into superhumans as a result of an accident. The ordinary citizens of the Marvel Comics universe seemed to have no problem accepting these heroes and their powers. However, it seemed that people were prejudiced against mutants—individuals *born* with powers through a genetic twist. Lee and Kirby's new group, the X-Men, were mutants, the so-called "Homo Superior" who were the next stage of evolution, and genetic heirs to the world. The X-Men were named after their mentor, the telepathic Professor X, and because of the fact that they had *ex*-tra powers. The X-Men made their debut in 1963, the same year as Dr. Martin Luther King, Jr.'s March on Washington. Although the X-Men were all Caucasian, the fear and hatred the mutant heroes experienced was a metaphor for racism and bigotry against anyone who was different.

The teenaged X-Men operated secretly out of an exclusive upstate New York school, where Professor X secretly trained mutants to use their powers for good. The first issue introduces the boys of the student body—the handsome winged Angel, an acrobatic brute called Beast, a slim youth named Cyclops who fires powerful beams from his eyes, and a young teen named Iceman. The Professor assembles the boys to meet the last member of the team, a pretty redhead wearing a prim suit and white gloves. Her name is Jean Grey, and she has telekinetic powers—the ability to move objects with her mind. Professor X issues Jean the codename Marvel Girl, and the same unisex black and yellow costume that the boys wear. Although the costume was not particularly flattering, Marvel Girl muses "Whoever designed this costume could have given Christian Dior a run for his money," as she surveys her own "new look" in a mirror. Perhaps Professor X hadn't considered recruiting a girl for the team, otherwise he might have picked a less gender specific name for the group. However, Marvel Girl is so devoted to the charismatic Professor X and his cause that she ignores the slight of being part of his X-*Men*.

As a heroine, Marvel Girl is more serious than Invisible Girl and Wasp. She is dedicated to the cause of freeing her people from oppression, and this noble goal gives her life purpose. Marvel Girl also has a more aggressive power than the other two heroines, making her useful in a scuffle. "Don't worry, boys! I won't let you down!" the teen mutant cries, as she fearlessly rushes into battle beside her school chums. Within the dynamics of the X-Men, Marvel Girl is also at a slight advantage compared to her sister heroines. The mutant teens are all around the same age, so the outspoken Marvel Girl can boss the boys around a bit, especially when they get a little overanxious about impressing the only girl in the school.

But like Invisible Girl and Wasp, Marvel Girl lets men dominate her life. She falls in love with the shy, duty bound team leader Cyclops, and basically pines for him until he makes the first move. "If only we were ordinary humans . . . free to follow the urgings of our hearts! But, I mustn't allow myself such hopeless dreams . . ." Marvel Girl laments, expressing the double whammy of being both a woman and a member of an oppressed minority. Looking to glean any bit of attention from the stony Cyclops, she thrills when he praises her telekinetic prowess. "Somehow when he says 'good girl,' it's better than Richard Chamberlain saying 'my darling'!"

But by far, the man who holds the most sway over Marvel Girl is the team's psychic headmaster, Professor X. Their relationship is yet another twist on the younger girl/older man theme popular in Marvel's other superhero teams. In this case, Marvel Girl and Professor X are student and teacher, but she is just as much in his power as the other two women are with their beaus. "But, without you, we'd have remained misfits, in a world that could never understand us—with no purpose, no goals!" Marvel Girl tells the professor, who she clearly feels has given her life meaning. Since she and Professor X both have mental powers, she works closely with him as his assistant and confidante, often surreptitiously working behind her teammates' back to carry out the great man's sub-rosa assignments. This protégé and tutor bond took on a creepy quality when Professor X reflects in an early issue how he is secretly harboring feelings of love for his much younger student.

Despite their limited heroic horizons, the women of 1960s Marvel Comics were written as generally satisfied with their lot. Like costumed glitterati, the Marvel heroes all rubbed elbows, and Invisible Girl and the Wasp were the socialites in the center of this superhero social whirl. Like the sensitive intellectual that she was, Marvel Girl preferred the Greenwich Village coffee houses to uptown cocktail parties. Marvel's pantheon of superheroes lived in a realistic and recognizable New York, not a fictional city like Metropolis. In Marvel Comics' Manhattan, all the lights were bright, just as Petula Clark promised. Invisible Girl and Wasp were like the glamorous girlfriends of famous men. They were portrayed as women who found fulfillment in their relationships, with little need for power or independence.

Marvel's comic book revolution came at a pivotal point in

American pop culture. The Beatles' 1964 arrival in New York heralded America's real launch into the modern age, as new, multicolored styles and ideas cleared the last drab, vestiges of the 1950s away. America may not have landed on the moon yet, but it began embracing all of those things that seemed to say that the futuristic Space Age was within its reach. Marvel's distinctly New York sensibility gave its comic books a signature irreverent sense of humor and a cynical smarty-pants edge that suited the times. By 1965, Marvel was billing its comics as "Pop Art Productions" to attach itself to the international art scene exploding with the cartoon inspired works of Andy Warhol and Roy Lichtenstein. Comic books looked beyond the sphere of children's entertainment to make their magazines part of the larger pop culture scene.

This shift in culture began a new era for women as well. Helen Gurley Brown became the editor of *Cosmopolitan* magazine, in 1965, and was credited as being one of the forces to kick off the sexual revolution, telling female readers that they could have it all: "love, sex, and money." Boyishly built model Twiggy became the modern beauty to emulate, relegating the bosomy bombshell to the pages of *Playboy* and strip clubs. Women were beginning to enjoy a new independence, unhampered by the mores of the past. However, Marvel's style of comic book realism did little to reflect this change. While competitor DC Comics was perceived as being more straitlaced, its stories raised the question as to which company was truly more forward thinking as far as women were concerned.

Marvel's new style of comic book storytelling meant serious competition for DC. 1963's *Doom Patrol* was perhaps DC's most clear reaction to the Marvel style. The Doom Patrol, besides featuring one of the coolest team names in comics, was composed of misfit heroes who bickered, took an unorthodox approach to fighting crime, and were led by a wheelchair-bound genius. The team debuted in *My Greatest Adventure* #80, a few months before the X-Men, also a group of outcasts with a paralyzed leader. The similarity left fans to debate whether it was merely coincidence, or if one concept had influenced the other. A mysterious scientist known only as The Chief gathers a trio of rejects, offering them a chance to start their lives anew. First is Robotman, a daring racecar driver whose brain is housed within a mechanical body after a horrific accident robs him of his human form. Next is Negative Man, a former pilot whose body has been ravaged by radiation, giving him incredible energy powers. Finally, there is movie star and former Olympic gold medal swimmer Rita Farr, who suffers an accident while making a film in Africa. After being exposed to mysterious volcanic vapors, Rita finds that she can grow to amazing heights, or shrink to a miniscule size. Because of her size-changing powers, Rita is called Elasti-Girl. The Chief convinces the three to band together to show the world what a team of "fabulous freaks" can do, and the Doom Patrol is born.

While DC's *Doom Patrol* had the same irreverent humor and "anything can happen" attitude of Marvel's Fantastic Four or X-Men, its female member was a sharp contrast to the women of those teams. The titanic Elasti-Girl is the powerhouse of the team, wrestling dinosaurs, opening bank vaults with ease, and often carrying her male comrades to the scene of a battle in her giant hands. She displays the level of physical strength that only Wonder Woman or Supergirl is allowed, and she has fun doing it. Elasti-Girl enjoys her power, and one story shows the heroine taking a trip to the zoo to "commune with nature." Grown to gigantic size, Elasti-Girl gently nuzzles the zoo's fiercest lions and tigers as if they are harmless housecats. As onlookers gape, a confused child asks, "Daddy—how come she's so much bigger than you if she's only a girl?"

Despite her accident, Elasti-Girl still maintains her glamorous movie star looks. But although she is the pretty member of a trio of freaks, Elasti-Girl is truly a part of the team. Her strength lets her take on the same risks as the men, and she often saves her male teammates at the last crucial moment. Her wisecracking teammate Robotman dubs her "Stretch Sox," as if to say that she is not the token girl of the team, but just one of the guys. When Robotman gives Elasti-Girl a hard time about being late for a mission because she was at the hairdresser, she retorts, "I'm just as much a part of the team as you are and I do my share!"

Within the familial dynamic of the Doom Patrol, Elasti-Girl is like a sister to her teammates Robotman and Negative Man, albeit a sister who could grow to a staggering height and crush them under the heel of her spike heeled boot should they draw her ire. Elasti-Girl is indebted to the paternal Chief for giving her life newfound purpose, but he doesn't have the same Svengali-like hold over her that the X-Men's Professor X does over Marvel Girl.

Elasti-Girl is an adult woman who had a career before becoming a crime fighter, which also sets her apart from the Marvel Comics heroines. She is a devoted member of the Doom Patrol, but she still retains her independence and life outside of the team.

Marvel's heroines were consumed with thoughts of romance and marriage, perpetuating a dated 1950s female stereotype. DC's fighting females were also not impervious to Cupid's arrows, but mixing love and crime fighting was more of a challenge for them. Elasti-Girl is wooed by the fabulously wealthy superhero Mento, but keeps him at giant arm's length for a long while, lest he interfere with her superhero lifestyle. In a rare team up story featuring two heroines, the January 1965 issue of *The Brave and the Bold* tells a tale called "Revolt of the Super-Chicks!" Supergirl and Wonder Woman, tired of missing out on glamour and romance, move to Paris and put their heroic lives on hold to embark on whirlwind romances with suave Frenchmen. When perils arise, the heroines must go behind their new boyfriends backs to perform amazing super-feats. ". . . I'll no longer look feminine to him!" Supergirl thinks, at the prospect of letting her Gallic beau see her use her mighty powers. In the end, Wonder Woman and Supergirl realize that they can't escape their destinies as heroines. Both women have vowed to use their incredible powers to improve the world. Romance would have to be placed on the back burner. Marvel's treatment of heroines like Invisible Girl and the Wasp was much different. The burden of responsibility was on their male teammates; the women just came along for the ride. DC's next addition to their roster was a new Batgirl who represented the next generation of both superheroine and real world female—the career woman.

Batgirl was originally created as a supporting character for the wildly popular, campy 1966 *Batman* TV show. By the third season, the show's ratings were sagging, and the addition of Batgirl was a ploy to lure female viewers. She did little to perk up the *Batman* show's ratings, and it got the axe in 1968. The comic book incarnation of Batgirl, however, was here to stay. While she embodied the spirit of a new wave of liberated superheroines, in the backdrop of the history of comic books, Batgirl carried on the tradition of the gutsy female vigilantes of the 1940s who struck out on their own to right wrongs.

Unlike many of the other superheroines of the day, Batgirl's alter ego Barbara Gordon was an adult woman with an actual career. Hearkening back to the lady crime fighters of the 1940s, Barbara is a prim and proper bespectacled librarian on the outside, and a redheaded bombshell on the inside, waiting to be released: "The whole world thinks I'm just a Plain Jane—a colorless female 'brain'! I'll show them a far more imposing girl tonight!" thinks Barbara, as she pours herself into a sexy Batgirl costume that she has whipped up for the Policeman's Masquerade Ball. En route to the party, Barbara becomes embroiled in a fight between Batman and a villain that gives her a taste of an adventurous life, and leaves her wanting more. Her restless spirit drives Barbara to train her body, assemble an arsenal of weapons, and once more don the guise of Batgirl. But now, Batgirl's goal is not to turn heads, but to fight for justice.

As expected, Batman tries pulling his usual macho trip on the new Batgirl. "This is a case for *Batman* and *Robin*! I'm sorry—but you must understand that we can't worry ourselves about a girl . . ." But, the tenacious Batgirl is not one to be put off so easily, and she proves to the skeptical Batman that she can be a good crime fighter. "From what I've seen, she doesn't take a back seat to anybody!" the stuffy Batman later admits to Police Commissioner Gordon, who is unaware that Batgirl is in fact his bookish daughter "Babs." Like the heroines of the 1940s, Barbara dons her glasses to resume her wallflower persona, and the world never suspects that she is the "dominoed daredoll" Batgirl.

If Batgirl's origin sounds like standard comic book fare, it was. But it was her motivations that set Batgirl apart from her sister heroines of the '60s. Batgirl goes on a personal campaign to rid her home, Gotham City, of crime. Plain and simple, and as pure a motive as any man might have. She doesn't don a costume and throw herself into danger to prove her love for Batman. Yes, she wears his symbol on her chest, but she is not his girlfriend or faithful handmaiden. Certainly Batgirl wants Batman to respect her as a detective and an agent of justice, but she doesn't require his validation or protection. She is a creature of more enlightened times, and there was no way that Batman could have belittled or controlled Batgirl the way he had Batwoman a few years earlier.

A big factor here is that Batman did not have power over Batgirl's emotions. While Batman could manipulate Batwoman through the love she felt for him, he does not have this advantage with Batgirl. In a 1967 story, the feline villainess Catwoman assumes Batgirl is her competition for the Caped Crusader's love.

But as the coolheaded Batgirl later explains, "I don't consider myself a rival of yours, Catwoman! I have absolutely no romantic interest in Batman!" This was, perhaps, the key to Batgirl's liberation. There is nothing that Batgirl would ever want more from Batman than to trade crime-solving tips; she isn't interested in marrying him or stealing his precious freedom. Because of this, Batgirl is a female who Batman can actually regard as a brilliant peer and a partner in the war on crime, the same way he would a male.

These two different treatments of women bring to light one of the great ironies about the comic books of the 1960s. Marvel gets most of the credit for invigorating the world of comic books during this decade, and for making the medium more adult and sophisticated. And much of that praise is valid. Marvel laid the groundwork for what would be the modern comic book, and the mainstream press promoted the idea that these comic books about superheroes with real life problems weren't just for kids anymore. DC's comic books, conversely, were often viewed as more traditional, simple superhero stories aimed at a more juvenile audience.

However, like Elasti-Girl and Batgirl, many of the DC's female characters got better treatment than the heroines featured in Marvel Comics. Scanning a comic book rack in the '60s, the covers would tell two different stories about the women starring within those pages. Wonder Woman and Supergirl starred in comic books that featured their names on the covers. These heroines were often seen performing great feats of strength like battling monsters or stopping missiles with their bare hands. Batgirl's name might be featured prominently on a cover of *Detective Comics*. The Doom

Patrol's Elasti-Girl was shown in the thick of battle fighting side by side with her male compatriots. On the Marvel Comics covers, Invisible Girl, Wasp, and Marvel Girl were shown struggling in the clutches of a villain, or watching helplessly from the background as their male teammates took care of business.

Independent and powerful superheroines faced the same question that career women in the real world would face going into the liberated 1970s: did their success and competency limit their options as women? DC's Wonder Woman, like her cohorts Superman and Batman, had to have her personal life remain in permanent stasis, since career came first for these heroes. Although Batgirl was sleek and sexy in her formfitting black costume, her serious nature didn't make her a real hot ticket in the superhero dating game. The heroines of Marvel Comics may have suffered from a lack of heroic opportunities, but they were allowed to grow in their personal lives. Invisible Girl and Mr. Fantastic married in a lavish 1965 wedding attended by all of the Marvel superhero pantheon. The wedding turned into a gigantic battle royal when all of the major villains crashed it, creating a tradition in which most superhero nuptials to come would be marred by a slugfest. Three years later, Invisible Girl's pal Wasp slipped into a Saks Fifth Avenue gown for her own march down the aisle with her insect beau Ant-Man, who now went by the name Yellowjacket.

Once married, both women are content to settle down to lives as married ladies, free of superheroics. "I want to be involved with supermarkets . . . instead of super-villains!" Invisible Girl laments. "I'm sick of living in a ridiculous costume! I'm a woman!

I want feminine dresses . . . foolish hairdos!" Mr. Fantastic quickly appeases his new bride by allowing her to go shopping for a new wardrobe, adding that, "Wives should be kissed . . . and not heard!" Once the couple have a baby in 1967, Invisible Girl is more than happy to take a break from the Fantastic Four, and devote her time to motherhood. The Wasp is equally happy to let her heroic career take a back seat to that of a suburban wife.

Meanwhile, the Doom Patrol's Elasti-Girl, continues to display her characteristic strength of character by juggling a superheroine's role with marriage. Even at the conclusion of her 1966 wedding to Mento, Elasti-Girl postpones going on her honeymoon in order to join her fellow Doom Patrollers on an important mission. "I'll do anything you say, dear!" she tells her new husband with a smile, "But we can't let that plane blow up! See you later!"

1967 began the era that, to most people, epitomizes the whole of the decade—hippies, Haight Ashbury, psychedelia, drugs, civil rights uprisings, campus unrest, and the antiwar movement. It wasn't as radical a shift as it may seem in hindsight; the so-called counterculture movement had been evolving, below the surface, from the roots of the Beat Generation for many years. But it went mainstream with 1967's Summer of Love, and mod futurism gave way to flower power. And this is where comics drew the line. Up to this point, comic book heroes had tried to keep up with the latest styles. But by the late 1960s, kids were still the main consumers of comic books, which still had to abide by the rules of the Comics

Code Authority. Superheroes represented law and order, and the hippie movement's connections with free love, the sexual revolution, rampant drug abuse, and revolutionary radicalism were taboo. As it was, superhero comics had pretty much steered clear of the Viet Nam War since the mid 1960s. There were plenty of war comics on the stands, but superheroes did not fly off to Southeast Asia to fight the Viet Cong the way they had whipped the Nazis twenty years before.

Superhero comics stayed away from the antiwar question as well. Wonder Woman, whose mission was to bring peace to "man's world" did not jump on the antiwar bandwagon, but remained a loyal member of the military in her alter ego of Lt. Diana Prince. Ironically, Wonder Woman was the only heroine to flirt with the counterculture. In 1968, with the sales of her comic book so low that it faced cancellation, Wonder Woman "dropped out." DC stripped her of her powers, tiara, eagle emblazoned bodice, and starry briefs. She becomes Diana Prince, a normal human woman in a white Courrèges pantsuit, using only karate and her wits to fight evil. Diana Prince opens a mod boutique in New York's Lower East Side, certainly not an area she'd have frequented in her days with the Justice League. "I'm a butterfly on the first day of spring!" Diana Prince proclaims, as she revels in the sights, sounds, and emotions she is experiencing in her new bohemian life.

Likewise, kid sister Wonder Girl was embracing the new world that was dawning in America. Wonder Girl was a foundling that Wonder Woman had rescued from a fire some years earlier. She took the child to Paradise Island to be raised by the Amazons, who bestowed a portion of their fantastic powers on her. In 1965, she joined the Teen Titans, a group made up of fellow youthful sidekicks Robin, Aqualad, and Kid Flash. The Teen Titans helped their fellow juveniles, and most of their stories were lighthearted romps, with Camelot era messages about staying in school, joining the Peace Corps, or doing the right thing. In Wonder Girl's first adventure with the group, she is seen leaving Paradise Island for Man's World, as Wonder Woman and Queen Hippolyta wave goodbye with a word of warning. "Be careful, Wonder Girl . . . despite your Amazon powers—you're just a girl amongst male superheroes!" Wonder Girl's response shows that she is a little more up with the liberated times than her mother. "Oh mother. Stop babying me! I can do anything any boy can do—and better!"

Wonder Girl had led a life of drastic extremes—raised among only women, and then immersed into a group of adolescent males as the lone female. She is stronger than all of her boy comrades, and never feels guilty about it. Wonder Girl represents the new teenage girl—fun loving, free, and confident in her abilities. When the Teen Titans visit a hippie neighborhood in 1968, it's Wonder Girl who tries to get her young cohorts to shed their clean-cut images and their "middle class junior superhero background." When Kid Flash rejects the idea of going hippie and growing a beard, a frustrated Wonder Girl replies, "Excuses, excuses! That's all a girl gets these days! This is the love-in generation, and I'm being left out—!"

By the end of the 1960s, the culture of the day reached an apex that asked a big question about what would happen tomorrow.

The Beatles, no longer the sweet moptops the world had fallen in love with a few years earlier, gave their last public performance. Woodstock showed the world a new vision of a nation of people united by music and love. Despite the peace anthems of the Summer of Love, the ongoing war in Viet Nam and the 1968 assassinations of Robert Kennedy and Dr. Martin Luther King, Jr. seemed to be saying that love might not save the day after all. The decade drew to a dark close in 1969 with the infamous Altamont Free Concert, where a spectator was killed during the Rolling Stones' performance. The grisly murder of actress Sharon Tate by the Manson Family cast a somber pall over the so-called counterculture movement.

In 1969, a man walked on the moon. The greatest goal of the day had been achieved, leaving the bigger question of what was left to strive for now? Likewise, the Silver Age of Comics began to wane as the decade drew to a close.

As the 1970s approached, the Wasp had exited the superhero scene, and was living the life of a dutiful wife. Invisible Girl was spending more time pushing a stroller through Central Park than she was fighting evil in her blue jumpsuit. When the heroine went on maternity leave from the Fantastic Four, Crystal, a teenage girl with elemental powers, replaced her as the team's token girl member. The elfin Crystal hailed from a lost race called the Inhumans, and was the girlfriend of the Fantastic Four's Human Torch. Despite her exotic background and powers, Crystal's goals in life were very old fashioned, and showed that the 1960s had done little to affect Marvel Comics' view of women's aspirations.

Attending the 1968 wedding of Avengers Wasp and Yellowjacket, Crystal sighs, "Gosh . . . I always cry at weddings! Mainly because they're not my own!"

The coming decade held promise for some of the liberated heroines of the 1960s. Batgirl looked forward to a decade where her efficient, take-charge attitude might not be so unusual for a woman. Her alter ego Barbara Gordon, miraculously no longer in need of glasses, was looking sexier, just in time for a new era where such things would matter. Sadly, the lovely, capable, and powerful Elasti-Girl, who perhaps best epitomized the emancipated heroine of the 1960s, never lived to see the beckoning days of Women's Lib. *The Doom Patrol* was cancelled in 1968, and DC literally sent the team out with a bang. Given the choice between saving themselves and sacrificing the lives of fourteen innocent people, The Doom Patrol members chose a heroic death, and were blown to kingdom come. Like her male teammates in the Doom Patrol, Elasti-Girl died with her boots on. Except hers had high heels.

The '60s were over. America needed to take stock of itself. And superheroines needed to figure out for themselves where they were going next.

Girls Together (Outrageously)

The victory party was in full swing. The walls of the Legion of Superheroes clubhouse reverberated with wild music. Inside, five teenage girls in colorful costumes dance madly in celebration, while their leader Saturn Girl shakes with triumphant laughter. "Operation Betrayal" was a success.

Earlier that day, the girls had eagerly carried out their grim assignments. Each had selected one of her male teammates to eliminate. Saturn Girl's orders had been clear, "We'll sneak attack them with our charms and super-powers . . ." The girls of the Legion were usually demure young ladies, but they gleefully transformed into coy seductresses in order to cruelly enthrall, and then destroy their boy compatriots.

Light Lass was first. Using her feminine wiles, the redheaded teen teased the socially inept Element Lad, leading the boy on with promises of kisses before turning her gravity powers on him. Next came Triplicate Girl, aided by her friend Shrinking Violet, whose meek demeanor had given way to a taste for cruelty. Splitting herself into three separate bodies, Triplicate Girl beguiled Invisible Kid, Brainiac 5, and Cosmic Boy with pledges of love and devotion, then shrank the three boys and joyfully imprisoned them in a tiny box.

And more males were marked for destruction. Saturn Girl feigned adoration of Superboy in order to lure him into a cave where he was exposed to deadly Green Kryptonite: "Die . . . trying to understand what changed me, your friend, into an unrelenting foe!" Meanwhile, Superboy's pretty blonde cousin Supergirl taunted the orange-skinned, antennae-sporting Chameleon Boy with kisses, while Phantom Girl led on the doltish Star Boy with the prospect of a make-out session. Once the boys were entranced by their feminine wiles, both young heroines heartlessly turned on them.

Later, the young heroines-turned-scoundrels make merry at the thought of their male victims. The girls dance like frenzied Maenads of old, overjoyed that they've eliminated the tiresome males from their lives. "We'll change the club constitution so no boys can join, ever!— Ugh! How I hate them!" cackles Supergirl, as she madly does the Twist.

We are reading this story in 1964, although the Legionnaires live a thousand years hence, in 2964. The Legion of Superheroes has faced the threats posed by the Time Trapper and the Legion of Super-Villains. But nothing could prepare them for "The Revolt of the Girl Legionnaires." Who could contend with a united force of teenage girls, with power and sexual charms at their disposal, exploiting their male teammates' greatest weakness—hormones?

Absolute power may be a scary prospect, but what could be more terrifying than power in the hands of teenage girls, out for revenge?

Girls Together (Outrageously)

The Legion of Superheroes was first introduced in 1958, when three teenagers from the 30th Century traveled back in time to visit Superboy. The teens—Lightning Lad, Cosmic Boy, and Saturn Girl—had come to invite the Boy of Steel to join their exclusive club for superpowered adolescents. Superboy joins the trio in their Time Bubble, which whisks them a thousand years into the future. There, after enduring a number of tests, Superboy is awarded membership in the prestigious team. The Legionnaires hail from different planets across the galaxy, although they all look humanoid and are predominantly white-skinned. By the time that cousin Supergirl is offered membership in the Legion of Superheroes in 1960, its ranks had swelled to include several female members. The Legion of Superheroes earned a regular feature in *Adventure Comics* beginning in 1962, and developed one of the most loyal fan followings in comic book history.

There was something inherently dorky yet absolutely endearing and captivating about the Legion of Superheroes. The founding members of the Legion—Cosmic Boy, Lightning Lad, and Saturn Girl—had saved the life of the richest man in the galaxy, who bankrolled the club for superpowered teens as a show of gratitude. They had twenty odd members, not including The Legion of Substitute Heroes, and the Legion Reservists. There was even a Legion of Super-Pets. They met in a strange clubhouse that looked like a rocket ship that had crashed into the ground, and they flew around in clunky looking ships. On the plus side, each member got one of the coolest accessories in the history of comics—the Flight Ring. As the name indicates, the rings allowed Legionnaires to fly, and were much better than the snazziest car. The Legion of Superheroes boasted the nicest kids in the galaxy, maybe a little square, but truly dedicated to making the United Planets a better place. They were involved in sweeping science fantasy epics on fantastic, exotic worlds, and fans were absolutely devoted to them.

While the Legion of Superheroes may have seemed like the strait-laced honor roll kids of the comic book world, their series broke one of the major rules of the industry. Superhero teams usually had one token female member. In the Justice League, Wonder Woman was always the odd girl out, and circa the early 1960s, most other superhero teams held to the same membership rules. That meant that the Fantastic Four had only the Invisible Girl, The Avengers had the Wasp, The Doom Patrol had Elasti-Girl, and so on. Of the almost twenty-five superpowered teen members of the Legion of Superheroes, a third of the members were girls. This meant that readers, including female ones, could see more than one heroine in a story. This also meant that the distaff members of the Legion had friends of their own sex to pal around with, and in some cases, conspire with. This was especially important, given the distribution of powers among the members.

Most of the boys have romantic titles that spoke of their powers—Sun Boy, Ultra Boy, Star Boy, Invisible Kid. Others have awkward, if not descriptive names—Chameleon Boy, Element Lad, Chemical King. Some Legionnaires have absurd powers, like the rotund and buoyant Bouncing Boy, or Matter-Eater Lad, whose alien digestive system allows him to safely eat anything. As far as heroics go, the girls' powers are another story. While the boys' names spell out what their impressive powers can do, the girls are given more dainty abilities.

The girl Legionnaires are mainly useful for diversion or spying. Triplicate Girl can split into three bodies, Phantom Girl can walk through walls, Shrinking Violet can . . . shrink. Princess Projectra can create illusions, and Shadow Lass projects darkness. The telepathic Saturn Girl, with her pragmatic *sangfroid*, shows the most strength and confidence of any of the girls. Saturn Girl becomes the team's first female leader in 1964, well before any other comic book heroines hold positions of authority. But Supergirl is the first girl in the club who exhibits any power comparable to the boys. The only other heroine to come close to Supergirl in sheer strength is Night Girl, whose satiny black costume, towering beehive hairdo, and dangling earrings make her look much older than her teenage years. Night Girl doesn't avoid sunlight to preserve her pearly white skin; she only has superhuman strength after dark. Unfortunately, Night Girl's limited powers only earned her a spot in the second-string Legion of Substitute Heroes.

When founding member Lightning Lad is killed in battle in 1963, his twin sister Ayla replaces him. In a Shakespearean move, she first tries to impersonate him, but her cross-dressing is eventually exposed. Outfitted with the gender appropriate name Lightning Lass and a pair of high heel pumps, Ayla wields deadly electrical powers, certainly more formidable than most heroines of the era. But it is not to last. Lightning Lad is revived from the dead, and since the bylaws state that each Legionnaire has to have a unique power, Lightning Lass has to go. An accident changes Ayla's electrical power to the ability to make things super-lightweight, hence her new name Light Lass. Kind of a step down from the Olympian power of hurling lightning bolts, but Light Lass accepts her new name and power downgrade with no argument, showing a lack of emotion typical of the early Legion stories. In a shocking 1966 tale, a giant rampaging killer machine named Computo destroys one of Triplicate Girl's three bodies. Rather than be traumatized or go into shock, the plucky Legionnaire simply announces to her teammates that from now on she will go by the name Duo Damsel, since she can now only split into two.

The large teen heroine cast made the Legion of Superheroes a bit like high school, with all of the archetypes. This especially became the case beginning in 1966, when fourteen-year-old fan Jim Shooter began writing the Legion's adventures, modeling the girl's personas after some of his schoolmates. Telepath Saturn Girl is the brainy class valedictorian. The intangible Phantom Girl is the cheerleader with the boyfriend from the bad part of town. Duo Damsel is the girl next door who harbors a crush on B.M.O.C. Superboy. Shrinking Violet is the shy wallflower. Light Lass is the girl with the worst taste in boyfriends. Supergirl is the popular beauty who picks the class nerd to date. Dream Girl is the gorgeous blonde who dresses too old for her age. Princess Projectra is the rich girl, and Shadow Lass is the black girl. Well, she's actually blue-skinned, but the original intention in 1968 was that Shadow Lass would be the Legion's first black member. Plans for integration were scrapped, and her skin was colored blue instead.

But, in a group of white girls, Shadow Lass' blue skin and exotic background essentially make her the ethnic girl of the school.

The token females of most superhero teams often had to suppress their femininity in order to be taken seriously by their male compatriots. When heroines like Invisible Girl or Wasp do display an interest in traditionally female pursuits like love, fashion, or the latest hairstyle, their male teammates chide them for being frivolous females. But the girls of the Legion have strength in numbers. Like typical teenage girls, they talk about clothes and boys and the latest dance craze from a distant planet. But although the boys outclass them in the power department, the girl Legionnaires take their jobs seriously. Writer Shooter made the girls more courageous and allowed them to contribute to the team more, despite their weaker powers. "Don't think you can keep *me* on the sidelines!" Shadow Lass announces to her male comrades before a suicide mission. The boys treat their female teammates with respect, although they don't seem to see them as their equals. When the super powerful Legionnaire Mon-El learns that the trio of Princess Projectra, Dream Girl and the White Witch has thwarted the evil sorcerer Mordru, he chuckles, "How ironic that he was foiled by three girls!"

Perhaps it was this attitude that sparked stories like 1964's "Revolt of the Girl Legionnaires," which shows what happened when the girls used their feminine charms to augment their weaker powers to turn against the boys. The "revolt" turns out to be the result of a post-hypnotic suggestion planted by the queen of the planet Femnaz, a world inhabited by only women. Once freed of mind control, the girls naturally hurry to make amends with the boys.

Shooter explores a similar theme in 1968's "Mutiny of the Super-Heroines!" A female ambassador from the matriarchal planet Taltar comes to Earth, and plants her seeds of dissension among the girl Legionnaires. The ambassador uses radiation to boost the girls' powers, making them dramatically stronger than the boys. Concerned leader Invisible Kid, thinking the girls have contracted a space bug, attempts to quarantine the females. "Well, of all the gall! You and your masculine pride! Just because we're mightier than you . . . ," an irate Light Lass proclaims. The girls overthrow the boys, and decide to spread their female superiority across the galaxy, gleefully shouting, "Hooray! Down with men!" The cool-headed Supergirl shakes off the scheming ambassador's brainwashing, and the status quo returns to normal. "Our powers are back to normal . . . but so are our minds . . . and that's the important thing!" says a somber Princess Projectra, trying not to sound disappointed by this turn of events.

While all seemed egalitarian in the utopian future of the Legion, it only took a little pushing to get the girls not only to turn on their male teammates and boyfriends, but also to willfully subjugate them, and take great pleasure in it. While the girls' revolts were shown to be the products of manipulation, the heroines also displayed a proto-feminist attitude even when not under any sinister influence. In a 1966 story entitled "The Super-Stalag of Space," a team of Legionnaires is captured and incarcerated in superhero prisoner of war camps—one for males and one for females. When the team's resident genius Brainiac 5 telepathically contacts Saturn Girl in the girls' camp to tell her not to attempt an escape, she coolly rebuffs him with a thought, "You and your masculine ego! Just be ready for a break . . . tonight!" She rallies the girl Legionnaires with the challenge, "We'll show the boys!" and hatches her plan to outwit the guards and liberate the male Legionnaires.

These stories of teenage girl insurrections indicate a shift in the image of the young heroine. No longer complacent and retiring, these girls could be not only confident and powerful, but also willful and vindictive. And, despite the fact that the girls were duped into turning on their male teammates and boyfriends, their all too convincing resentment hinted at a seething dissatisfaction with their inferior status within the team. But, a gathering of teenaged females could have its downside, and bring out other emotions besides feelings of sisterhood. Just as in high school, jealousy and competitiveness would rear their ugly heads among the girls of the Legion. When the glamorous but haughty oracle Dream Girl joins the team and gets the boys to wait on her hand and foot, her fellow females get upset. " . . . I know you resent all us girl Legionnaires, and would like to get rid of us!" a livid Triplicate Girl snaps at the platinum blonde Dream Girl. But nowhere is this jealousy and female rivalry more telling than in 1963's "The Condemned Legionnaires." In this story, a mysterious purple-clad masked female named Satan Girl threatens to kill all of the girl Legionnaires with the deadly Crimson Virus. Supergirl is the only girl Legionnaire immune to the effects of the Crimson Virus, and able to defeat Satan Girl. Unmasking the would-be murderess, the Legionnaires see that Satan Girl is actually . . . Supergirl? Under the always-unpredictable effects of Red Kryptonite, Supergirl had split into two beings—one good and one evil. The evil Supergirl was an expression of the Girl of Steel's subconscious desire, which in this case was to eliminate her female rivals for the honor of being the most popular girl in the class.

By the 1970s, the Legion of Superheroes still boasted the same large cast of superheroines, with the winged Dawnstar joining the group after Supergirl resigned in 1974. But there was less interaction among the team's female members. The focus of the girls' emotional connections became their boyfriends, who were usually also members of the Legion. When the rotund Bouncing Boy discovers he has lost his powers, he proposes marriage to his girlfriend Duo Damsel. "Oh, Chuck . . . you don't know how long I've waited for this moment!" she gushes, apparently feeling it was more important to settle down rather than travel the cosmos righting wrongs.

The Legion of Superheroes hit their peak of popularity in the 1980s, but the girls were still, for the most part, fragmented. Phantom Girl and Shadow Lass were written as friends, presumably because they had the same taste in boyfriends. But in general, boyfriends were still the focus of the girls' lives. Eventually, Light Lass gets tired of her emotionally unavailable boyfriend, Timber Wolf, and leaves him. Shrinking Violet, meanwhile, is kidnapped and tortured by rebels from her homeworld. As it happened with many heroines in the 1980s, her post-traumatic response is to cut her hair and adopt a tough and aggressive demeanor. She also dumps her boyfriend Duplicate Boy. It is only after Light Lass, (now with her Lightning Lass powers and title restored) and Shrinking Violet are romantically unattached from boys that they are allowed to develop a friendship. When Lightning Lass' attempts to spark a romance with younger member Magnetic Kid are rebuffed, her fellow female Shrinking Violet is there to lend support. "Just *remember* who your friends are, lady," the formerly meek heroine tells her teammate.

By the end of the 1980s, the Legion of Superheroes finally grew up and became adults. They stopped using their "girl," "boy," "lad" and "lass" names. Some members died, some got married and had kids, and the whole series became more serious. And Shrinking Violet and Lightning Lass embraced a different kind of sisterhood, becoming lesbian lovers.

In 1968's "Mutiny of the Super-Heroines," a mind altered Supergirl comments to her fellow girl Legionnaires, "I've been thinking about how great it would be if the world were ruled by women!" While the assumption at one time may have been that a team with more than one female would turn into a treacherous coven of witches out to overthrow the men, the results never turned out to be that disastrous. By the '70s and '80s, superhero teams relaxed the lone female member rule, with organizations like the male-centric "X-Men" often boasting a female majority. But for a few years, it was the female "lasses" and "damsels" of the Legion of Superheroes, in their futuristic girls' dormitory, who kindled the fires of sisterhood for generations of heroines to come.

1970s: Sirens and Suffragettes

Power Girl was irritated, once again. This should have been a happy day for the formidable young heroine. She had finally become an official member of the Justice Society of America, and earned the respect of her male teammates. But, as usual, it was men who were the source of Power Girl's frustration.

First, there was her cousin Superman. Like him, Power Girl had been placed in a rocket as an infant to escape the destruction of Krypton. But her journey to Earth took sixty years. Within the confines of the tiny ship, Power Girl remained asleep and youthful in suspended animation for all of those years, emerging a young woman of twenty. Power Girl felt stifled when Superman tried to control her life, resenting him for keeping her existence a secret. She didn't want to live in his shadow. "Don't patronize me, cousin! And don't give me any more orders, either!" she would say, jamming her elbow into the famous red "S" on the chest of the father of all superheroes. "I deserve my chance, too!"

Then, there were the men of the Justice Society of America. The venerable group of august male superheroes dated back to the 1940s. They doubted Power Girl's abilities because of her age and sex, and it was only because she was Superman's cousin that they gave her a chance. "I'm sick of being considered a child—especially by men," Power Girl thought, as she constantly struggled to prove her worth to the skeptical males.

But now the day had finally come when Power Girl was inducted into the Justice Society. Her teammate Star Spangled Kid had no idea what hit him when he offered Power Girl a gift to commemorate the event. It was an emblem to decorate Power Girl's white costume. The sight of the red crest caused the heroine to seethe. "Why you little chauvinist piglet! That's just a Superman emblem with a P instead of an S! I thought you understood—I may be Superman's cousin, but I'm not his carbon copy! I'm my own woman!" Power Girl shouts, as she crushes the emblem to powder in her mighty blue-gloved fist.

Power Girl's cousin stands silently, watching her display of rage. Superman calmly explains to the young woman that she has proved herself and has earned her place in the Justice Society. "Stop fighting so hard," Superman says, "you've won."

It's 1977. Queen Elizabeth II is celebrating her twenty-fifth anniversary as ruler of the United Kingdom. TV heroines Wonder Woman and Charlie's Angels take a sexy bite out of crime each week in millions of American homes. *Star Wars*, featuring the commanding white clad heroine Princess Leia, is the highest grossing movie of its day. And another heroine in a white costume is trying to make her mark in the world of male superheroes. Power Girl is tough, tenacious, and has a message for Superman and his caped brethren: "I'm gonna be around for a long time!"

In 1969, a heroine was born who would embody many of the qualities of the coming era's comic book females. Her name was Vampirella, and she began her career in September of that year as the star of her own adult black and white horror comic. Billed as "Captivating Comics about Fantastic Females," *Vampirella* was created by independent publisher James Warren to recapture the gruesome glory of EC horror comics of the 1950s, now updated with sexuality not restricted by the Comics Code Authority. Vampirella's origin was standard comic book fare. She hailed from the distant planet Drakulon, where rivers flowing with blood instead of water nourished its people. When the blood streams dried up, Vampirella stowed away on a convenient rocket ship and set out to find a new home on Earth.

While her origin was reminiscent of Superman's, Vampirella's costume was enough to make the upstanding hero blush. Originally designed by underground comic book artist Trina Robbins, the costume was an eye-popping creation. Comic books had produced few outfits as blatantly daring as Vampirella's red swimsuit. With its cutaway front that laid her breasts and stomach bare, the costume consisted essentially of two straps and a g-string, with a tiny gold bat appliqué perched coyly above the crotch. A pair of spike heeled boots and long black dominatrix tresses completed the look. While initially presented more as bloodsucking airhead than deadly seductress, over a short period of time Vampirella's character evolved into a mysterious sexpot. For the first time in almost twenty-five years, the comic book femme fatale was alive, sexier than ever, and living on the magazine rack at the local 7-11.

Vampirella's greatest superhuman ability seemed to be that she could move in her costume without falling out of it. But in spite of her scandalous attire and ripe form, Vampirella was really more bark than bite. She drank a blood substitute to keep her natural cravings in check, and only occasionally dispatching a deserving foe with her deadly bite. Most of her time was spent using her powers to battle demons and mystical forces, while always staying one step ahead of overzealous vampire hunters. She was basically virtuous, and her racy attire belied her sweet nature.

Vampirella was the classic good girl with a naughty streak archetype, as adorable and alluring as the fresh faced coeds who displayed their charms in the centerfolds of *Playboy* every month. In truth, for underage boys in the early 1970s, *Vampirella* was the next best thing to reading *Playboy*. Clearly, her main appeal was that flimsy costume, and storylines continuously contained scenes of sharp nailed ghoulies clawing at her shapely posterior or wooden stakes aimed between her heaving, half-covered breasts. Vampirella existed in a fantastically erotic world meant to fuel male sexual fantasies. She battled an array of female menaces, from voodoo priestesses to queens of lost civilizations, who all shared her taste for scanty attire.

Strangely enough, none of the characters that Vampirella met in her adventures ever seemed the least bit fazed by her peek-a-boo swimsuit. In fact, there was a strange air of innocence about Vampirella's frankly revealing costume. In 1971, Aurora Toys even produced a model kit of Vampirella, as part of their Monster Scenes line, a somewhat questionable collection of toys that featured Frankenstein, a mad scientist with various torture chamber devices, and a girl victim in tattered hot pants. The controversial line was pulled from the market shortly after its introduction, but for a while, Vampirella, in all of her breast baring glory, graced the shelves of the local suburban toyshop alongside model airplanes and the Visible Man. While few heroines would show as much skin as Vampirella, she sent a shockwave through the world of comic books, announcing that a new era of sexual freedom had arrived. Following in the footsteps of 1940s sirens like Phantom Lady and Sheena, Queen of the Jungle, Vampirella would lead the revival of the sexy image of the comic book heroine.

If Vampirella was the new dark princess of seduction for comic books, the following year would introduce an icy Teutonic beauty who represented the other end of the female spectrum. A 1970 issue of Marvel Comics' superhero team *The Avengers* featured a story entitled "Come On In . . . The Revolution's Fine!" In it, female Avengers Scarlet Witch and the Wasp, along with friends Medusa and Black Widow, get a crash course in feminism. A spear-toting female calling herself the Valkyrie assembles the quartet of heroines in order to enlighten them about their oppressed state. Valkyrie is a new kind of heroine—a woman who had been wronged by the chauvinistic ways of men, on a personal crusade to free her sisters from "the invisible shackles that men had placed" on them. Valkyrie's costume marked her as strictly No Man's Land. Valkyrie's all black Wagnerian garb, with its menacing silver nose cone breasts, sent a clear *verboten* message to any male she encountered. The glacial Valkyrie was the angel of death for male-dominated society, and anticipated the "I am Woman/hear me roar" ethos that singer Helen Reddy trumpeted two years later across radio airwaves. She was the Anti-Wonder Woman, and her message was the polar opposite of the loving coexistence of the sexes that the Amazing Amazon had advocated since the 1940s.

Valkyrie convinces the four heroines that their male compatriots have been subjugating them. Dubbing themselves the Lady Liberators, the women set out to trounce the male members of the Avengers in order to win back their rights. OK, so maybe the name sounded more like a women's softball team, but it was 1970, after all. In the aftermath of the resulting battle, Valkyrie is revealed to be the Avengers' old foe, the Enchantress, who had manipulated the unwitting females into defeating the more powerful male heroes for her. After the women learn the truth and vanquish the Enchantress, the boorish Avenger Goliath chides his female teammates, hoping that ". . . you birds finally learned your lesson about that women's lib bull!" The Scarlet Witch and Wasp, however, did not seem so convinced. While they did not rush out to burn their bras, the seed had been planted. Valkyrie's feminist message, sham as it may have been, would resonate throughout the coming decade. The '70s would see established heroines question the roles that they had been placed in, and finally begin to strike out on their own.

Welcome to the 1970s, where the comic book world underwent another series of revolutions. Vampirella and Valkyrie represented two extremely different visions of the comic book heroine, but they were merely examples of the changes that the industry would go through in the coming decade. The major comic book publishers faced a new reality at the dawn of the 1970s. Comic books, as a medium, had celebrated their thirtieth birthday, and some felt it was time to start growing up. Many of the veteran artists and writers had begun to retire, passing the torch to a younger generation of bearded and shaggy headed creators, who began infusing stories with more topical, controversial subject matter pulled from real life. In the era where pop music was producing rock operas and TV sitcoms had messages, comic books were starting to be looked at as a serious American medium, with serious things to talk about. The 1970s was the decade when the comic book let its hair down and entered the real world.

The world where superheroes lived was growing darker, and their eyes were opened to the realities of modern life. Drug dealers, slumlords, and corrupt politicians replaced the super spy foes and mad scientists of the 1960s. Readers learned that Superman's pristine home of Metropolis had a ghetto. The Manhattan where Marvel Comics' heroes dwelt began to grow more dirty and gritty, expanding beyond the 5th Avenue shops where Wasp and Invisible Girl shopped for their frocks to the mean streets of Harlem and the barrios uptown. The cosmic superhero Green Lantern paired with the ultra liberal and volatile Green Arrow to embark on an *Easy Rider* inspired road trip that exposed the problems that were "destroying America"—drug addiction, overpopulation, racism, heartless corporations, and the suffering of the under classes. Even Captain America, disillusioned by the corruption of the American government, gave up his star spangled citizenship and took on a new nationless identity—The Nomad.

The face of superheroes was literally changing. The introduction of the African hero Black Panther in 1966 opened the doors for more black heroes like the Falcon, the bulletproof soul brother Luke Cage, Hero for Hire, and Black Lightning. A new superhero team called The Defenders perhaps best expressed the laidback sensibilities of the "me" decade. Formed by outsiders Sub-Mariner, Dr. Strange, and the Hulk, the Defenders were a loose association of antiheroes, often described as a "non-team." Members came and went casually, without the formal rules and bylaws that teams like the Justice League and the Avengers adhered to. The times were a'changin', and these new heroes were setting the tone for the new decade.

So, what did the 1970s hold in store for women in comic books? While the Valkyrie's assessment of the heroines' role as victims of male heroes' chauvinism seemed harsh at the time, it was not really that far off base. Throughout the '60s, nothing much had changed for superheroines. The '70s began as the '60s had, with Wonder Woman, Supergirl, and Lois Lane as the only women in the superhero world who starred in their own comic books. But as the decade progressed, the role, and consequently the image, of the comic book heroine, would begin to evolve to keep up with the times. The heroine of the '70s was no longer content to be the devoted but ineffectual girlfriend or assistant, making coffee or sewing costumes for her male teammates. The era of the emancipated superheroine had arrived.

Feminism was a tricky subject for comic books to handle.

Initially, comics of the early '70s used the more outré aspects of feminism like the aggressive viewpoints of the Valkyrie, as novelty story material. These treatments of the "battle of the sexes" never went beyond the sort of "girls are just as good as boys" debates that could be heard on most episodes of the *Brady Bunch*. Even romance comics tackled the dilemma of how to juggle liberation and love in stories like 1970's "No Man Is My Master." But generally, the tone of these stories suggested that the male writers didn't take women's liberation seriously.

A cover of a 1969 comic book shows a defeated Batman ensnared in the villainess Catwoman's bullwhip. "It's all over Batman! You just lost the Battle of the Sexes!" Catwoman announces. Assembling a gang of female felons that she dubs the Feline Furies, Catwoman decides to go on a crime campaign tinged with women's liberation. "Men! It was men who led us astray—men who put us behind bars like caged tigers! Now I give you a chance to strike back—with bared fangs and clawed paws!" In the end, Catwoman's lust for sparkling jewels gets the better of her, and her own slavish desires cause her to abandon her campaign to emancipate her sisters. Stories like this suggested that Women's Lib was a passing fancy, like a new skirt length or hairstyle.

There was even the implication that it was perhaps dangerous to upset the status quo. 1971's *Savage Tales*, Marvel Comics' foray into adult oriented black and white comic books, featured a story about the Femizons, a warlike society of women, or "vicious voluptuaries," who ruled 23rd century America with an iron fist. But a Femizon named Lyra makes the mistake of falling in love with a slave boy and learns the error of her ways: "When a man is but a slave—it is the woman who lives in bondage." But as Americans watched *Maude* and a new era of independent TV heroines espousing the merits of Women's Lib weekly, it should have come as no surprise that a less sensational version of these sentiments should eventually infiltrate the comic book pages. The early 1970s began a period of reinventions of superheroines, as these women attempted to, in the jargon of the day, "find themselves," and be regarded as respected partners in the fight against evil. But was the predominantly male comic book world ready for the liberated heroine?

The 1970s would be the era of liberation for the comic book heroine, as the fires of revolution lit a new path for her. But, if the women's liberation movement created a new, emancipated persona for the superheroine, it would be the sexual revolution that would provide an image that would make her new liberated role more palatable to the still mostly male comic book audience. The social changes of the '60s counterculture movement heralded a new era of sexual freedom and expression. Sexual freedom was a topic, and in a sense a trend, that permeated popular culture in the early 1970s. If comic book readers were not of the age to be engaging in sex, they were certainly aware of its allure. The birth control pill was redefining relationships, and marriage was no longer seen as the only option for women. Racy page-turners like *The Happy Hooker* and *Fear of Flying* burned up the paperback racks. Movie stars bared more flesh than ever before, and the male centerfold debuted on the pages of *Cosmopolitan* and *Playgirl.* Homosexuality, bisexuality, androgyny, and wife swapping became topics of suburban American conversation. Even innocent animated cartoons went X-rated with 1973's *Fritz the Cat.* Freewheeling sex was rampant. What better way to draw young, pre-pubescent males into reading comics?

The 1970s was the great makeover decade for superheroines. Vampirella's erotic costume was the first shot fired in the sexual revolution of the comic book heroines. Feminism and the sexual revolution became strange bedfellows in the evolution of the superheroine. Just as a movie star like Jane Fonda could be an activist and still reignite her career by taking on a racy, sexual role, a superheroine could appear to be liberated and still sport a sexy and revealing new costume. Cher had removed the taboo of the exposed female navel on her weekly TV show, so it was OK for the comic book crime fighters to also show some skin. As heroines took on more emancipated personas, necklines plunged, backs and legs were laid bare, and high heels made a comeback. The prim skirts of the '50s and the unisex space age looks of the '60s gave way to sexy, flesh baring costumes. Sex appeal was the "spoonful of sugar" that helped the "medicine" of feminism go down. A liberated heroine who still looked sexy would be less threatening to the male readers of comic books.

The Black Widow was one of the first heroines to be reinvented as a sexy and liberated character in the '70s. The Black Widow had been introduced in 1964 as a Communist agent and foe of Iron Man. She later reformed and defected. By 1970 she is simply Madame Natasha, the worldly and glamorous jet setter. Bored with her privileged existence, Natasha decides to get back into the superhero game. Black Widow dumps her bouffant hairdo, mask, and fishnets for a new look that is, as she said, "more in keeping with the swingy Seventies." Her new image owed much to Modesty Blaise, the sultry, dangerous adventuress from British newspaper comics. The costume was a shiny black leather jumpsuit that fit like a second skin—sleek, sexy, and minimal. The outfit was also practical, accented with wristbands that fired her deadly widow's bite, and a power line that allowed the martial arts mistress to swing from the skyscrapers of New York. Surveying her new look in the mirror, Black Widow muses that her costume would "be the envy of my jet set crowd from Jackie on down!"

Black Widow's new costume fit her perfectly, in every sense. Unlike the heroines of the previous twenty years, Black Widow was a thrill seeker who chose the life of a crime fighter for the excitement it brought her. She didn't do it to aid a boyfriend, didn't hide behind a wallflower alter ego, and lived her life with a freedom usually reserved for men. In keeping with the issue-conscious '70s, she descended from her penthouse to battle loan sharks and came to the aid of Puerto Rican youth groups. Rather than swing across the Manhattan skyline like Spider-Man to reach a crime scene, the chic Black Widow would often have her chauffeur drive her there in her limo. Black Widow's sexy costume defined her independent way of life and reflected the new freedom that women were seeking in the 1970s. Black Widow was unquestionably sexy, but, as with everything else in her life, it was on her terms. Still, the liberated heroine had doubts. "Is there really a place for her in a world such as this?" Black Widow thinks in 1970, of the newly independent persona she has created for herself.

Black Widow's uncertainty about her role in life was common for women at the start of the '70s, when many felt that they were at a crossroads. In singer Carly Simon's 1971 hit "That's The Way I Always Heard It Should Be," a young woman faced the idea of marriage, a home, and a family with suspicious trepidation. Women were exploring what kinds of lives they wanted, and for the first time, these types of characters were appearing in comic books. Many of the heroines of the '70s pursued a life of crime fighting in order to find themselves. Marvel's Spider-Woman was a mysterious beauty who used her powers to discover the secrets of her past, fighting evil in the process. These women became superheroes to benefit society and themselves, not to win a man's love.

The story of the woman leaving her old way of life behind to embark on a new one was a popular subject of 1970s entertainment. Think of the Mary Tyler Moore TV sitcom, or 1974's *Alice Doesn't Live Here Anymore*, and you'll get the picture. Black Canary brought her version of this story to the comic book page. She had been retired in 1951, but re-entered the superhero scene full-time in 1968, when her martial arts skills and newly acquired, ear splitting "canary cry" earned the high profile position as the sole female member of DC's Justice League.

By the 1960s, DC Comics had created the concept of multiple parallel Earths to explain why their heroes were perpetually youthful. The heroes who had first appeared in the 1940s lived on Earth 2, while their youther, present day incarnations that had begun fighting crime in the late 1950s lived on Earth 1. Black Canary moved from Earth 2 to Earth 1 after her husband Larry died, and still looked as dewy as she had in 1947. Astride her motorcycle, the image of the modern "Blonde Bombshell" was remolded from '40s girl daredevil to '70s biker chick. Groundbreaking artist Neal Adams drew her as a karate chopping *Playboy* centerfold, with a long platinum blonde wig, frosty pink lipstick, and heavy black eyeliner. "You make Raquel Welch look like Little Orphan Annie!" her Justice League teammate Green Arrow tells Black Canary.

Black Canary's adventures show a woman with no man in her life to depend on, making her way on her own. "This widow lady has to find a job!—And that won't be easy! I'm an expert at judo—that's all!!" Black Canary thinks as she scans the newspaper's help wanted ads, giving voice to the realistic tone that had now entered the world of 1970s superheroes. The hotheaded bowman Green Arrow quickly falls for the dazzling blonde heroine, and professes his love. But for a change, it is the female Black Canary who keeps the male Green Arrow's amorous advances at bay, rather than leaping at the prospect of landing a man. Black Canary says that she needs space to figure out who she is, and doesn't want a boyfriend around to complicate things. At the end of a Justice League mission, she gently lets down the lovestruck Green Arrow while also focusing on her crime fighting career. "Perhaps in a while . . . I'll be able to . . . discover myself! For now, let's be grateful that we saved your Earth!"

When she does discover herself, the Black Canary of the '70s evolves from weepy, insecure widow to full-fledged liberated heroine of the day—tough, independent, yet still sexy. Even when she and Green Arrow do become romantic and crime fighting partners, Black Canary still retains her freedom. "It's not as if I can't take care of myself, Mr. Domineering Male!" Black Canary tells her lover in 1973.

Black Canary's "no strings" approach to love indicated a new shift in comic book relationships. Superheroines had often been defined by their romantic liaisons, and many of these were facing new, modern complications as well. Black Widow abandoned both her crime fighting and romantic partnership with fellow hero Daredevil when she was offered prestigious membership in the Avengers, echoing the hard personal choices that the '70s career woman was facing. Even the Fantastic Four, Marvel Comics' first family, was not immune to the changing times, as Invisible Girl saw her idyllic marriage to Mr. Fantastic begin to unravel in 1973. Tired of being overlooked as a heroine, she lashes out at her husband, "…in the heat of battle, you didn't think of me as a member of the team…only as the 'mother of your child'!" Packing up their child, she leaves Mr. Fantastic, rebounds into the arms of former flame, the Sub-Mariner, and files divorce papers. While the couple eventually patches things up, young readers of the '70s could draw parallels to events that were taking place in their own family dramas. Wasp, on the other hand, faced different strains on her own marriage when she rejoined the Avengers in 1976, but her husband Yellowjacket didn't. "He's his own man, and I'm my own woman," thinks the miniscule heroine. But a year later, her husband's increasing schizophrenia causes Wasp to turn on the sexual heat to save her troubled marriage. In a transformation no doubt inspired by Marabel Morgan's self help book for wives, *The Total Woman*, Wasp designs a skimpy, stomach baring costume and slathers on purple eye shadow to keep Yellowjacket interested in their union.

In some cases, a heroine's romantic life spurred her on towards a liberated persona. The Scarlet Witch debuted in 1964 as a member of the Brotherhood of Evil Mutants, led by the X-Men's arch foe Magneto. Like Marvel Girl in the X-Men, the Scarlet Witch suffered from being in a group whose name sounded like a boy's club. The Scarlet Witch was a mutant gypsy girl from an eastern bloc country who had crazy unpredictable hex powers. She basically made things go wrong—she pointed at a wall, it fell on someone. She pointed at an opponent's gun, and it exploded. Scarlet Witch and her brother Quicksilver, who could run really fast, were coerced into joining Magneto's terrorist organization, but once the fiend was defeated, the twins joined the more altruistic ranks of the Avengers.

The Scarlet Witch had always yielded to the whims of her overbearing brother with a resigned, "I shall do as you wish, my brother." But by the early 1970s, Quicksilver had hotfooted it to greener pastures, leaving his sister the Scarlet Witch in the enviable position of being Marvel Comics' premiere superheroine. Marvel had done little to establish a strong female superstar, so as the sole female of Marvel's high profile Avengers, Scarlet Witch won immediate star status. Free of her overprotective brother, she began a relationship, and eventually married, her teammate the Vision. This caused an uproar because Scarlet Witch was a mutant and the Vision was an android—an artificial human. The super couple's embattled relationship was a metaphor for the problems that interracial couples faced in the real world. Faced with opposition from all sides, the Scarlet Witch loses her timid reserve and lashes out: "All right, if it's the *two of us* against the world, that's the way it will *be!* But look out, world!"

While the established heroines were spreading their wings and speaking their minds, a new breed of female entered the comic book world in the 1970s. Due to their aggressive natures and unorthodox personalities, many of these women were initially presented as threats. One of the first was a seven-foot drill sergeant named Big Barda.

Along with writer Stan Lee, artist Jack "King" Kirby had masterminded the Marvel Comics revolution of the 1960s. After a falling out with Lee over creative control, Kirby jumped ship and went over to competitor DC Comics. Given carte blanche by DC, Kirby unveiled his Fourth World series, a trio of interlocking comic book titles that told the operatic tale of the war between the benevolent "new gods" of the planet New Genesis and the evil gods of the dark world Apokolips. One of the "new gods" was Scott Free, an idealistic young deity who fled to Earth to become Mister Miracle, Super Escape Artist. In her youth, Big Barda, a lieutenant in the fearsome Female Furies, had aided Scott in his escape from the dread prisons of Apokolips. Years later, she joined him on Earth, now an armor clad commander in the heartless legions of Apokolips.

Big Barda represented perhaps the ultimate male fear of women's liberation. She was massive and powerful, with the gruff temperament of a battle hardened warrior, but a jaw dropping body, and inadvertently sexy air. "I'm not so bad!—A little rough, maybe!—But once you get to know me—I can be a real pussycat!" she coyly says on her arrival on Earth. Big Barda was an equal to Wonder Woman in sheer physical power, but lacked the Amazon princess's cool demeanor. She shattered walls with a touch, bent steel with ease, and commanded the Female Furies, a freakish band of merciless, kinky killer women. Big Barda's initial reaction to a bad situation was destroy first, ask questions later. Her partnership with the levelheaded Mister Miracle skewed the traditional male/female relationship in comics. Big Barda is the physically stronger, reactionary masculine half of the duo who felt inclined to protect Mister Miracle, the gentler, philosophical feminine half of the pair. Barda's oppressive military training had caused her to suppress her emotions so much that for some time she wasn't even aware that she was in love with her comrade, Mister Miracle.

At the end of one mentally brutalizing ordeal at the hands of a foe from Apokolips, the balance between Big Barda and Mister Miracle was flipped, presenting a cautionary tale for the liberated heroine of the 1970s. This time, it is Mister Miracle who saves Big Barda. Helpless in Mister Miracle's arms for the first time, Barda begs forgiveness for what she considers to be failure on her part. "Scott—!! Scott—forgive me!! I-I was afraid! For us! I—a warrior ..." The cool Mister Miracle eases Big Barda's fears with a dose of reality. "You're *better* than that, Barda!! You're a *woman!!*"

This presented a question for the liberated heroine of the '70s. Would she have to become less of a woman in order to fight evil like a man? This was the dilemma posed to Marvel's liberated heroine of 1972, the Cat. She was part of Marvel Comics' attempt to launch comic books that would appeal to a female reader. *The Claws of the Cat* was the most obvious attempt to produce a Women's Lib heroine, and boasted a female writer and artist, a rarity in those days. Editor Lee reflected that he liked the comic's "obvious awareness of the new spirit, the new mood of independence of women everywhere."

The first issue of *The Claws of the Cat* introduces Greer Nelson, a pretty young policeman's widow from Chicago, having to fend for herself for the first time. As her father attempts to console her at her husband's gravesite, a teary Greer laments, "Daddy, I don't know how to be strong! All my life there's been someone more than willing to take care of me!" Without a college degree or work experience, Greer finds her job prospects extremely limited. Eventually, Greer becomes the lab assistant of her old physics professor Dr. Tumolo, and gains a newfound confidence. "Dr. Tumolo really makes me proud to be a woman. I can't let her—or myself—down," Greer thinks, as she resumes her studies, and begins to rebuild her life.

Dr. Tumolo reveals to Greer that she has invented a device that would "make it possible for any woman to totally fulfill her physical and mental potential—despite the handicaps that society places on her." The doctor secretly begins conducting experiments on Greer, enhancing her assistant's intelligence, strength, and agility, while giving her a heightened empathy. Dr. Tumolo later learns that the sinister man bankrolling her experiments plans to use the device to create an army of perfect, strong, and obedient female killers, all dressed as deadly cats. She tries to blow the whistle on his plans, but winds up dead. A vengeful Greer steals one of the cat costumes, and goes hunting for male rats.

The Cat's costume was not particularly striking—a yellow leotard with a cat's paw emblem on the chest, blue gloves and boots, and a mask with ears and whiskers. The retractable claws on the Cat's gloves enabled her to swing from rooftops or scale the sides of buildings. Greer's enhanced physical powers made her a good fighter. Rather than face the Cat's deadly metal claws, Dr. Tumolo's killer commits suicide. "I almost feel sorry for the madman—almost," the Cat thinks as she stands over his body. Despite her earlier thirst for revenge, in the end the Cat is wracked with guilt over her actions. "All our plans for the betterment of womankind—! I did what I set out to do, and I did it well—but have I misused my powers? Have I become a stronger woman—only to become a poorer human being?" In order to be an effective foe of evil, would a woman have to betray herself?

This was not a question that Greer would have to wrestle with for long, since *The Claws of the Cat* only lasted a disappointing four issues before Marvel pulled the plug. The heroine never found the female readership she was intended to attract, and her feminist undertones and existential struggles may have put male readers off. The Cat disappeared into comic book limbo but returned as Tigra in 1974. Readers learned that the Cat had contracted fatal radiation poisoning while fighting a terrorist organization. Her mentor Dr. Tumolo turns out not to be dead after all, and comes to the Cat's rescue. The doctor, always full of secrets, reveals herself to be a member of the Cat People, a hidden race descended from felines rather than apes. In the subterranean home of the Cat People, Greer is offered a radical choice to save her life. "Life is precious to me, Dr. Tumolo—in any shape. Do what you must." And so, Greer undergoes a ritual that transforms her into Tigra, the Were-Woman.

If Greer's Cat identity was born out of the women's liberation movement, her Tigra persona seemed made for the sexual revolution. Tigra's lithe body was covered with orange and black striped fur, her hands and feet were like paws with sharp claws. Her hair was now a big mane that looked like one of Tina Turner's old wigs. Tigra wore a tiny black bikini because the Comics Code wouldn't allow her to wear nothing but her furry pelt. Her facial features were feline and savage, with fangs and mysterious green eyes. And her transformation was not just physical. As Tigra, Greer now possessed a wild nature that made her a ferocious fighter, increased her strength and speed, and filled her with animalistic passions. As she battles a foe, Tigra notices the changes that have come over her. "I stopped thinking right about then . . . as the deepest, strongest, most consuming, bestial hatred and bloodlust I have ever felt swept over me."

Where Greer had fizzled as the Cat, she sizzled as Tigra. While the Cat was written as serious and long-suffering, Tigra burned with a lusty appetite and a raw sexuality. Any aspirations of

Greer becoming a scientist flew out the window. Maybe it was too difficult to handle test tubes with claws anyway. Tigra didn't seem to be concerned about her new feline body as it freed her to pursue a life as a fulltime crime fighter. As Tigra, Greer enjoyed a long career as a superheroine and member of the Avengers. Clearly, comic book fans were more interested in a wild and sexy creature than an earnest suffragette.

One of the problems facing the liberated superheroine was that she often wound up being written as the Superbitch. The Superbitch was a new archetype that arose in the 1970s. These were fierce women, loyal only to themselves, and brimming with an air of superiority. "To your feet, you who are lower than a swine! Face the fury of—Mantis!" the mysterious kung fu mistress declared, as she made her entrance in a 1973 issue of the Avengers. The former Saigon bargirl/hooker didn't come from a conventional background like the heroines who had preceded her. Her teammates were never sure if the enigmatic Mantis was an enemy in their midst, especially when she tried to steal the Vision away from the Scarlet Witch. The men of the Defenders were joined by a new incarnation of the Valkyrie in 1972. This one was heroic, but no less strident than the one who had battled the Avengers two years earlier. When asked by her teammate Sub-Mariner whether her reputation as a man-hater is deserved, Valkyrie responds, "I do not hate men, Sub-Mariner. I merely know I'm as good as they are." A seven-foot, chain wielding female warrior named Thundra declared her own battle of the sexes by stating her female superiority, "…scamper back to your rabbit-holes like the miserable male rodents that you really are—and let Thundra do your fighting for you!"

The Queen Superbitch was Power Girl, who made her debut in 1976. Like Black Canary, Power Girl hailed from the parallel world, Earth 2. She was the younger cousin of the original Superman of 1938. Like Superman, Power Girl was infinitely strong, impervious to pain, and could fly. By the time that Power Girl arrived on Earth, Superman was a graying champion who had already been fighting tyranny for over forty years. Superman was inclined to act fatherly towards his young cousin, but those years of being cooped up in that ship gave Power Girl a nasty temper and a restless spirit.

While some superheroines toyed with feminism in the '70s, Power Girl was the real deal. She was strong, confident, outspoken and unapologetic. When she began her career as a member of the Justice Society of America, she demanded that the sometimes stodgy older male heroes treat her as an equal, and defied any man to try and put her down. "I--am--not--a-- 'broad!'" Power Girl tells the sexist pugilist Wildcat, as she slams a door in his face. Where Supergirl had accepted her fate and role as Superman's helper, Power Girl wanted her freedom. She had no interest in being perceived as a copy of her cousin Superman, and refused to wear his symbol on her chest or bear his name. "I'm not as strong as my cousin Superman—but I'm still ten times stronger than any mere man ..." Romance was never the motivation for any of Power Girl's actions, since she didn't expect a man, including Superman, to complete her life. Power Girl was a young, independent woman of her times who stood up for herself. As a result, her character often came off as a bitch, as was often the case with strident feminists.

Given Power Girl's militant feminist stance, her costume was a bit incongruous. Sure, the emancipated Power Girl wore her blonde hair in a breezy short style, unusual for a superheroine at the time, reminiscent of Olympian Dorothy Hamill. Power Girl's body, however, was not that of a figure skater. Power Girl had a powerful statuesque figure poured into a form fitting red, white, and blue costume, just perfect for America's Bicentennial. The design of her costume featured a circular cutout on the chest that drew the reader's eyes to the main attraction, Power Girl's massive cleavage. To put it bluntly, Power Girl was stacked. She may have lived her life as a powerful independent woman, but her D-cup breasts and revealing costume took some of the thunder out of her feminist manifesto. Power Girl's tough demeanor and rejection of her cousin Superman's values represented a new superheroine archetype that chose not to sit idly by and watch men run the world. But no matter how much she may have roared, there was always the impression that her male comrades, and readers, were sniggering behind her back as they looked at her chest.

As was the case with Power Girl, the two concepts of feminism and sexual freedom didn't always mesh up well. One of the worst casualties of the 1970s sexualizing of comic book heroines was Red Sonja, a flame haired female warrior who crossed swords with Conan the Barbarian in 1973. The legendary hero of pulp fiction, Conan was the king of the "sword and sorcery" craze popular in the early '70s comic books, featuring lusty sword-wielding heroes saving half-clad harem girls from unspeakable horrors, usually with a strongly implied sexual reward. Red Sonja was the exception —a beautiful, fierce female mercenary who had sworn that she would only surrender her charms to the man who defeated her on the battlefield. Even Conan met his match with Red Sonja, and fans demanded to see more of her. Well, they certainly got their wish. Red Sonja got her own comic in 1975, but instead of the sexy, confident Amazon in the curve-hugging chain mail shirt who strode the bloody battlefields two years earlier, the cover featured a busty redhead spilling out of a tiny silver metal bikini, with heavy black eyeliner and big pouty lips. Red Sonja might have been billed as "She-Devil with a sword," but now she looked more like a stripper.

Perhaps the quintessential superheroine of the 1970s was Storm. The decade had given the world the first black Bond girl, the first black model on the cover of *Vogue* magazine, and, in 1975, the first major black comic book superheroine. Ororo Munroe was the daughter of a Kenyan princess and an African American photojournalist, born in Harlem and later orphaned in Cairo, where she became a pickpocket and expert thief. As a teenager she wandered to the Serengeti, where her powers to control the weather made her the object of worship among the native people. Ororo was recruited by Professor X to join the new incarnation of his X-Men, and to find her place in the world. "You are no goddess, Ororo. You are a mutant—and have responsibilities," the professor tells her. "Come with me, child. Taste the world outside. You may find its flavor bitter—or surprisingly sweet." With these words, Professor X lured Ororo from her life of isolation to discover a new one. The limitless promise of a new world of sights and sensations was what women in the real world were experiencing as new doors opened for them, allowing them a new life of exploration.

Ororo was code-named Storm, one of the first heroines to bear a modern *nom de guerre* that didn't use "girl," "woman," or "lady." After her would come a long line of woman with names like Apparition, Mystique, Mirage, and Fahrenheit. Tall, stately and elegant, with a mane of long white hair, angular exotic features, and blue eyes, Storm eschewed the blaxploitation aesthetic of the times by forgoing hot pants and giant afros. Storm wore a typically sexy costume of the early disco era—a shiny black swimsuit with skin baring cutouts and thigh high boots with heels. But, the costume didn't look sleazy or salacious due to Storm's regal air of confidence and power. She was sexy without being overtly sexual—her allure came from her powerful persona, and goddess-like quality.

Marvel Comics created this new version of the X-Men with an international cast to better appeal to foreign markets. The demonic Nightcrawler was German, Colossus was Russian, Banshee was from Ireland, Sunfire hailed from Japan, and Wolverine was Canadian, with leader Cyclops and Thunderbird rounding out the group as the resident Americans. Storm was far from the token girl of the new X-Men. She commanded the respect of her teammates with the same ease that she controlled lightning, wind, and rain. Even the feral berserker Wolverine bowed to Storm's serene strength. In an early adventure, she stops him from attacking team leader Cyclops with a touch of her hand and a simple command, "You will do nothing, Wolverine . . . not now. Not ever . . . or you will answer to me." Atypically, Storm did not fall in love with any of her fellow X-Men, as usually happened in superhero team comics. While Nightcrawler and Colossus jokingly compete for the honor of escorting Storm to dinner, she responds with her usual goddess-like poise, "I am no one's 'date' . . . I enjoy being with both of you. Which means that the three of us will go into dinner together as equals. Agreed?" Storm was the start of a new generation of smart, coolly sexy, and powerful heroines born more for the sleeker disco days that closed the '70s than the more radical times that started them.

Storm's strength of character was the product of Chris Claremont, whose debut as X-Men writer in 1975 began a sixteen-year run on the series, taking it from cult status to the number one selling comic in the industry. Claremont's trademark was strong heroines, and he became best known for Storm's fellow X-Woman and best friend, Phoenix. When Professor X recruited his new team of X-Men, most of the original team from the 1960s went off to build new lives. Jean Grey, once the telepathic X-Men member Marvel Girl, left the confines of the X-Men's school to find herself. She got an apartment in Greenwich Village, and the next time that readers saw her, she was a cool '70s chick. Artist Dave Cockrum wanted to get rid of what he called Jean's "young Republican" wardrobe, and started dressing her in sexy, flowing *Cosmopolitan* magazine styles. Cockrum gave Jean the essential cool hairdo for 1976—the feathered Farrah Fawcett mane. Jean was the prototypical suburban girl from the '70s, who moved to the big city to lead a slightly bohemian, Carly Simon sort of life of romance and self-discovery. Claremont even wrote a flashback story that showed good daughter Jean put her parent's framed photo into the drawer of her nightstand as she planned her first time sexual encounter with boyfriend Scott.

Jean's problems stemmed from Scott. He was also Cyclops, the X-Men's leader, and the only one of the original members to remain on the team. Jean's relationship with Cyclops keep pulling her back into the X-Men's adventures. In 1976, the X-Men and Jean are stranded aboard a space station that is about to blow up. In order to save her friends, Jean takes matters into her own hands and pilots the X-Men back to Earth in a space shuttle. The only hitch is the massive solar flare that the ship has to fly through. While Jean hopes that her mental powers can shield her from the solar radiation, she knows it is a suicide mission. And so, Jean dies to save her friends.

Except that the story didn't end there. When the X-Men are safely back on terra firma, they are shocked to behold their friend Jean resurrected. "Hear me, X-Men! No longer am I the woman you knew! I am fire! And life incarnate! Now and forever—I am Phoenix!" she proclaims, rising from the ashes and restored to life, resplendent in a green and gold costume with a swirling sash, and sporting a blazing nimbus of red hair. Jean had bonded with the Phoenix Force, one of the primal entities of the universe, the fire of life itself, and it lived within her resurrected form.

There had never been a superheroine like Phoenix in comics

before. She was powerful on a cosmic, almost godlike level. She could read minds, pull asteroids out of orbit, battle the toughest opponents with blazing fiery blasts, travel across the galaxy—this girl did it all. "There's power surging through my body that I never dreamed existed!" Phoenix thinks, as she blazes over New York's Washington Square. Phoenix's power was described as a "song within her . . . a passion beyond human comprehension." As her boyfriend Cyclops nervously watches Phoenix do her thing, he notes the change that has come over her. "My . . . god. Jean used to be the *weakest* X-Man."

Sounds great, right? Well, as Lord Acton wrote, "Power tends to corrupt, and absolute power corrupts absolutely." This seemed to be the fate of Phoenix. The incredible power that she now wielded makes her hungry for more, and gives her a savage, destructive nature. "My power—it's hitting me like a drug. I've never felt such . . . ecstasy! God in heaven, what have I become?" Good question indeed, since Phoenix was in fact second to God in power. Things get worse when Phoenix single-handedly saves the universe from destruction and bonds with the very heart of creation. Phoenix experiences the ultimate rapture, cosmic ecstasy, a universal orgasm, the biggest of all Big O's. In that moment, Phoenix transcended to another level, and life just wasn't the same for her after that. She longed for more.

The sexual revolution of the 1970s cast a new light on women's intimate needs, and specifically, the quest for the orgasm. 1976's *Hite Report on Female Sexuality* found that only 30% of women had experienced orgasm. Every month *Cosmopolitan* magazine, with its cleavage baring cover models, promised new secrets to achieving the elusive orgasm. In the cocaine-fueled disco days of the late '70s, the search for pleasure became all-consuming. Such was the fate of Phoenix. When she falls under the influence of the villainous Mastermind, Phoenix really lets herself go. First she is transformed into the lascivious, corseted dominatrix called the Black Queen. A treacherous wanton, the Black Queen is a slave to her desires. She revels in using her powers to inflict cruelty, especially on her teammates in the X-Men. Jean eventually shakes off Mastermind's mental seduction and comes to her senses, but it is too late. The thrill of evil has taken hold of the heroine. Now clad in blood red, Jean becomes the flaming goddess of death, Dark Phoenix. After crushing her fellow X-Men, Dark Phoenix flies off into space in search of something to satisfy her hunger—the ultimate cosmic orgasm. "She craves that ultimate sensation . . ." the text reads, as Dark Phoenix devours a sun, killing billions of innocent aliens in the process. Jean Grey went from a beloved superheroine to one of the worst villains to ever appear in comics, all because she wasn't able to control the powers that coursed through her body. "I . . . hunger, Scott . . . for a joy, a rapture, beyond all comprehension. That is part of me, too. It . . . *consumes* me." Dark Phoenix tells her boyfriend Cyclops, as she battles to control her passions.

Dark Phoenix's struggles were a parable for the late '70s, where the hedonistic search for pleasure and gratification led to addiction, and ultimately death. The glamour of Studio 54 and the wild delights of the nightlife were dimmed in the early '80s, when the first reports of the "gay cancer" that would become

AIDS began to surface. Many felt that it was atonement for the bacchanalia of the '70s. Phoenix too had to atone for the genocide that she had committed in her quest for pleasure. A cosmic empress orders Phoenix to stand trial for her crimes. Writer Claremont's original plan was for Phoenix to have to undergo a psychic "lobotomy" that would have removed her powers. But Marvel editor Jim Shooter felt that her punishment needed to be stronger. Rather than have to water down Phoenix' story, Claremont decided on a more final judgment. Knowing that she can never control the inhuman hungers of the cosmic entity that lives in her body, Phoenix makes the tough decision. "I'd have to stay completely in control of myself every second of every day for the rest of my immortal life." Rather than risk one more death on her conscience, Phoenix heroically destroys herself.

The story that became known as the Dark Phoenix Saga was like the "Bohemian Rhapsody" of comic books—an epic tale of cosmic triumph and tragedy. It put a cap on the space operas that filled comics of the '70s, and gave a glimpse into the dark days ahead in the '80s. The 1980 demise of Phoenix also removed the most powerful superheroine from Marvel Comics' roster. Despite scoring success with males like Spider-Man, the Hulk, and Captain America, Marvel had never created what it considered to be its own iconic superheroine. In 1977, Marvel Comics wanted to develop an iconic female superhero that could headline her own title, the way DC's Wonder Woman did. But rather than try to create a strong female character from scratch, Marvel Comics decided instead to snap off a rib from one of their male heroes to create their Eve.

Carol Danvers had been introduced in 1968, as a NASA security chief, and love interest of Captain Marvel. This was not the original Captain Marvel from the 1940s, but instead a new, extraterrestrial superhero that Marvel Comics had created in 1967 when they obtained the rights to the name. By 1977, Carol was no longer a government agent, but was now the editor of woman's magazine. She was a gutsy, Frye boot wearing Candice Bergen type by day, a sophisticated beauty in a Halston gown by night. Carol was such a hip '70s woman, she even saw a therapist. Carol would get nasty headaches that caused her to black out. Unbeknownst to Carol, when she is unconscious, she transforms into Ms. Marvel. It turned out that years before, Carol had been exposed to radiation that altered her DNA and gave her powers just like Captain Marvel. Sort of like super herpes— one encounter, but you have it for life. Ms. Marvel could fly, had super strength, and a "seventh sense," a sort of super female intuition. She had a hairdo like a '70s female tennis player, and wore a red costume like Captain Marvel, only it was uglier and exposed her navel. The first issue of her comic announced "This Female Fights Back!" Off to a good start? Well . . .

First, the good stuff. Ms. Marvel was very much of an idealized career woman of the 1970s. She was hip, liberated and confident. And despite sharing his name and powers, Ms. Marvel had almost no connection with Captain Marvel. She wasn't his girlfriend or partner, and didn't take orders from him. Except for a few chance encounters, the Captain and the Ms. didn't even stay in contact. In an interesting twist, the character's alter ego, the tough talking editor Carol Danvers, was much cooler than her rather bland, somewhat one-dimensional heroic persona, Ms. Marvel. Carol didn't even know that she was Ms. Marvel for a while, until her psychologist figured it out while she was under hypnosis.

But there were some problems. Despite Marvel Comics' claim that they wanted to create an iconic female character, it didn't seem like they were really that sincere. First off, rather than create a strong original female character, they made a female version of one of their conceptually weaker, less popular male heroes. Then, once they had this strong woman, they didn't seem to know what to do with her. Here was a woman who wanted to use her great powers to help humanity, just as a man would. But she didn't fit the mold of how a superheroine should act. Ms. Marvel wasn't overtly sexy, and wasn't consumed with romance, as many female characters were. Since she was independent and liberated, she was written as a bit of a cold bitch. Ms. Marvel joined Marvel Comics' big superstar group, the Avengers, but never really fit in. She wasn't a pushover, so her male teammates didn't get her, and she never developed much of a rapport with her female teammates. Ultimately, Ms. Marvel didn't make too many friends among readers, either. In 1979, she got a sexy new black costume in order to boost some interest with male readers, but it was too late. Ms. Marvel's comic book was cancelled after just two years. After that, she just appeared as a minor member of the Avengers.

This is where her story gets weird, because what happens next almost seems like a decision to punish the Ms. Marvel character for being exactly what she was created to be—an independent, strong woman. When the Scarlet Witch contemplates having a baby with her android husband, the Vision, she gets some advice from her "sister Avenger" Ms. Marvel. In classic career woman mode, Ms. Marvel doesn't understand why the Scarlet Witch feels that her being a mother would be better than the thrill of being a superheroine. "Surely you find that more 'fulfilling' than any silly stereotype of having a baby?" the pragmatic Ms. Marvel says. Minutes later, Ms. Marvel collapses, and after being rushed to a hospital learns that she *herself* is three months pregnant. This could have been a groundbreaking story—the hardnosed '70s career woman who finds that she's pregnant, and has to decide whether or not to have the baby.

The original story was that Ms. Marvel had been impregnated by an alien intelligence, but the version that was published is even more bizarre. Within days of learning that she's pregnant, Ms. Marvel has gone full term. Her fellow Avengers react in a strange way, as though embarrassed by the aftereffects of what they think may be the debauched life of a single woman. "I think it's great! Gosh, a real baby!" Wasp gushes. Rather than try and figure out how their teammate could deliver a full grown baby after three days, the Avengers coo over the newborn boy, and buy him gifts. Ms. Marvel suffers from more than post-partum depression; she is convinced that her body has been violated. Her fellow Avengers are mystified by what they perceived as a lack of maternal feelings on Ms. Marvel's part.

"He's not my son! I don't want to have anything to do with that . . . that thing!"

When Ms. Marvel finally musters up the courage to see her "son," she is surprised to see that he has grown to adulthood in a matter of a few hours. He is Marcus, a resident of the timeless dimension of Limbo. Marcus reveals that in order to escape his world and journey to Earth, he had transported Ms. Marvel to Limbo, used his technology to seduce her, had sex with her, planted his essence in her, wiped her memory of the events, and sent her back to Earth, none the wiser. Hmmm, sounds kind of like rape, right? Marcus had basically used Ms. Marvel's uterus as mode of transportation, and she was now his mother/lover. Something goes wrong with Marcus' plan, and he has to go back to Limbo, lest his presence on Earth were to cause time itself to unravel. Inexplicably, after hearing this whole story, Ms. Marvel decides to return to Limbo with her son/lover/rapist, because she thinks she loves him. ". . . I've been denying my feelings for quite a while. Maybe it's time I started following them." Her fellow Avengers never raise a finger to stop her. Iron Man simply asks Ms. Marvel if she's sure that she's doing the right thing, rather than saying, "But . . . um, he raped you." The thunder god Thor uses his magic hammer to transport Ms. Marvel and Marcus back to Limbo. And, with that, Ms. Marvel was gone. All of the efforts to create a strong female character destroyed on the most basic level imaginable with one story. Could it get any worse?

Well, it could, because by this time, the grim and gritty era of 1980s comics was upon us. In the '80s readers found out that things hadn't turned out so idyllic for Ms. Marvel and Marcus in Limbo. After she made her way back to Earth, a bitter Carol Danvers retired from the superhero world. Unfortunately the mutant villainess called Rogue finds Carol, steals her powers, memories and persona, and throws her body into the San Francisco Bay. So, you see, it did get worse. Ms. Marvel had gone from being the '70s ultimate liberated "Female Fury" to the tragic Frances Farmer of comic books.

Ironically, the heroine who benefited the least from the 1970s superheroine liberation wave was the original comic book feminist herself, Wonder Woman. In 1972, editor Gloria Steinem put Wonder Woman on the cover of the premiere issue of *Ms.* magazine, declaring the heroine an early feminist icon. By the following year, Wonder Woman had tossed out her old white pantsuits, and was back in the old strapless stars n' stripes. But the transformation was probably not what Ms. Steinem had in mind. Since this was 1973, the red, white and blue swimsuit was now a little smaller and sexier. Wonder Woman was drawn less as a robust Amazon and more as a pretty fashion model. She was not restored to the full feminist icon of Ms. Steinem's girlhood memories. The cover of one 1973 issue showed Wonder Woman hog-tied to a giant phallic missile, a clear indication that this comic would not be a primer on feminism.

But, it was the sexual revolution rather than feminism that would wind up having more lasting effects on Wonder Woman, and give her more power. When she made her transition to TV in 1976, Wonder Woman was remade into an object of male fantasies.

The somewhat sexless Wonder Woman of the comics had always been a bit of a turnoff to most males. But Lynda Carter's stunning, sparkly-eyed portrayal of the Amazing Amazon pushed the character into the realm of idealized sex object that males could be comfortable with. The good thing is that millions of girls growing up in the 1970s were able to look beyond the cheesecake appeal of the show to be inspired by Wonder Woman's pro-female message of beauty and power, and finally have a heroine to look up to.

The sexual revolution was able to thrust Wonder Woman into the pop culture spotlight, from being the threatening dyke of comic books, to an icon able to take her place in mainstream stardom beside Superman and Batman. But the times were changing in the industry where these three titans had reigned for almost forty years. Beginning in the 1980s, comic book publishers would now sell directly to comic book specialty stores, rather than to newsstands. Just as the industry had opened its doors to the world at the beginning of the 1970s by bringing realism to stories, now it was closing a door by making it harder for the public to find comic books. The days of kids buying comics off the rack at the drugstore were gone, and as a result the audience for comics became older, and stories became more mature.

The superheroines of the 1970s had enjoyed their last twirl across the dance floor of the disco. As they stepped outside to greet the new decade, these liberated ladies felt a chill. Maybe it was time to put on some less revealing costumes, and slip on a black leather jacket to prepare for the cold days ahead.

Wonder Woman's Extreme Makeovers

Achilles speared Penthesilea in their first encounter, and dragged her from the saddle by the hair. As she lay dying on the ground, the Greek soldiers cried: "Throw the virago to the dogs as a punishment for exceeding the nature of womankind!"

*Dictys of Crete, chronicle of
the Trojan War*

In 2006, the United States Post Office issued a set of stamps showcasing DC Comics' greatest superheroes. The stamp featuring Wonder Woman described her as "the most recognizable female character in comics." 2006 was the same year that Wonder Woman's comic was relaunched with a new first issue. Ironically, the title of the story featured in that first issue of "the most recognizable" female character's comic was "Who is Wonder Woman?" This was the ninth time that the Amazon princess had started her life over. It wouldn't be her last.

Despite the fact that Wonder Woman has been part of the American pop culture landscape for over seven decades, there seems to be some confusion as to who she actually is. When most people think of Wonder Woman, they probably recall the image of the gorgeous Lynda Carter deflecting bullets from her Amazon bracelets on the 1970's TV series. Perhaps some will think of the stalwart female member of Saturday morning's *Superfriends*, with her high heeled boots and Jackie Onassis hairdo. Or some may simply regard her as a modern embodiment of female strength and beauty. Wonder Woman is one of a small group of female superheroes who has mainstream recognition. But beyond the eagle bra, star spangled panties, and tiara, what is the essence of the most famous female character, or icon, in American comics? An even more interesting question, perhaps, when you compare her to her male counterparts in the pantheon of comic book legends.

Comic book fans reverently refer to them as the Big Three. They are the three original icons of American superhero comics—Superman, Batman, and Wonder Woman. They are the source from which all later inspiration would come. Aside from Superman, the other two may not have been the first of their kind, but they surely did it the best, warranting their legendary stature. Now, most people would easily be able to describe the essence of the two male heroes. Superman is faster than a speeding bullet, upholder of truth, justice, and the American way. Those not that steeped in comic book lore can still tell you that Superman is the last survivor of the planet Krypton, largely as a result of TV and movies. He is the last hope; the guardian angel always looking out for mankind. Batman is the dark nemesis of evil, the gadget-wielding vigilante, the detective mastermind. Though some may not remember that he fights crime to avenge his murdered parents, they will recall

all of the trappings of his world—the sweeping leathery cape, his sidekick Robin, the Batcave and Batmobile, the giant bat signal illuminating the night skies of Gotham City.

But what is Wonder Woman's shtick? Where does she come from, and what is her mission? Superman protects Metropolis, Batman patrols Gotham City. Wonder Woman lives in . . . Washington DC? New York? Chicago? Why are Wonder Woman's male counterparts so easy to define, while she is known mainly for her costume?

In the language of modern comic books, the Big Three are also referred to as the Trinity. In Catholic terms, that would make Superman the Father: the alpha, the supreme and infinite power. Batman would be the Son: born of man, the earthborn champion of justice, the teacher, and architect of scientific miracles. So that would make Wonder Woman . . . the Holy Ghost. That's the mysterious figure that everyone's heard of but that no one quite understands. The Holy Ghost is purported to be a powerful being, but where did it come from, and what does it do? The same questions could be asked about Wonder Woman. So, how did the most famous superheroine in comic books wind up in this position after seven decades?

Superman and Batman were born in the late 1930s, springing from the old pulp magazines—Superman owing much to Philip Wylie's *Gladiator*, and Batman influenced by vigilantes like The Shadow and The Spider. Wonder Woman debuted in 1941 as a reaction to the onset of World War II. With her star spangled costume and crusade to crush the Axis powers, Wonder Woman represented America more than Superman and Batman did, and her comics carried more philosophical messages about the need to overturn oppression and domination in order to save the world. But what to do once the war had been won? Veterans, with their medals, war stories, and foreign brides, came home to a nation where their blood and sacrifices hadn't necessarily earned them a place in the new postwar society. It was easy enough for Superman and Batman to go back to their prewar civilian do-gooder activities. With the Axis defeated, many of the wartime superheroes simply disappeared, and Wonder Woman's mission in "man's world" was about to become significantly diminished.

With the 1947 death of Wonder Woman's creator Dr. William Moulton Marston went all of the messages of equality and love that were meant to inspire young female readers. Although Wonder Woman's comics sold well, girls were a smaller percentage of the comic book market. Since Wonder Woman was not as big an income generator, she didn't graduate to another level of success the way Superman and Batman did. The war years had been good to the two heroes. Superman and Batman were featured on toys and cereal boxes, and had also transcended comic books to make the jump into movie serials and radio programs that gave them greater fame. At a time when toys for girls were focused on training future wives and mothers, there was not much call for a Nazi bashing Wonder Woman doll. And Wonder Woman never made the transition to movie serials the way Superman and Batman did, a sign for what the future would hold for her.

If Wonder Woman the warrior was no longer needed, what

about her role as a woman? With a rallying motto of "We Can Do It," the women of America had done their part to support the war by working in war plants, building the airplanes that their men would fly to preserve freedom. But after the war, women were ready to retire their unflattering overalls and be pretty and feminine once more. In this new era, Wonder Woman had no choice but to soften her look as well. She traded her high-heeled war boots for pseudo-Roman sandals that looked more like ballet slippers. Artist Irwin Hasen began drawing comic book covers that put a more girlish gloss on Wonder Woman. Her figure was more shapely now, her face softer and more glamorous, like that of movie star Ava Gardner. Wonder Woman and her boyfriend Col. Steve Trevor looked as young and fresh as the lovebirds seen on the covers of the new popular romance comics. Even the *Sensation Comics* logo was softened and feminized to look like a romance comic. The stories inside were something else. Although original artist Harry G. Peter continued to draw Wonder Woman's adventures, he was in his seventies, and age was taking its toll on the quality of the artwork. In contrast to the glamorous creature shown on the cover, the heroine seen inside the comics appeared stiff and unfeminine.

The 1950s brought changes in taste, and superheroes were falling out of fashion. By 1951, most of the superheroes of the '40s had been given their walking papers. That year Wonder Woman lost her starring role in *Sensation Comics* when it became *Sensation Mystery*, now featuring tales of the supernatural. Wonder Woman still had her own eponymous comic book to fall back on, and along with Superman and Batman, was one of the few survivors left standing after the postwar demise of the superheroes. Superman continued to thrive throughout the 1950s, and as his power grew for the new modern age, he traveled through time and space to now become a universal defender of freedom. As portrayed by the square jawed actor George Reeves, the Man of Steel conquered the new world of television, which made him more recognizable than ever. Meanwhile, Batman was distancing himself from his old dark vigilante persona, as he became increasingly friendlier and more upstanding. His stories became lighthearted colorful capers, and as the space age beckoned, Batman and Robin even began traveling to other worlds for weird sci-fi adventures. Superman and Batman were now best friends and comrades in arms, starring in the team-up comic *World's Finest*.

Conversely, Wonder Woman was a pariah who never mixed with Superman or Batman. The mighty Amazon was not allowed to play with the boys, and had to stay on her side of the sandbox. The 1950s were not very kind to the Amazon princess, as was the case for a lot of American women. When Marston passed away, most of the fantasy elements of Wonder Woman's adventures disappeared as well. She no longer journeyed to strange worlds to save oppressed women and her foes now consisted of spies and mobsters. Her female sidekicks Etta Candy and the Holliday Girls were long gone, as were the diabolical and powerful female foes. Stories now focused on romance, presumably to provide the appropriate kind of entertainment for impressionable girls. Featurettes about courtship customs around the world replaced the profiles of famous women in history.

Wonder Woman's charmless boyfriend Steve Trevor was now the focus of her world. He was always trying to trick Wonder Woman into believing that the world no longer needed her so that she would retire and marry him. Why was this man so eager to get married? Wonder Woman was a virgin, like her namesake, Diana, chaste ancient Roman goddess of the hunt. Wonder Woman had already forsaken her immortality to be with Steve in "man's world," and by submitting to him, she would be surrendering the last of her power. Steve, the military man, is eager to consummate their relationship, conquer new territory, and put Wonder Woman in her place, which presumably was the kitchen.

The 1950s saw America swept up in anti-Communist paranoia, where everything considered "Un-American" was under scrutiny. Similarly, Wonder Woman felt herself put under the microscope in her own comic. The mighty Amazon, who had come to "man's world" to beat the Nazi menace, now found herself the object of suspicion. Numerous stories focused on the world's obsession with learning Wonder Woman's secret identity in an effort to find her weakness. Imposters were a common threat to Wonder Woman, as scientists created robot versions of her that promised to be just as good as the original. These challengers threatened to steal not only Wonder Woman's title, but Steve's heart as well. Besides making her beau seem like a fickle cad, these stories gave the impression that Wonder Woman was not that unique, and easily replaceable. Her very right to be called Wonder Woman seemed to always be in question, as her Amazon sisters constantly tested the heroine to see if she still had the right to bear the title. Wonder Woman handled all of these threats from a defensive position, displaying none of the confidence she'd shown a few years prior.

While the Big Three continued to be published throughout the 1950s, the decade signaled an ending of sorts. After Dr. Frederick Wertham's 1954 exposé *Seduction of the Innocent* triggered an outcry that comics were too violent, too sexual, and too subversive, the Comics Code Authority was instituted to censor questionable content. Wertham's demonizing of Wonder Woman cut to the core of the character:

> She is physically very powerful, tortures men, has her
> own female following, is the cruel, "phallic" woman.
> While she is a frightening figure for boys, she is an
> undesirable ideal for girls, being the exact opposite
> of what girls are supposed to want to be.

The Comic Code Authority made sure that all of the bondage elements in Wonder Woman's comic were eliminated, as well as feminism and anything that smacked of lesbianism. In the aftermath of the comic book cleanup, DC Comics' began to introduce modernized versions of some of their old 1940s heroes, like The Flash and Green Lantern. While Superman, Batman, and Wonder Woman were never officially "reintroduced" to the readers, subtle changes were made to update the three heroes, who now approached twenty years of publication.

In Wonder Woman's case, the changes began in 1958. By this time, artist Peter had also passed away, and the last tie to the Amazon's original history was gone. New artist Ross Andru updated Wonder Woman's look, making her slim, pretty, and girlish. But the changes to Wonder Woman's appearance were just the beginning. Over the next years, her origin would undergo a sanitization to make it more appropriate for the conservative era of the Comics Code Authority. The Amazon queen Hippolyta was now a pretty Grace Kelly-type blonde in a diaphanous gown, rather than the hearty brunette warrior monarch she had been previously. Readers were told how centuries ago, Hippolyta gave birth to a daughter begat by an unseen consort. There was no trace of the child having been magically created solely by a woman and female divinities, as in Marston's original 1941 story, as single mother parentage might confuse impressionable young minds. The baby Diana was given gifts of strength, wisdom, speed, and beauty by the Olympian gods. Cut to a scene years later, where the queen is shown lamenting that all of the Amazons' men have been wiped out in wars. Her wailing subjects in attendance look more like the tragedy stricken widows from Euripides' *The Trojan Women* than the female warriors of myth. Queen Hippolyta tells her daughter Diana, now a ponytail-sporting teenager, that she must be brave, befitting a princess. The following day the Amazons board a ship for their new island home, far from the wars that killed their men. It was "war" that was bad, not the men themselves.

What followed went beyond sanitization—it was more like suburbanization. The goddess Athena appears to tell the Amazons that they are immortal as long as they remain on Paradise Island, and that Princess Diana will grow to womanhood, but no older. Readers were now treated to zany adventures of Wonder Woman as a teenager that showed growing up on Paradise Island to be not that different from a normal adolescent's life. The Amazon homestead looks like ancient Greece, but the women possess futuristic technology, and some even wear eyeglasses. The teenaged Wonder Woman has two boyfriends, the amphibian Mer-Boy and the winged and feathered Bird-Boy. Since neither beau can set fin or talon on Paradise Island lest the Amazons lose their powers and immortality, young Diana's virtue is not at risk. That, and the fact that neither boy has any detectable genitalia buried under their scales and fluffy down. The boys are always competing for the teenage princess' attention, as they try to get her to go on dates to underwater dances or avian parties. Later came the addition of Wonder Tot, who was the Amazon princess at the age of a baby-talking, mischievous toddler. Readers must have been totally bewildered by "imaginary" stories that would throw the tot, teen, and adult versions of Wonder Woman into madcap adventures together. This concoction was called the Wonder Woman Family, and their wholesome adventures were a far cry from Wonder Woman and the Holliday Girls wreaking havoc on the Nazis just fifteen years earlier.

All of these new developments seemed intended to distract readers from what more moralistic times must have deemed Wonder Woman's sordid past. In this modern, cleaned up, and simplified version, Wonder Woman's mission was minimized. Athena now commands Queen Hippolyta to select the strongest Amazon to go to "man's world" to fight crime and injustice. "Only when her services are no longer needed—can she think of herself." Wonder Woman now only needs to stop crime, not end war and teach men about love and peace. There is no mention of fighting for the rights of her fellow women. In "man's world," Wonder Woman is still Lt. Diana Prince, except now she lacks the acerbic wit that she had in the 1940s. Instead she is just a mousy Plain Jane in large harlequin eyeglasses, desperate for any attention that Steve Trevor might pay her.

Where did this leave the mighty Amazon princess? The answer is that, after leeching so much of the original magic from the Wonder Woman character, there was not much left. Aside from her costume, the Wonder Woman of the late '50s and early '60s bore little resemblance to her confident wartime persona. Beginning in 1960, Wonder Woman fought side by side with the men of the Justice League of America. The Justice League represented the egalitarianism and optimism of the Kennedy era, and Wonder Woman had an equal seat at the table with her male comrades Flash, Green Lantern, Martian Manhunter, and Aquaman. But in her own comic book, things were not so peachy. Now Wonder Woman seemed to merely be reacting to events inflicted on her, rather than taking on a decisive role. When she wasn't cavorting with her makeshift "Wonder Woman Family" in high-spirited adventures, she faced danger with boyfriend Steve Trevor.

Many critics called Steve Trevor a "male Lois Lane" since Wonder Woman spent as much time rescuing the Army colonel as Superman did saving his snoopy reporter girlfriend. But unlike Superman, Wonder Woman didn't exert any powerful authority to control Steve. Instead, she dutifully plucks Steve out of harm's way when he insists on tagging along on her missions, all the while worrying about keeping him happy. Once a messenger of love sent to abolish war, Wonder Woman now works essentially as a tool of a US government that by the early 1960s was getting embroiled in conflicts in Viet Nam. Where she once battled the mighty war god Mars, now she faces ludicrous enemies like the diminutive Mouse Man, or the diabolical Egg Fu, the Oriental Egghead. And though she is still portrayed as supremely strong, Wonder Woman uses her lasso only to perform feats of derring-do, and rarely to exert what was probably her greatest power—the ability to make men tell the truth.

Despite the emphasis on her romance with Steve, there was an implication that Wonder Woman's great strength made her an inhuman machine, and somehow less of a woman. Superman flew through time and space saving countless lives, and was hailed as a guardian angel of the universe. Wonder Woman raced around performing similar feats of kindness and bravery, but was somehow suspect. In 1964's "The Revolt of Wonder Woman," the Amazon princess is like a harried mother of a needy world, overwhelmed and exhausted by trying to keep it running smoothly. As Wonder Woman works feverishly to avert one crisis after another, the response that she gets from the public is less than flattering. "She's as tireless as a machine! She doesn't need to eat—or drink—or sleep! Wonder Woman's not human!" She finally reaches her breaking point and falls to her knees in anguish. "I--I--m-might as well be a—a—robot—a m-machine for all anyone cares! Isn't there someone wh-who wants me—for myself alone?" Even her fellow females seem to think of Wonder

Woman as a freak. In a 1968 issue of *Brave and the Bold*, Wonder Woman and Batgirl become rivals when they inexplicably develop mad feelings of love for Batman. As they compete to win Batman's affections, Batgirl refers to Wonder Woman as a "muscle-bound Medusa," saying, "An Amazon is incompatible with a normal, human hero . . . but I'm not!"

A 1965 story entitled "I Married a Monster" shows how far Wonder Woman had deviated from her original incarnation. The Wonder Woman Family is aghast when the Amazon princess agrees to marry the hideous, woman-hating beast Mr. Monster, thinking that her love can redeem him. The Amazon's love transforms the monster into a handsome prince, but his own bad nature has him green and ugly again in no time. As the hateful monster storms off in a huff, a tearful Wonder Woman thinks, "The way to a man's heart is through his stomach! I'll ask mother for recipes that will make the monster act like the dreamboat he became for a few moments!" Now, let's review. Once Wonder Woman's mission was to save the world by ending war and violence, and teaching mankind about the power of love. The idea of her putting on an apron to whip up some spanakopita to win over a mean-spirited guy made it apparent how much of a shadow of her former self she had become.

Things needed to change, and they did, abruptly. All of the secondary characters like Wonder Tot and Mer-Boy were "retired," and Wonder Woman's comic book moved in a stripped down direction that would return the Amazon to her 1940s roots. Her origin was restored, and Wonder Woman was once again the magical creation brought to life by goddesses, and not the product of a man's loins. But everything else in these bizarre, pseudo 1940s stories was played as camp, and did little to push the Amazon to new heights of glory. Wonder Woman's comrades, as usual, were faring better at this time in the 1960s. By 1966, Superman was a true American icon who had become the subject of a Broadway musical, while Batman became a sensation with the debut of his wildly popular, campy TV series in 1966.

The Amazon continued to flail. A rejected 1967 Wonder Woman TV pilot by *Batman* TV producer William Dozier, shows Wonder Woman as a myopic heroine. She sees her reflection in the mirror as an Amazon beauty, when in reality, she looks schleppy and ridiculous in her patriotic costume, and is an inept heroine. This depiction of a lame-brain Wonder Woman showed that her legend had truly faded by this time. She was now a sad joke. While the comic book world of the late '60s was caught up amidst the swirling frenzy of go-go and psychedelia, there was one prominent female strangely missing from the discotheque's dance floor. Sitting sadly in the corner was Wonder Woman. With her spit curls and starry bloomers, she looked like a relic from a bygone era, which, by that time, she was indeed. With opposition to the Vietnam War and the US government's involvement growing, Wonder Woman was still draped in stars and stripes. Could she be any less cool? With her comic on the verge of cancellation, DC tried a new approach—a new Wonder Woman.

"Forget The Old … The New Wonder Woman is Here," declares the cover of *Wonder Woman* #178. In the issue's story, Steve Trevor is framed for the murder of a pretty blonde he is attempting to seduce behind Wonder Woman's back. This fact is quickly ignored. Wonder Woman realizes that she can do more good for Steve in her Diana Prince persona, so she undergoes a transformation into a mod '60s chick who can infiltrate the "swinger set." Diana sets her glasses aside, gets a groovy wardrobe to go with her new *Valley of the Dolls* hairdo, and goes undercover. She manages to get the goods on the spies who have framed Steve, then makes a quick change into her dull old Wonder Woman garb and captures the crooks. Once freed, the doltish Steve admits to Wonder Woman that old maid Diana has really surprised him, and that he now finds her very attractive. Wonder Woman is perplexed at the thought of being in competition for the first time with her own secret identity. This would be the least of her problems.

In the next issue, Steve is in trouble again, but Wonder Woman has a bigger issue to deal with. Queen Hippolyta informs her daughter that the Amazons have to travel to another dimension to renew their powers. Wonder Woman says that she can't leave Steve behind in his hour of need, so she makes a tough decision. She relinquishes her costume, bracelets, lasso, and powers in a somber ceremony. The Amazons fade away, and with that, Wonder Woman is no more. Shortly after this, Steve is tragically killed, leaving Wonder Woman high and dry, alone for the first time in her life, with no powers, family, or man.

In her newly powerless Diana Prince persona, the heroine

finds herself wandering the streets of New York's Lower East Side. There she encounters a blind Asian elder named I Ching. As one might predict, he is a wise martial arts master. Under I Ching's tutelage, Diana becomes a karate-chopping dynamo. Wonder Woman, raised by ancient female warriors, is now trained by a man. Yet another new life had begun for Wonder Woman.

Diana becomes an international woman of mystery, taking on evil scientists and romancing dangerous men in exotic locales. She was a female James Bond, minus the endless sexual conquests. Her base of operations is New York's Lower East Side, where she opens a clothing boutique. Because of Diana's eventual penchant for wearing monochromatic mod attire, this period is often referred to as the "white pantsuit" period. This new direction had almost no relation to Wonder Woman's old persona, except for the occasional trip back to visit her mother and the Amazons to help them fight some menace or another.

When DC Comics was trying to figure out how to retool Wonder Woman's image to make her cooler, they looked at another Diana—Diana Rigg. Rigg had caused a stir as Mrs. Emma Peel when the British TV series *The Avengers* was imported to the US in 1966. Mrs. Peel defined the heroine of the mod '60s—brilliant as she was beautiful, witty, champion fencer, martial arts expert, modern artist, crack shot with a pistol, and fearless secret agent. Attired in sleek black leather catsuits or mod body stockings, Emma Peel was a true force to be reckoned with, combining beauty, brains, and power. And, apparently a new role model for Wonder Woman.

"I've always felt that some day Superman might marry her...now they've lost each other!" thinks The Flash, as a powerless Wonder Woman sadly resigns from the Justice League. This was an odd comment, since there had never been any indication of romance between the super duo. But it indicates that as a powerful heroine, Wonder Woman could have been a suitable mate for Superman. If it seems like the new powerless, white pantsuit wearing Wonder Woman was taking a giant step back, the answer would be yes, and no. True, she no longer was an indestructible warrior, but on the other hand, this new direction gave readers something they hadn't seen in Wonder Woman in the preceding years—a personality. Wonder Woman regained the sense of humor and confidence that had gone missing for almost twenty years. But most importantly, she was actually treated like a real person with emotions, fears, and desires. The other difference with the new Wonder Woman was that she now had a male mentor. Diana had always gone to her mother for advice. Now, she had the sage council of I Ching to guide her through this period of her life. For the first time Wonder Woman had a paternal figure in her life.

There was still an implication that when Wonder Woman had her powers, she was an inhuman fighting machine. But in her new powerless incarnation, she was considered to be more like a real woman. "When I was an Amazon princess—as Wonder Woman—I had perfect control of my emotions! As plain Diana Prince, I'm *human*—too *darn* human!" Oddly, it was implied that power and emotions cancelled each other out, and that they couldn't exist simultaneously inside Wonder Woman. "I want to hurt him . . . I want him to feel what *I'm* feeling!" Wonder Woman cries, as she lashes out with deadly fury at a spy who has cruelly tricked her into falling in love with him. This was a new Wonder Woman indeed, ready to enter the hedonistic, self-absorbed "me decade" of the '70s.

While most of Wonder Woman's new adventures were standard 1960s spy intrigue, some revived old themes. In 1969, Diana encountered "Them," a trio of vicious, sadistic lesbians who enslaved a young runaway, and marched her down the street wearing a dog collar. While this story may seem shocking for the times, in theme it was similar to the bondage, submission, and implied lesbianism of the Wonder Woman stories of the 1940s. The only difference was that now servitude was shown as bad, and not Dr. Marston's "loving submission." Bondage once again became a recurring element in Wonder Woman's adventures, as covers regularly showed Diana in chains and at the mercy of her adversaries. Along with the bondage came a return of brilliant and diabolical female foes, which had been conspicuously absent for two decades.

Wonder Woman's image change came at a time when comics were striving to become more "relevant" to what was happening in the real world. Soon, Superman and Batman would undergo changes as well. Superman's alter ego Clark Kent began to sport purple suits and wide ties when he became a TV newsman. A more hip looking Clark was featured in TV commercials for the "Dry Look" men's hair spray. Batman turned his back on his campy TV persona and returned to his dark, vigilante roots. But neither of these changes was as drastic as the one that Wonder Woman underwent. DC Comics editors didn't just alter Wonder Woman's persona, they replaced it. Equally perplexing was the New Wonder Woman's reaction to topical subjects. Issue #203, from 1972, was written by noted science fiction writer Samuel R. Delaney, and was billed as a "Women's Lib Issue." When asked why she doesn't get more involved with the Women's Liberation Movement, Diana Prince replies, "I'm for equal wages, too! But I'm not much of a joiner. I wouldn't fit in with your group. In most cases, I don't even like women." Considering the fact that Diana grew up in a society that was 100% female, her comment was particularly mystifying. Ironically, Women's Lib would shape Wonder Woman's next metamorphosis.

The new Wonder Woman was finally cool, but to some people, she just wasn't Wonder Woman. In July of 1972, the premiere issue of *Ms.* magazine declared "Wonder Woman for President." The cover depicted the Amazon princess in her famous tiara, bracelets, and full star spangled glory, coming to the rescue of a war torn world. Editor Gloria Steinem praised the 1940s Wonder Woman as a feminist role model for women of her generation. She urged DC Comics to restore the Amazon princess to her former glory, although low sales on the *New Wonder Woman* comic were probably the real motivator. In an abrupt change of direction, Diana's mentor I Ching is struck down by a sniper's bullet, and Diana suffers a blow to her head while attempting to capture the gunman. An amnesiac Diana manages to instinctively make her way back to Paradise Island, where the Amazons use their wondrous devices to restore her memory and powers. Well, part of them anyway, but more on that later. Her powers miraculously restored, and clad once more in her red, white and blue regalia, Wonder Woman is back, as though nothing had ever happened. The story was called "The Second Life of the Original Wonder Woman." Another new start.

The restored Wonder Woman underwent a few updates to make her seem more up with the times. She was drawn youthful and pretty, with free flowing hair, and a costume that looked more like a modern swimsuit. In order to seem more hip, Wonder Woman was even given a black twin sister named Nubia. Wonder Woman was now billed as "Superheroine Number One," but she may not have been exactly what Gloria Steinem hoped for.

The 1970s should have been a great time for the Amazon to flourish. The Women's Liberation movement was in full swing, and American society had finally begun to embrace the feminist manifesto that Wonder Woman had preached in her comics thirty years earlier. But the Amazon's comeback had a few missteps. The oddest thing about Wonder Woman's "reintroduction" was that she was treated like a *tabula rasa*. Queen Hippolyta casually omits Steve Trevor's death, the entire non-powered, white pantsuit period and I Ching from her daughter's memory, and sends her back to "man's world" none the wiser. There, Wonder Woman becomes a United Nations translator in her Diana Prince identity. Because she wears glasses and occasionally spouts feminist viewpoints, Diana is treated as bitter. "Like all homely women who can't get a man—they hate beautiful women—men—themselves," observes her chauvinistic UN boss.

By 1974, there was yet another drastic change in direction, this one totally serious in tone. Wonder Woman's Justice League teammates inform her of the several months of which she has no memory. An anguished, if not slightly racially insensitive Wonder Woman exclaims, "I want to know about I Ching, the blind old Chinaman you say became my mentor . . . and what happened to Col. Steve Trevor . . . my poor, sweet, darling Steve!" When Wonder Woman confronts her mother, Queen Hippolyta admits to tampering with her daughter's memories. "We restored your memories completely—omitting only the period you'd spent in "man's world" without your wondrous powers!" When the queen tells her daughter that Steve Trevor is indeed still dead, a tearful Wonder Woman turns her back on her mother and decides to get tough.

The Wonder Woman who emerged from this period was stronger, and began to live up to her potential as a feminist heroine of the Women's Lib era. Readers saw a return of the moralistic Amazon princess, who upheld a high standard for human behavior. As she swats The Cavalier, a villain who seduces and enslaves females, Wonder Woman declares, "You epitomize every repulsive thing I've dedicated my life to defeating—and I won't let you make a mockery of that!" As a member of the Justice League, Wonder Woman was strong and opinionated, often clashing with her male teammates. In *Justice League of America* #143 Superman has a chat with Wonder Woman after hearing complaints about her bad attitude. When she responds that the men of the team are patronizing her, Superman chalks it up to being a "Women's Lib thing." Wonder Woman angrily snaps back, "It is not! It's a Wonder Woman thing--! I've got my confidence back, Superman! I'm just as much a part of this team as anybody else ..." Wonder Woman's alter ego Diana Prince now worked for the United Nations Crisis Bureau. She was resourceful and feisty once again, and with her long streaked hair, oversize tinted glasses, and pantsuits, she looked conspicuously like Gloria Steinem.

The 1973 Saturday morning cartoon *Superfriends*, with its cleaned up, kid-friendly version of the Justice League, introduced Wonder Woman to a much wider audience. The *Superfriends* Wonder Woman was sexy but slightly butch, a good overall distillation of the Amazon's allure. Wonder Woman's foray into primetime television was a bit more difficult. A failed TV pilot from 1975 starred blonde former tennis star Cathy Lee Crosby in a red white and blue costume that made her look like an Olympic gymnast. The following year, another pilot featured a brunette Amazon princess who was closer to her comic book sources, played by former Miss World contestant Lynda Carter. Premiering in 1976, amidst America's huge bicentennial celebration, the *New, Original Wonder Woman* series took place during World War II, and featured a blend of patriotism, camp, and bondage. The Amazons were gorgeous women who ran around in pastel colored baby doll nighties, making Paradise Island looked like a toga party at the Playboy Mansion. The TV series catapulted Wonder Woman to heights of fame and made her a character with worldwide recognition. As portrayed by Carter, Wonder Woman wasn't a strident, threatening virago, but displayed a quiet confidence and poise mixed with power. Carter's looks and statuesque curves ushered Wonder Woman into the new status of pinup and male fantasy, while still making good on the character's original mission of inspiring young girls with the Amazon's combination of strength, and messages of female empowerment. Wonder Woman was finally catching up to her male counterparts, Superman and Batman, in terms of widespread recognition. For the first time, this meant that Wonder Woman was a big licensed character, with a flood of products hitting the market.

But too much of a Women's Lib message might have hurt sales of dolls, Halloween costumes, and Pez dispensers, so Wonder Woman's comic book drifted back to a series of safe adventures. To better tie in with the World War II time period featured in the TV show, the focus of the comics switched to the 1940s era Wonder Woman. She was back fighting the Nazis again, although the bizarre, kinky foes and malevolent females of the 1940s were replaced with more conventional, mostly male comic book villains now. When the TV series switched to a modern day setting, the comic also changed back to the Wonder Woman who lived in present day. However, the Amazon didn't regain the feminist edge that she had just two years earlier.

"Where's my life going? What's to be my next mission? Where do I go from here?" the modern day Wonder Woman mused. Interesting questions, especially in light of what was happening with her male contemporaries. By 1979, Superman had achieved even greater iconic status when he conquered the silver screen, played as a noble farm boy by Christopher Reeve. Batman continued down a darker path of crime stories, and was establishing a reputation as an obsessive authoritarian. Wonder Woman, however, was back to being adrift. The TV show was over by 1979, and while it had raised the Amazon's pinup appeal, it hadn't really done much for her credibility.

"If you haven't already driven WW crazy, you're at least coming close to turning *us* into raving lunatics. At this rate you might want to consider renaming this comic *The Lost World of Wonder Woman*," a frustrated reader wrote in a letter column, echoing the sentiments of many fans. All of the revisions of Wonder Woman's origin and changes in direction were testing the readers' patience, and weakening the character. Even though Wonder Woman was supposed to be the original independent heroine, her writers didn't seem to know what to do with her unless she had a boyfriend. In the space of four years, Steve Trevor had been revived from the dead, killed again, and revived once more. The heroine was constantly being manipulated by her mother and the gods of Olympus. By 1980, readers were again told, "It's a brand-new start for the Amazing Amazon..." But this would be the last makeover for *this* Wonder Woman.

By the mid 1980s DC Comics decided that it was time to face the future. After forty years of history and multiple versions of their heroes, it was getting harder for readers to keep things straight. The DC Universe needed to be streamlined to make its characters more accessible to new, younger readers. An epic mini-series called *Crisis on Infinite Earths* would redefine the

DC superheroes and change them for modern times. But as a character, Wonder Woman had been through so many changes and reincarnations that she was seemingly beyond repair. In the final issue of her comic, Wonder Woman and Steve are married at last, in a ceremony officiated by Zeus himself. Later, dressed in a filmy gown, Wonder Woman gazes out from her Olympian honeymoon suite. What a strange journey the last forty-five years had been. The mighty Amazon then surrenders into the arms of her new husband, ready to finally make the ultimate submission to her man. And that's where her story ends. In the 1986 *Crisis on Infinite Earths* climax, Wonder Woman is blasted by the rays of the fearsome Anti-Monitor, and seemingly blown to atoms. But in fact, she had simply been erased from existence. After *Crisis on Infinite Earths* was over, no one remembered that Wonder Woman had ever existed, and the DC universe went on as though nothing had ever happened. Wonder Woman did not appear in a comic book for almost one year.

In 1988, the new Wonder Woman was re-introduced to the DC universe. The basic story was the same, except that now, everything made sense, and there was an added element of Political Correctness. The Amazons were now a race of peaceful, racially diverse female warriors, reincarnations of women unjustly killed by brutal men. After being enslaved and brutalized by Hercules and his men, the Amazons once again fled "patriarch's world" to live immortal lives on their new island home, now called Themyscira rather than Paradise Island. This time, the Amazons' island home is like ancient Greece, without any futuristic science. Queen Hippolyta is the reincarnation of a murdered pregnant woman. Centuries later, she feels the pangs of motherhood and the call of the unborn soul within her. She forms a baby out of clay, which is brought to life by the Olympian goddesses. The addition of a soul was an effort to make the new Wonder Woman a real person, and not just an inhuman magical creation. The queen names her daughter Diana, after a heroic American Air Force pilot who had crashed on the island in the 1940s, and died aiding the Amazons. When Princess Diana is grown, the goddesses decide that one Amazon must go to "patriarch's world" to stop the war god Ares from consuming the world in the flames of battle. Princess Diana wins a tournament held to pick the greatest Amazon. She is presented with a costume bearing the colors and emblems found on the jacket of the fallen American pilot. Basically, this was a rational way of explaining why the young princess was now dressed like the American flag.

So, the new modern Wonder Woman was here. She was still strong, brave, and powerful, but now she was an inexperienced young novice rather than a seasoned adult heroine. Despite any retooling of their histories and personas after *Crisis on Infinite Earths*, Superman and Batman remained established heroes. Batman's transition to big screen star in 1989 would make him an even bigger star than Superman. Batman's dark persona was more suited to the cynical times than Superman's eternal optimism. But what chance did Wonder Woman have now? She was no longer on the same level as her two male counterparts. All of Wonder

Woman's history and experience had been flushed, and she had to once more work to reestablish her reputation as "Superheroine Number One."

The new Wonder Woman was less a superhero and more of an ambassador of her people. She was regarded as a foreign dignitary, and addressed the United Nations rather than working as an interpreter there. Her mission to bring peace to a troubled world was first and foremost to her. There was no more Diana Prince alter ego, so she was Wonder Woman all the time. Most significantly, there was no more boyfriend in the picture. The Steve Trevor of the new series was now a military man in his fifties—a friend and ally, but not a love interest.

The new Wonder Woman was powerful and capable, she just wasn't always that much fun. Writer/artist George Perez was trying to make the reintroduced Wonder Woman friendly to female readers. She had a strong, muscular body that wasn't overly sexualized, and no longer wore high heels. For as strong and powerful as she was, Wonder Woman was presented as an outsider from the ancient world, beholden to her Olympian gods, and catering to their every capricious whim. There were plenty of messages about female empowerment and sisterhood that her creator Marston would have approved of, but overall the new Wonder Woman lacked the smiling confidence and sense of humor that she had displayed in the 1940s.

Wonder Woman seemed a bit out of step with what was going on in comics, and the world. The industry had been swept up in the "grim and gritty" trend, with violent storylines and morally conflicted crimefighters who were almost as dark as their foes. Many established superheroines had adopted tough-as-nails attitudes, and these rough girls made the sensible Wonder Woman look like a Pollyanna. By the 1990s, as world wars loomed on the horizon once more, Wonder Woman's message of love and peaceful coexistence should have been that much more potent. But the world had grown darker and more violent, and no one wanted to hear about getting along, either from Rodney King or Wonder Woman. The Amazon needed to toughen up again to be reestablished as a formidable crime fighter. In 1992, readers were promised the "stunning return of comics' greatest heroine!" as Wonder Woman's image was reworked yet again. Although stories now focused on Wonder Woman as a superhero and less as an educator, fans winced as the mighty Wonder Woman was reduced to taking a job in a fast food restaurant in order to support herself.

Marketing had infiltrated the comic book world in a major way by the 1990s, and much-hyped sensational stories brought big changes to old established characters as part of an effort to increase sales. In Wonder Woman's case, this involved adding two surefire American moneymakers—sex and violence. New Brazilian artist Mike Deodato, Jr. turned the sexual heat up by giving readers a Wonder Woman with big breasts, tiny waist and thong clad butt, long supermodel legs, and a tousled mane of hair. She switched to a new all-black costume that consisted of a bra and a pair of spandex bike shorts decorated with stars, held together by an assortment of belts and straps. With her severe new black dominatrix hairdo, Wonder Woman looked like an S & M aerobics instructor. She also relaxed her famous nonviolent beliefs to adopt a fiercer attitude. The sex and violence hype paid off, and sales on Wonder Woman's comic rose. Wonder Woman was now no longer a role model for females but was instead, like *Playboy* magazine, "entertainment for men."

Having been embraced by a male audience, Wonder Woman was poised to take her rightful place beside Superman and Batman in the Trinity of superheroes. In 1996, writer Grant Morrison re-imagined the Justice League as modern day equivalents to the godly pantheon of Olympus. Superman was the king of the gods, Zeus, while Batman was analogous to Hades, the lord of the underworld. Wonder Woman's counterpart was Hera, the queen of the gods. Since 1991's Gulf War, American female military personnel were engaged in actual enemy conflicts, so the nation had grown more accustomed to the idea of a woman soldier. Wonder Woman still preached peace, but her warrior's heritage was played up considerably now. She was the ultimate soldier, and new artist and writer John Byrne dressed her for battle. Byrne's 1995 run on Wonder Woman's comic was billed as yet another "Beginning of a bold new era!" Byrne's Wonder Woman had a little more of everything: bigger muscles, bigger bulletproof bracelets that were now giant gauntlets, bigger tiara, bigger armor plated chest, and even bigger hair. Byrne strove to establish Wonder Woman as second in strength and power to Superman, and also to show her as an indomitable war machine. The ultimate goal was to restore Wonder Woman to her former glory as the premiere comic book superheroine and Amazon, and not a glorified humanitarian.

But, despite these upgrades, it seemed like Wonder Woman herself was becoming less vital to her own series. The question was whether Wonder Woman was merely the red, white and blue swimsuit, or the actual woman inside of it. Eventually Wonder Woman was even killed off, and the gods of Olympus resurrected her as the divine Diana, goddess of truth. Her mother, Queen Hippolyta, decided to get into the family act, squeezed into the eagle-emblazoned bustier, grabbed a sword and shield, and succeeded her late daughter as the new Wonder Woman. The members of the Justice League hardly seem to notice any difference when mom Hippolyta starts showing up at their meetings, as she was written as essentially the same character as her daughter. Superman's persona was noble, Batman's was grim. Wonder Woman was just a crown, some wristbands, and starry panties; it didn't seem to matter who was wearing them. Wonder Woman eventually got tired of cooling her heels in Olympus, gave up her godhood and reclaimed her mortality and title. But she still lacked personality.

Wonder Woman was still often written as the cold, untouchable, inhuman warrior princess. When the Justice League met their descendants from the far-flung 853rd century, all of the various members except Wonder Woman had flesh and blood futuristic counterparts. Her future incarnation was a living marble statue, which indicated how much of a real woman writers considered her to be. Part of Wonder Woman's dearth of personality stemmed from her indefinable sexuality. For as jaw dropping as Wonder Woman was drawn at the dawn of the 21st century, she was still the inviolate virgin goddess who was somewhat sexless. Since women had found it necessary to adopt a sexual persona in order to remain successful in modern popular culture, Wonder Woman had to be seen as desirable in order to become more popular. While Wonder Woman had not had a love interest since being reintroduced in 1988, by far her deepest and most revealing relationships had been with her male counterparts Superman and Batman.

In order to establish Wonder Woman as a true equal to Superman and Batman in the eyes of male readers, she had to become sexually attractive to both. When Superman first meets the newly reintroduced Wonder Woman in the 1980s, he is thunderstruck by the vibrant Amazon beauty, and asks her out on a date. This '80s Superman was now portrayed as a nice Kansas farm boy who happened to have godlike powers, while the new Wonder Woman was a perfect woman who regularly communed with gods. The pair decide that they are worlds apart, better off as allies than lovers. Meanwhile, in a 2002 adventure, Batman and Wonder Woman share a kiss on the eve of a suicide mission, leaving them wrestling with the question of whether or not to pursue a relationship. While Wonder Woman admired Superman's goodness and virtue, her warrior's nature was drawn to Batman's passion, and presumably the prospect of athletic sex. "He's brilliant. He's driven. A warrior in the classic sense," she thinks as she considers a life as Mrs. Bruce Wayne. Ultimately the duo decides that they are also better as lifelong friends than as romantic partners. In the past, when Wonder Woman's sexual allure was deemphasized she was seen as less than a woman, and inferior to

Superman and Batman. Her reputation as a powerful hero was well established, but Wonder Woman needed to be acknowledged as a woman by her iconic peers to enter their stratosphere of fame.

So where did this leave the Wonder Woman in the 21st century? She was still an anomaly—the warrior from an ancient world who believed in peace, an armor plated activist helping the world's downtrodden, the perfect woman plagued by doubts about her place in the universe. In the era of deceptive government officials and corrupt corporate heads, one of Wonder Woman's abilities was more terrifying than ever—the power to compel men to speak the truth. She had taken her message of peace and love global by opening embassies around the world, and in the post 9/11 world, was often seen helping *burqa* clad women in unidentified, desert countries who were being brutalized by tyrannical men. As might be expected, a despotic leader offered to stop waging war and withdraw all of his forces if Wonder Woman would spend one night with him. But despite the fact that she advocated the power of love, Wonder Woman's goal was not to sleep her way to world peace.

Because Wonder Woman was still presented as a champion of peace, her fans were outraged when she became a killer in 2005. In order to stop widespread death across the globe, Wonder Woman calmly and coolly snapped a villain's neck. Pals Superman and Batman didn't approve of these extreme measures, Wonder Woman's credibility was shot, and her mission of peace was pretty much down the toilet.

The most famous female in comic books once more entered

the revolving door of personalities for another reinvention. This time around, there was an answer to the question Wonder Woman had been grappling with for decades—could she be a "wonder," and still be a "woman" too? "I think the only way I can accomplish my mission is if I don't have to be Princess Diana of Themyscira or Wonder Woman. If I can just be me," she tells Batman, as she assumed her new secret identity of Special Agent Diana Prince. Eventually Diana reclaimed her Wonder Woman role, but with a twist. An enchantment caused the indestructible Wonder Woman to turn into a normal, vulnerable human being when she switched to Diana Prince, thus fulfilling her wish to understand what it is to be a regular person: "To be part of the human race, not just standing outside of it."

The cover of *Wonder Woman* #14, from 2008, didn't carry a banner announcing a "brand-new start" for the Amazon princess. But this particular issue featured perhaps the most significant changes in Wonder Woman's history. For the first time in over six decades, a woman was the regular writer of Wonder Woman's monthly comic book. Amid a flurry of media fanfare, Gail Simone took over the reins of Wonder Woman's adventures. Known for her complex and realistic female characters, Simone gave readers a Wonder Woman who was noble and courageous, a brilliant and confident warrior: a role model for her fellow superheroines. This version of Wonder Woman was warm, human, and, amazingly enough, had a sense of humor. But since this was Wonder Woman, this new version wasn't meant to last.

In 2011, readers saw Wonder Woman reinvented yet again.

Now she was an angry warrior in a leather jacket on a quest for vengeance against the men who had killed her mother and slaughtered the Amazons. But it didn't stop there. Later that year DC Comics announced they were going to give not only Wonder Woman, but all of their superheroes a makeover. In September of 2011, DC's New 52 presented the newest version of Wonder Woman, intended to be more modern and accessible. She wore a variation of the same costume Wonder Woman had sported for decades, although now her skin was a bit darker. She lived in London, frequented dark nightclubs, and was rather glum and humorless. Wonder Woman was officially "edgy."

But there were more fundamental changes made to this new Wonder Woman. She was no longer the creation of just her mother Queen Hippolyta, but was now the product of a tryst between the Amazon monarch and the god Zeus. Instead of being loved by her Amazon sisters, now Wonder Woman was the object of their scorn. Wonder Woman had always embraced the ways of peace, as the sworn enemy of Ares, god of war. Now Ares was the mentor who had trained the young Wonder Woman to fight. When Ares was eventually killed, Wonder Woman assumed his place as god of war. The new version systematically eliminated every female-focused element from Wonder Woman's character. The result was a harder, more masculine, warlike version of Wonder Woman. Ironically these changes came at a time when publishers were supposedly trying to attract female readers

Blockbuster superhero movies were box office moneymakers at the beginning of the 21st century, and both Batman and Superman were back on the big screen. When it was announced that Wonder Woman would appear in 2016's *Batman v. Superman: Dawn of Justice*, fans waited nervously to see how their beloved heroine would be portrayed. As played by actress Gal Gadot, the cinematic Wonder Woman is introduced as Diana Prince, a mystery woman who deftly outwits master manipulator Batman. "I don't think you've ever known a woman like me," she confidently tells Bruce Wayne after his combination seduction/intimidation ploy fails to work on her. But it was Wonder Woman's dramatic first onscreen appearance in full costume that had audiences cheering. While the majority of film critics gave *Batman v. Superman* unfavorable reviews, most agreed that Wonder Woman's big screen debut was the heroic highlight of the movie.

No doubt Wonder Woman will continue to be reinvented time and again, since after seven decades most writers can't seem to see beyond the costume to understand the woman wearing it. A 2011 Wonder Woman TV pilot starring Adrianne Palicki presented one of the more off-base interpretations of the heroine—powerful corporate CEO by day, violent crimefighter by night. Although misguided, one scene in the pilot encapsulates the challenge that many people, especially comic book writers, seem to have with Wonder Woman. Frustrated by the way the world sees her, the heroine declares, "Wonder Woman's perfect. Perfect tits. Perfect ass. Perfect teeth…She always does everything right. God forbid she make a mistake. It's not like we should expect the world to accept her being human."

1980s : The Dark Road

Storm was desperate. The mutant mistress of lightning, the weather witch, the wind-rider, was feeling the weight that came with responsibility, and she didn't like it. Storm had taken over the leadership of the outlaw team of mutant superheroes known as the X-Men, and she was feeling the weight of that job. The burden of making the right choices to keep her team safe and alive was a heavy one.

The past few months had been an endless series of tests of her resilience. On her first mission as leader, she lost control of her awesome powers. Turning against friends and foes alike, Storm proclaimed herself a terrifying elemental goddess, giving in to her most selfish desires, and unleashing a mighty hurricane. She finally came to her senses. But her passions had been stirred. What followed were more trials for Storm. She became a bloodthirsty slave of the vampire lord, Dracula. Her body became the host for an evil parasite alien embryo that pushed Storm, who cherished life, to the brink of suicide.

The turning point was when the X-Men met the Morlocks, a tribe of freakish mutants who lived beneath the streets of Manhattan. The Morlocks were hideous, disfigured outcasts who dressed in leather, rags, and spiked collars. Their leader was a lethal eye-patch-wearing woman named Callisto who challenged Storm to a duel. Her fellow X-Men watched in fear as their leader became locked in a deadly knife fight with Callisto, knowing that Storm had vowed never to take a life. That fear turned to shock when they saw Storm coldly and efficiently bury the knife in Callisto's heart. As the winner, Storm claimed Callisto's black leather vest as the symbol of leadership over the Morlocks.

Despite her victory, Storm was nearing her breaking point. She felt her duties as the X-Men's leader were forcing her to become a different woman, with beliefs that went against everything she held dear. Storm felt resentful that the team's mentor, Professor X, caused the moral crisis. "It is because of you that I became an X-Man, old man—and that decision is destroying me!"

While on a mission with the X-Men in Tokyo, Storm's life changes forever. After a night of fighting and near death, the usually calm Storm feels liberated. "I have never used my powers to deliberately inflict pain," she says, feeling a tide of temptation sweep over her. The next day, her teammates are shocked to see their leader's transformation.

Storm wears the Morlock black leather vest instead of her sweeping black cape. Her shiny black swimsuit costume is also gone, replaced by skintight leather pants and boots. Leather belts encircle her hips, a studded collar wraps around her neck. The flowing waist length white hair is also gone; in its place is a mohawk. Severe black eye makeup arches across her face like claw marks, completing the metamorphosis.

It's 1983. MTV, the 24-hour music television channel was introducing America to new artists in leather jackets who sang of alienation and urban angst. The world was dancing to a different beat, and Storm had decided that it was time to toughen up her act.

As the 1980s dawned, a new administration moved into the White House, with a message that America needed to comb its hair, sit up straight, and put on a clean shirt. Stern parents Ronald and Nancy Reagan were intent on cracking down on what they saw as years of drugs and negligent behavior that the nation had engaged in throughout the '70s. They cast an eye on the rest of the world as well. The implication was that America had to get tough, and take a stronger approach to dealing with the threats to its democracy, even if that meant creating weapons that would rain destruction on our foes. The days of Cold Wars and playing nice were over. It was time to face the future.

In the world of comic books, superheroines were facing the future as well, and finding that cold and harsh days were upon them. Twenty years had passed since superheroines had returned to the pages of comic books, and they were in for some rude awakenings when the '80s began, ushering in a new tone of dark realism. The X-Men's Phoenix had found that "having it all"— beauty, love, and, in her case, infinite power—was not the answer, and that a woman might have to pay the ultimate price for striving for the heavens. Batwoman, whose ambition it was to marry her idol Batman, was cruelly killed in 1979, a needless leftover of a more frivolous time. Supergirl, the crown princess of comic books, also met her demise in the '80s, but for much crueler reasons. After two decades of tireless heroism, she was deemed unnecessary, and eliminated. Out of style, Wonder Woman was also erased.

And the 1980s brought even more misfortune to superheroines. Ms. Marvel was a victim of rape. The Avengers' Wasp found that storybook endings didn't always last when her husband Yellowjacket went from superhero to wife beater. Wasp got a black eye, Yellowjacket got kicked off the team and they both took a trip to divorce court. The Fantastic Four's Invisible Girl found that the radiation encountered on a mission with her team was the cause of her miscarrying her second child. While the Black Canary claimed she didn't want to be a mother, injuries that she suffered at the hands of drug dealers rendered her unable to bear children. Heroines had spent the 1970s fighting to be treated as equals to men. The new decade delivered a barrage of agony that would test these women's strength in new ways. They cut their hair, ditched their high heels, and hunkered down to face this cold decade. Would the new heroines born into this brave new world be different from their sisters who had come before?

Two vastly different superheroines made their debuts at the start of the decade, and each in her own way would give clues to the direction that female characters, and the comic book industry itself, would develop over the next several years. The first was Dazzler. When Dazzler first appeared in 1980's *Uncanny X-Men* #130, most comic book fans thought that she already seemed out of date. The X-Men first encountered the sparkly mutant singer in a run down Lower Manhattan disco. The story's tone and the punky habitués of the club seemed to imply that disco was on its last legs. Dazzler could turn sound into a stunning light show that she used as part of her musical act. She wore a skintight silver jumpsuit with a low cut neckline and hung a miniature mirrored disco ball around her neck. To disguise herself, Dazzler painted her face with wild makeup like the rock band KISS. To complete the disco theme, Dazzler would put on a pair of shiny chrome roller skates that helped her to zip around and blind bad guys with her light powers. While amusing, she seemed like a one-off novelty character that readers would probably never see again.

Dazzler may have seemed dated, but in reality she represented where the comic book industry was heading. The '80s would see marketing and co-branding infiltrate the comic book industry, reaching a pinnacle of hyped up excess in the '90s. The decade would be dominated with interconnecting series and carefully orchestrated crossover storylines that ran across several comic book titles. The major comic book publishers teamed up with toy manufacturers to produce series that tied in with collectible superhero dolls, or "action figures," to use the newly coined, male friendly term. All of these marketing blitzes were designed to get readers to buy more comics featuring their favorite characters, but didn't always concentrate on telling good stories.

In Dazzler's case, Marvel Comics had partnered with Casablanca Records in the late '70s to produce a comic book about a disco superheroine. Marvel had already published two comic books starring the biggest stars in Casablanca's stable, the heavy metal band in Kabuki makeup called KISS. The plan was that Casablanca would produce a recording artist named Dazzler who would then be featured in a comic book, with a potential movie to follow. The process of working with Casablanca on Dazzler's design caused long delays for the release of the comic book. Eventually, the record company dropped out of the project, and plans for a movie fell through as well. Dazzler guest starred with popular Marvel characters like the X-Men and Spider-Man to build up some excitement about the disco superheroine. But by the time Dazzler's comic finally debuted in 1981, disco definitely seemed like yesterday's news. In the first issue of her comic book, seven people were listed as having shaped Dazzler's concept, indicating that she had been a corporate committee creation, rather than a spark of genius from one writer or artist. The studio executives behind the ill-fated movie wanted Bo Derek to play Dazzler, so in the first story the heroine was drawn to mimic the *10* actress' dramatic bone structure. The truth of it was, with her shimmery laser light powers and roller skates, Dazzler reminded readers more of Olivia Newton-John in the campy movie musical *Xanadu*.

While the plan to promote Dazzler may have been inspired, it suffered from bad timing. Marvel's "Shining Superstar" was already a relic from the dying disco era, and her career had just begun. A few months after the premiere of Dazzler's comic book, MTV hit the airwaves, bringing a hard-edged new sound into American homes. Pat Benatar's "You Better Run" was the second video to be played on the channel, and her powerful voice and tough rock chick persona made silvery disco queen Dazzler look like a lightweight.

MTV served up a 24-hour nonstop supply of new bands with leather jackets, torn t-shirts, and a harder sound and attitude that created a soundtrack for a world that was moving beyond the hedonism of the '70s towards angst, detachment, and cynicism. The proliferation of nuclear weapons in the hands of the world powers made people worry how long it would be before the Cold War heated up for one last bonfire. AIDS, crime, and drug addiction were ravaging the cities of America, casting a pall of fear and paranoia across the nation. Comic books began reflecting this new mood of apprehension and desperation, as stories became more violent and heroes became more morally conflicted.

The second heroine to debut in 1981 was well suited for this world of fear. Writer/artist Frank Miller is often credited with starting the "grim and gritty" trend in comic books when he began working on Marvel's C-list *Daredevil* series in 1980. Daredevil had debuted in 1964, telling the story of Matt Murdock, a blind lawyer who possessed heightened radar senses that allowed him to "see" and fight crime as Daredevil, the red-clad, acrobatic enemy of evil. Daredevil had dwindled into standard superhero fare in the '70s, but Miller's noirish storytelling style and hard-bitten crime stories revitalized and transformed the hero into one of Marvel's hottest titles. A big factor in Daredevil's renewed popularity was a cold-blooded killer for hire named Elektra. She would define a new kind of comic book female for the '80s.

Elektra was Matt Murdock's college sweetheart, and the daughter of a Greek diplomat. When Elektra was unable to prevent her father's death at the hands of terrorists, her old way of life ended. "I used to love the world . . . now I can't let it touch me. Ever again," Elektra said, as she turned her back on Matt, and part of her soul, to take up a bloody path towards revenge and destruction. Martial arts expert Elektra allied herself with The Hand, an order of mystical ninja assassins, who trained her to be a deadly killer. Elektra moved up the ranks of The Hand, mercilessly carrying out her grim assignments of death. When Elektra becomes an independent murderer for hire, she crosses paths with her old lover Matt, now the crime fighting Daredevil. Dressed in matching blood red, Elektra and Daredevil find themselves on opposite sides of the law, but still hopelessly drawn to each other. "No matter how much it pains me, I must hunt Elektra down . . . and bring her to justice!" Daredevil says, as his heart breaks.

Fans loved this violent, blood-drenched love story, and Elektra became the comic book "It" girl of 1981. Tragedy had played an integral part in Elektra's development; death, incest, madness, and lost love all made her a heartless killer. Unlike the earlier heroines who strove to find love, Elektra eliminated emotions from her life to shield herself from the tragedies she had endured. What was left was a grim, emotionally crippled, but incredibly sexy murderer—the ultimate *belle dame sans merci*. Brandishing her deadly daggers, Elektra cut an impressive figure with her long black hair, asymmetrically cut costume, and strap festooned limbs, ushering Ninja Chic into the world of comic books. Her debut came at a time when comics from Japan, as well as fashion, were starting to make a big impact in America. Elektra became a sensation, and made the comic book anti-heroine the style *du jour*. She seemed infinitely cooler than all of the noble heroines plying their trade in comic books, and her tragedy somehow made her more real. Unlike the dated Dazzler, Elektra's heartless persona seemed completely in fashion for the MTV '80s. Red was the new black.

Despite the fact that she was a remorseless bloody killer, writer Miller made readers think that Daredevil could find a glimmer of hope in the assassin's black soul. In a fitting end to this tragic romantic epic, Elektra was fatally stabbed by a rival assassin after an especially violent battle, and died in her lost love Daredevil's arms. And when ninja sorcerers of The Hand later attempted to resurrect Elektra as their ultimate weapon of destruction, it was Daredevil's love for the beautiful killer that purged her soul of its darkness, and set her on a path of righteousness. Elektra's demons had been exorcized, and so her story was over, for now. But her tale had shown how appealing corruption could be.

In the 1978 movie musical *Grease*, good girl Sandy, played by Olivia Newton John, trades in her cardigan sweater and circle skirt for red lipstick, spandex pants, and cigarettes. While Sandy's transformation is in part to win the love of bad boy Danny, she is also giving in to the thrill of flirting with her dark side. Comic books had used the "good girl gone bad" concept for years. Bad behavior could usually be chalked up to hypnosis or a mystic spell. No self-respecting heroine ever turned bad of her own accord. But tastes were changing, and a new archetype was reaching fruition. Throughout the '80s, comic book readers saw honorable heroines walk a dark path, resulting in either their salvation or destruction.

The saga of Dark Phoenix pushed the X-Men to the top of the industry, which meant tragic heroines translated to big bucks. But the mutant heroes didn't have the monopoly on tainted, corruptible heroines. *Uncanny X-Men's* biggest competition in the early '80s was DC Comics' *New Teen Titans*, an update of the old 1960s sidekick team. The original band of teenagers had faded into relative obscurity through the 1970s, but had been revived in 1980 with a new lineup. The members of the diverse new team were brought together by Raven, a mysterious young woman who appeared in a cloud of smoke, bearing premonitions of doom. Traditionally, comic book heroines made a decision to fight evil either for revenge or to make the world a better place. Raven was different. She formed the New Teen Titans to save the world from herself.

Raven was the misbegotten offspring of a human woman and a megalomaniacal demon named Trigon. She was raised to follow the ways of pacifism, which clashed with the gnawing darkness in her soul that was her sire's legacy. Raven had mysterious abilities, including the power to control emotions, and even made Kid Flash fall in love with her so he'd join the team. But it was her own emotions that Raven feared most, because if she followed her feelings, her father's evil would consume her. Raven was secretive and manipulative, and the other Titans never knew if they could trust her. She isolated herself from her teammates, hiding her inner torment and struggles from them: ". . . you mean well, but you do not understand the forces that churn within me," was Raven's response to the well-intentioned concern of her fellow Titans.

Draped in a voluminous midnight blue hooded cape, with a long flowing gown slit to the hip, Raven's look was pure old style comic book glamour, hearkening back to 1940s heroines like Lady Satan. But Raven's questionable motives straddled the line between good and evil. Her face obscured by shadow, Raven made readers wonder how long it would be before she succumbed to her dark heritage. Like the X-Men's Phoenix, Raven played the lead role in a morality tale about the price a woman must pay for power. Both Phoenix and Raven had power thrust upon them. In Raven's case, it was a result of her infernal parentage. Raven's awesome powers put her in a class with comparable male heroes, but those very abilities forced her to constantly wrestle with her own nature, lest she unleash an inferno on the Earth. Like Phoenix, Raven eventually gave in to temptation and let her darkness consume her, forcing her teammates to kill her. Was death the only outcome when a woman couldn't shoulder the responsibility of power?

X-Men leader Storm's 1983 transformation from disco Earth goddess to leather clad punk was indicative of a different kind of struggle. Two years earlier, Storm had become intoxicated by her own power, and almost wiped out the Eastern seaboard with a massive hurricane. The heroine's evolution into mohawked punk indicated less a submission to a darker side, and more a reflection of the dilemma of the modern career woman. By the 1980s, many women had reached their professional goals, but were struggling to maintain their identities in a more complex life. Storm was the leader of both the X-Men and the outcast Morlocks. She acted as surrogate mother to the X-Men's youngest member Kitty Pryde. Storm wielded the forces of nature and had an empathic relationship with the Earth itself, forcing her to constantly keep her emotions in check lest she spark a violent tempest: "I had no conception of the responsibility such power entailed." Last but not least, she was a woman used to living a life of freedom, who was now feeling unbearable pressure from the world around her.

Storm's black leather makeover of 1983 showed how much the world had changed in the eight years since the mutant heroine had been introduced. While women had always been pushed to the background in the macho world of rock 'n' roll, they were major stars of the so-called New Wave music popular in the '80s. New Wave was the way the record industry packaged the new music style that divorced it from the anti-commercialism overtones of punk rock. New Wave bands were heavily featured on MTV, and people not only heard but now also saw punk princesses like Debbie Harry and Siouxsie Sioux, angular androgynous beauties like Grace Jones or Annie Lennox, or tough swaggering rock guitar goddesses like Chrissie Hynde and Joan Jett. The new female rock stars projected a strength and hard attitude well suited for the urban jungle. Music featured disaffected, bored vocals heard over electronic synthesized sounds, giving a sense of alienated passion blended with apathy. "Let's play master and servant," Depeche Mode sang dispassionately in their 1984 hit, echoing the darker sexual thrills that had slipped into the mainstream to entertain the jaded masses.

The '70s were about sensation and pleasure; the '80s craved alienation and suppressed emotion. Storm used her new leather and studs fashion and the accompanying harsher attitude to build a wall around herself, to keep the world out. "The difference is not cosmetic . . . my appearance is an expression of something deep within me . . . I find myself casting aside the precepts and beliefs that gave my life meaning—and hardly missing them once they are gone," Storm tells Professor X, as she tries to cope in a world grown cold and forbidding.

Of the mainstream superhero comics, the X-Men perhaps best reflected the darkening 1980s. Writer Chris Claremont emphasized the X-Men's outsider status, playing up the idea that they were outlaw superheroes. Wolverine, the hard drinking, cigarette smoking, indestructible mutant with the razor sharp metal claws and blasé attitude toward killing, had become the team's most popular member. Despite the team's male-centric name, by the mid-'80s, the female members of the X-Men outnumbered the males. With the exception of the feral Wolverine, most of the male X-Men managed to remain sedate. But, it became a tradition, and eventually a cliché, that all of the team's heroines would go off the deep end and turn evil at some point.

It seemed to be a requirement that the women who wore an "X" on their costumes would eventually take a dip in the crazy pool at least once. Power intoxicated these women and made them cruel, maniacal menaces who cast aside loyalties to friends and lovers. Even when possessed by an evil entity, the implication was that a suppressed part of the heroine's soul was reveling in the rush of deviltry. "I must say, you pair are proving most delightfully difficult to kill. I suppose I'll simply have to keep trying ... till I get it right!" says the magnetically powered Polaris in 1987, once an X-Woman, now a bitter foe preparing to dispatch two of her former teammates. And like Storm, these women's trips down a dark path resulted in all manner of '80s MTV friendly attire from straps, spiked collars and giant shoulder pads, to rock 'n' roll hair. These were the daughters of Eve, that first woman to fall under bad influences and become a threat. These heroines-turned-villainesses represented the ultimate fear that men have about female power—the secret betrayer, the dormant evil waiting to awaken, the weak creature who can't handle power. These stories suggested that there was something tragic, yet expected, about a woman's inability to control her power. Despite the advances that women had made in comic books, there was still a message that they could not handle power as well as a man. They were powerful women giving in to their desires, regardless of the costs.

With all of the *Sturm und Drang* revolving around the women of the X-Men, it seemed that the beacon of hope in this darkness was the team's youngest member, Kitty Pryde. Introduced in 1980, Kitty was a thirteen-year-old girl from the suburbs of Chicago, a near genius level student, and a ballet fanatic. She was, perhaps, the first realistic teenage superhero ever seen in comics, with all of the flaws and charms that come with youth—spunky, brilliant, courageous, while also insecure, flighty, and immature. Kitty was almost as freaked out about her parents' impending divorce as she was about her newfound power to walk through walls. She was drawn as a gangly, skinny kid, not a curvy preteen vixen. She was also Jewish, which was something new for the WASP-y world of comic book heroes.

Readers got a different perspective on the weird, dangerous and frightening superhero world of the X-Men through the eyes of this normal suburban teenage girl. Kitty gave the X-Men an emotional core, and brought them back to their original purpose of helping young mutants to learn to use their powers. Team leader Storm became Kitty's mentor and older sister, while the burly Russian beefcake Colossus was the object of her schoolgirl crush. Kitty's innocence and youth softened the battle-hardened Wolverine's tough exterior, and he in turn taught her how to fight.

Kitty appeared at a time when American popular culture was rediscovering the cute but quirky, lovable teenage girl, through John Hughes' movies like *Sixteen Candles*, and the breakthrough TV sitcom *Square Pegs*. Although technically a student and not a member of the team, Kitty often snuck off on missions with the X-Men. With her ability to walk through walls and genius level computer skills, she quickly proved she could be a valuable member of the team. Clad in a soft green costume with flowing sleeves and fantasy makeup, Kitty was Ariel—a teen princess heroine, a sort of Stevie Nicks vision of a superheroine that a young teenage girl might come up with.

In Greek mythology, the seasons are explained by the story of Persephone, the maiden daughter of the Earth goddess Demeter. Persephone was abducted by Hades, the god of the underworld, and carried down to his dark kingdom. Each year, Persephone had to spend four months in the underworld, and the world grew cold and barren. Even though every spring Persephone was allowed to return to the sunlit surface world, her youthful joy was diminished. Of Persephone's darkened nature, Edith Hamilton wrote, "After the lord of the dark world below carried her away, she was never again the gay young creature who had played in the flowery meadow without a thought of trouble." Such was the fate of Kitty Pryde in the doom-laden '80s.

Kitty starred in her own Persephone tragedy when she was dragged down to the dank, abandoned subway tunnels inhabited by the Morlocks. There, Kitty was dressed in a tattered wedding dress and ragged veil for her marriage to the hideous Morlock Caliban. It was 1984, and she looked like she had fished some of Madonna's old "Like a Virgin" outfits out a dumpster. This was just the beginning of a series of tragic events that left Kitty feeling heartbroken and abandoned.

Kitty eventually falls under the sway of the Japanese sorcerer Ogun, who transforms her into a deadly assassin with ninja fighting skills. She is able to free herself from Ogun's mind control, but she has changed. She adopts a new, darker persona to go with her lethal abilities and spiky shorn hair. "I'm not the girl you brainwashed, Ogun. In some ways, no longer a girl at all. That Kitty's no more—and you have no power over a *Shadowcat*." Now wearing a midnight blue leather costume with studded armbands, Kitty's fatal new Shadowcat persona reflects the cold realities of life, and not the dreams of an innocent young girl. Like Persephone, Kitty can never quite shake the taint of her brush with the dark underworld. She may have seemed like her old cheerful self, but she threw out her Shetland sweaters and leg warmers in favor of spiked collars, leather jackets, and fishnets. She had lost her youthful outlook on life, and like the rest of the X-Men, became a harder, darker character.

The X-Men's Kitty Pryde spearheaded the return of the teen superheroine. Over the years, superhero teams like the Justice League, the Justice Society, and the Avengers would all add a "Kitty Pryde" type teenage girl to their ranks. While Marvel's X-Men seemed to epitomize corrupted heroines of the '80s, their main competition at rival DC would perhaps go a step further. When Terra was introduced in the *New Teen Titans* in 1982, fans may have thought that she was another young teenage heroine in the mold of Kitty Pryde. On the contrary, writer Marv Wolfman created the bucktoothed blonde teen as an "anti-Kitty Pryde," in response to the ongoing comparisons between X-Men and the New Teen Titans. Terra, a spunky girl of fifteen, was an "earth-mover," meaning she caused earthquakes, landslides, or made the ground split open. Unlike Kitty, Terra came from a tragic background, and had been shunned and ostracized all of her life. She clashes with the Teen Titans several times, and despite Terra's rebellious nature and insolence, they make her a member of the team. Terra was a new kind of teen heroine: angry, foul-mouthed and belligerent. The Teen Titans believed that she could be rehabilitated. "You've got a proud tradition to uphold," says team leader Robin, "but something tells me you're gonna do just fine."

Robin may have been a great detective, but he was a lousy judge of character. Terra may not have worn leather and spikes like the women of the X-Men, but her dark nature went beyond fashion. Under Terra's tough chick exterior was a truly amoral young woman. In actuality, Terra was spying on the Teen Titans for Deathstroke the Terminator, an enemy of the young heroes. "She's the best little sociopath I've ever known," gloats Deathstroke, relishing his imminent defeat of the Teen Titans. Deathstroke stokes the fires of Terra's hate for the Titans, who she refers to as "sanctimonious do-gooders." Especially sleazy are the boudoir scenes where the teenaged Terra makes her reports to Deathstroke, her master and much older lover. Readers were shocked when they saw Terra lounging in a kimono, dragging on a cigarette, her face heavily made up to look like a middle-aged woman. When Deathstroke tells Terra to tone the makeup down because it doesn't fit her "cute girl" superhero image, Terra's response is typically cold-blooded. "An' damn all cute girl super-heroes, too."

The women of the X-Men usually walked the dark path as a result of the manipulations of others, usually a man's. Terra was another story. She was just inherently bad; Deathstroke wasn't the catalyst for her corruption; he simply gave her opportunities to exercise her hatred for humanity. A climactic confrontation between the New Teen Titans and Deathstroke exposed Terra's ruse. Thinking that her lover Deathstroke had betrayed her, the psychopathic teen heroine cum villainess went ballistic with her powers, inadvertently killing herself. Terra was unrepentant to the end. Readers were shocked not only that Terra didn't reform, but that she was killed off. Writer Wolfman and artist George Perez intentionally crafted a sympathetic character readers would fall in love with to make her true nature more shocking. Comic books had never seen a heroine, much less a teenage one, who was this unrelentingly corrupt. Even the mass murderess Elektra was redeemed at the end of her life. Teenaged Terra was perhaps the most corrupt of the dark '80s heroines because she had not been led astray to moral downfall—she willingly chose that path herself.

Not all heroines were aware that they had a vendetta that could invoke a dark persona. By the 1980s, writer/artist John Byrne had taken over the reins of *Fantastic Four* with the goal of returning Marvel's sagging flagship title to its level of 1960s greatness. Under Byrne's hand, Invisible Girl became a stronger character, using her force field powers in innovative ways, including as a weapon to attack opponents. Even the Fantastic Four's pompous archenemy Doctor Doom had to acknowledge the Invisible Girl's new abilities. "For the first time I am even compelled to consider that you, whom I once thought weakest of the four, might actually survive a battle with Victor von Doom." Doom's assessment was correct. The potentials of Invisible Girl's abilities were hampered only by her resourcefulness, and once she began using her near-limitless powers in new ways, she stood to become the most powerful member of the team. When her husband Mr. Fantastic went missing, Invisible Girl took charge, saying, "With Reed missing, I am the acting leader of the Fantastic Four. We will do what I say."

In 1985, after the miscarriage of her second child, Invisible Girl slides into depression, tinged with bottled up rage and frustration. When she falls under the power of the manipulative Psycho-Man, Invisible Girl is transformed into Malice, Mistress of Hate. Dressed in a revealing gown and wearing a mask and collar studded with spikes, Malice is like a punk rock dominatrix on a revenge mission. Malice's rage and fury drives her to use her powers in lethal and ingenious new ways, making her almost unbeatable. When she has her "loving husband" Mr. Fantastic and "loyal brother" Human Torch at her mercy, Malice unmasks herself, burning with resentment for always being considered the weak member of the team. "But then, why would you even *consider* that your utter defeat could come at the hands of one for whom you have *no respect* . . . Susan Storm, the Invisible Girl!!!" Naturally the brilliant Mr. Fantastic uses the power that no woman can withstand—love—to restore his wife to her right mind. A wrathful Invisible Girl hungers for revenge against Psycho-Man, and lashes out at her husband when he asks her to once more put her personal feelings aside. "I've spent most of my adult life following you into countless battles, risking everything, everyone I love, to save the world one more time! Well, this time it's my turn!!" But the trauma of Invisible Girl's transformation into Malice forces her to take a look at herself and start to finally grow up. "There is no Invisible Girl anymore, Reed. She died when the Psycho-Man twisted her soul. From now on, I am the Invisible Woman."

Invisible Woman's evolution was typical of the journey that many heroines took in the 1980s. The innocence of earlier decades was gone. The newly divorced Wasp decided to take her life as a superheroine seriously and took command of the Avengers. The Legion of Superheroes' Shrinking Violet went from shy teen to hardened and bitter brawler, prompting her teammate Lightning Lass to comment, "Violet, you're one *tough* lady." Their fellow Legionnaire, the privileged Princess Projectra, avenged the death of her husband Karate Kid by executing his killer with her bare hands. Abandoning her throne, she became the enigmatic and terrifying Sensor Girl, hiding her beautiful face behind a featureless mask.

Only one heroine had a brush with tragedy, and never recovered from it. By 1988, Barbara Gordon had suffered a midlife crisis of sorts, and had hung up her Batgirl cape. In the one-shot *Batman: The Killing Joke*, Barbara is enjoying a quiet evening with her father, Police Commissioner Gordon, when Batman's archenemy, the Joker, breaks in. To her father's horror, the Joker shoots Barbara, then strips her and photographs her naked, bleeding body as she writhes in pain. Barbara awakes in a hospital bed and learns that she will be paralyzed for the rest of her life. After living a life as a successful career woman, politician, and strong costumed crime fighter, Barbara struggles with the cruel hand that fate has dealt her. "Worst of all was the fear—of being physically helpless, unable to defend myself. Of having no sense of self, of feeling that I meant nothing, that my life was over now." But after months of training to regain her confidence, Barbara reemerges with a new mission, and a new name.

By the following year, readers would see Barbara become the mastermind computer hacker and scourge of the underworld named Oracle. Oracle used her computer skills and complex information systems to amass information about criminal activities that she supplied to the world's superheroes, especially Batman. Though wheelchair-bound in a dark room with her monitors,

Oracle's reach was worldwide. She became Batman's ultimate ally, her unseen hands thwarting evil across the globe, and a perfect expression of his will. Oracle was a mysterious, faceless entity that could invade anyone's world through her sophisticated computer network, representing the cold technological place the world was becoming. She was ruthless, manipulative, ever vigilant, and terrifying, much like Batman.

Fans of Batgirl may have been outraged that their favorite heroine had been maimed in this way, but as Oracle, Barbara Gordon was much more powerful, and a greater force for good than she had been as the "dominoed daredoll." While Oracle didn't follow the same path of corruption that some other heroines did in the 1980s, the entity that she became lost some of her humanity. As Batgirl, Barbara had always been one of the more humane members of Batman's "family," and a counterpoint to his bleak persona. Batgirl had been a symbol of her times— the liberated '60s and '70s, when women were enjoying newfound freedom. Now robbed of her freedom and mobility, Barbara's new persona suppressed her emotional female nature in order to make herself stronger. As Oracle, Barbara was a picture of cold, emotionless male efficiency, a peer for Batman, and in an ironic sense, his ideal mate.

In the final analysis, Barbara Gordon might have been lucky that her encounter with the Joker left her alive. Other members of Batman's "family" were not as fortunate. By the 1980s, Batman's original sidekick Robin had grown up, put on long pants and adopted the new identity of Nightwing. He was succeeded by a new, younger and edgier Robin, who never really caught on with fans. In 1988, readers were invited to call a special 900 phone number to vote on whether the new Robin should live or die. Cynical readers gave the kid the thumbs down, and the Joker subsequently clubbed the new Robin to death. This much-hyped event was just another of the marketing ploys that the comic book industry cooked up in the '80s, although this one was tinged with the grimness that had stained the decade.

A 1986 cover of *Uncanny X-Men* showed the mutant heroes glaring defiantly at the reader with the caption "C'mon, mess with us—make our day!!" By the following year, the once upstanding Justice League glowered menacingly from their cover, as their member Green Lantern dared the reader with the question, "Wanna make something of it?" The dark, violent mood that was once cutting edge in comics was now the standard of the medium, and simply another way for the industry to make money. At the end of Alan Moore's acclaimed and masterful series *Watchmen*, heroes Nite Owl and Silk Spectre, contemplate a new life of adventuring together. The heroine, however, wants an image update. "'Silk Spectre's too girly, y'know? Plus, I want a better costume that protects me: maybe something leather, with a mask over my face... also, maybe I oughta carry a gun."

Amidst all of this grimness, it was often hard to see what a woman's (or for that matter a man's) motivation was for becoming a superhero. A proliferation of new superhero teams throughout the 1980s—New Mutants, Outsiders, West Coast Avengers, Justice League International, Omega Men, Infinity, Inc.—introduced scores of new heroes and heroines to comic books. Being a superhero became more of a lifestyle, rather than a noble crusade to help the world. As heroes became more conflicted, it became harder to understand what their real mission was. Comic book stories became less about foiling a bank robbery or a bid for world domination, and more of a series of feuds and vendettas between rival factions, like the Capulets and Montagues with masks and powers.

By the end of the 1980s, MTV wasn't a music revolution anymore, just another moneymaking venue in the entertainment business. Music video had now replaced radio as the means through which recording artists got exposure to the public. The channel was no longer the exclusive home of spiky-haired, avant garde artists, but was now frequented by smooth, commercial pop artists belting out overproduced power ballads. What were once the upstarts were now the establishment.

Likewise, Marvel's X-Men ended the decade at the top of their game. The dark horse team that had swept the comic book industry with groundbreaking characters and storylines had grown into a franchise of six X-related titles, and set the prevalent style among superheroes. Bonafide stars in the comic book firmament, the X-Men had lost some of their alternative angst. Gone were the studded armbands, and belts. Team leader Storm grew out her Mohawk and modeled a look that embodied the best style touchstones of the late '80s—big hair, giant *Dynasty* shoulder pads, and lots of black leather. She looked like a rock 'n' roll high priestess, or better yet, Cher. Bad girl Rogue was no longer a leather-clad punkette with spiky hair, but a gorgeous brunette with a killer body.

As a solo act, Dazzler turned out to be a one-hit wonder. The "shining superstar" never caught on, and was cancelled in 1985. Down on her luck, she got the best gig in the comic book world when she joined the number one act in the business, the X-Men. Dazzler, who was born out of a business deal, would attest that having powerful friends made all of the difference in the world. She had ditched her silver jumpsuit and roller skates some years ago, and modeled a costume that looked more like attire for an aerobics class instructor. Suntanned Dazzler brought a decidedly mutant Malibu Barbie look to the team, wearing sunglasses into battle to protect her eyes from the laser beams she fired.

Overall, the women of the X-Men didn't look as hard and angular as they had a few years earlier. They now had slim shapes, long limbs and perfect pretty faces. They didn't look like superheroines so much as supermodels.

Angst and rebellion can only take a girl so far. By 1989, the Berlin Wall had fallen, and a brighter future lay ahead for the world. Capitalism had won the day, and the best way to celebrate was to look hot, get breast implants, and sell more comics. Lots more.

The '90s were coming.

Sex and the Single Superheroine

Sex is a difficult subject for America. The nation's Puritanical roots continue to make themselves felt. While sexual expression has become more prevalent—some might say rampant—in American society, there is still shame around intimate matters. Sex still prompts a spectrum of responses, from nervous schoolyard titters to constraining federal legislation. Even after the various sexual revolutions of the past forty years, women still find there is a distinct double standard. And nowhere is this more evident than in the world of comic books.

Sex has always been the "elephant in the room" for comic books. The medium created a world of powerful, muscled Adams and perfect, luscious Eves. They cavort across heaven and earth dressed in skintight costumes that show off almost every detail of their idealized bodies. They are the apexes of humanity, the manifestation of sexual desire. Yet we are to believe that in their personal lives they are relatively nonsexual. The *raison d'etre* of superheroes is to make the world a better place. They just dress as they do to make themselves symbols of power, not to attract potential sexual conquests.

For females, this is where the sexual double standard of comic books comes into play. Superheroines are presented in a highly sexualized way, but we are told that their scandalous costumes don't represent their true natures. A female superhero may dress like a whore, but between those perfect breasts must beat the heart of a virgin. Crime fighting women of the 1940s, like Phantom Lady and Miss Masque, adopted seductive guises and flirted with men. But back in their everyday identities, these sirens crossed their legs and returned to their colorless identities as dutiful daughters or loyal secretaries. Comic books were intended for a young audience, and while women could look sexual to attract male readers, that was as far as it could go. The morals of the day declared that sex outside of wedlock was bad, and only lascivious wantons engaged in it. As a result, these girls could never be both noble heroine and sexual female.

Traditionally, the only women getting any action in the bedroom were villainesses. "I am P'Gell . . . and this is not a story for little boys!!" So spoke the ravishing French criminal when she was introduced in the pages of Will Eisner's *The Spirit* in 1946. Lounging on a divan in a darkened room, cigarette dangling from her red lips, and wearing a red gown that did little to cover her full breasts, P'Gell oozed seduction and slinky sexual menace. Temptresses like P'Gell offered sex, but there was a price. In the 1940s, many of these fatal femmes were Axis spies who gleefully lured good red-blooded American men to their doom, further establishing the connection between illicit sexuality and evil.

AIRBOY

The beguiling but treacherous Nazi aviatrix Valkyrie uses her charms to lure the heroic Airboy astray, *Air Fighters Comics* v.2 #2, 1943

Consorting with these carnal females required a descent from the straight and narrow path, and square jawed detectives like the Spirit did their best to steer clear. Villainesses were like the venereal disease of comic books—a hero could play, but he would pay.

But bad girls, like blondes, have more fun. And even the staunch Batman was not immune to the siren call of sex. Beginning in 1940, this winged rodent began a game of sexual cat and mouse with one of the most famous femme fatales in superhero comics, Catwoman. "Quiet or papa spank!" the Caped Crusader says, when he captures the masked jewel thief on their first encounter. When Batman catches sight of the unmasked beauty, he's taken aback. "Well . . . what's the matter? Haven't you ever seen a pretty *girl* before?" she snaps back. Obviously not often enough, as Batman "accidentally" prevents his youthful sidekick Robin from stopping the pretty thief when she escapes. "She had lovely eyes! . . . Maybe I'll bump into her again sometime . . . ," muses Batman, as Robin glowers disapprovingly. Catwoman had sunk her claws into Batman, and found his one weakness: his oft-suppressed male libido.

By the late 1940s, Batman had left much of his gloomy vigilante roots behind to become a smiling, kid-friendly defender of justice. Catwoman provided some much needed sexuality to Batman's adventures. Catwoman was both nemesis and temptress to Batman. Clad in a purple satin gown, with razor talons and wielding a lethal whip, she was the embodiment of female power blended with desire. She may not have been as powerful as Wonder Woman, but she drew her strength from her feminine powers of seduction, making herself the "Empress of Crime," and the "Queen of the Underworld."

Catwoman was perhaps the most overt dominatrix in the early comics, gravely glamorous in her gown and cape, demanding submission from all with her lethal cat o' nine tails. She represented the only kind of sexual nature a woman could have in comic books—cruel, forbidding, terrifying. Even Batman and Robin crouched apprehensively like trained animals in a cage when Catwoman raised her bullwhip. Sex with Catwoman wasn't just an innocent roll in the hay; it was a relinquishing of power to a mistress of sin. While Batman may have dismissed Catwoman as a troublesome kitty, a 1947 cover illustrates her power succinctly, along with the threatening dangers of sex: Batman rushes to the aid of the devoted Robin, who recoils in pain as Catwoman takes a swipe at the Boy Wonder with her sharp claws, slashing his little red jerkin, leaving gashes on his tender flesh. Bad women like Catwoman left their marks on good boys who made the mistake of dallying with them.

Unlike the virtuous "girls" who paraded through comic books of the 1940s, like Hawkgirl, Flame Girl, and Rocketgirl, Catwoman was an adult. She was a "woman," and *all* woman at that. Catwoman offered Batman a forbidden desire. Or at least a different one than he was rumored to be experiencing with his loyal pal Robin in the Bat-Cave. She was the libidinous counterpoint to the stoic Batman's masculine adherence to logic, detection, and duty. In *Seduction of the Innocent*, Wertham described the Batman and Catwoman dynamic this way:

A typical female character is the Catwoman, who is vicious and uses a whip. The atmosphere is homosexual and anti-feminine. If the girl is good-looking she is undoubtedly the villainess.

Catwoman's slinky ways were becoming too racy for conservative times. So, in 1950, readers learned that Catwoman was not really a malicious crime queen at all, but just simple Selina Kyle, a stewardess who had developed amnesia after a plane crash, and whose feline alter ego stemmed from a childhood love for cats. "Now I understand . . . while I had amnesia, I became a criminal! Ohh . . . how horrible . . . horrible . . ." moans a remorseful Selina when she learns of her nefarious, libidinous past. Catwoman's criminal record and her sexual history were cleared on the grounds of "amnesia." Selina opened a pet shop, and settled down to live her life as a good and moral woman. She made her last appearance in 1955, paving the way for Batman's new love interest, the more buttoned-up and sexless Batwoman.

The message in comic books about women and sex was this: powerful and intriguing women might be sexual, but it also meant they were bad. Once a woman began to behave herself, it meant a suppression of her sexual identity. The only women who seemed to be willingly engaging in sex were the jungle queens like Sheena. But they were savages at heart, and not subject to the same laws of proper society that civilized heroines had to follow. The jungle antics ended in 1954, when the Comics Code Authority cleaned up the bush and sent these libertines in bikinis packing.

Under the Comics Code Authority's watchful eye, the only

time a woman displayed a sexual nature was when good girls went bad. Writers loved to spin tales of Lois Lane, Supergirl, or Lady Blackhawk turning into heartless vixens. None of these women were intrinsically evil, more like housewives out on a rampage. But it was only in temporary villainy that these women had an opportunity to act out all the passion and sexual frustration that repressed 1950s society had kept bottled up. A race of immortal warrior women gave Green Lantern's girlfriend Carol Ferris a magical gem that, unbeknownst to her, transformed her into the ruthless Star Sapphire. Dressed in a hot pink costume, Star Sapphire engaged in skirmishes with Green Lantern that were like sexual foreplay. "I seem to be two people—one wanting to conquer Green Lantern—the other at the same time wanting *him* to defeat me!!"

★ ★ ★

Marvel Comics' "revolution" of the 1960s, with its realistic superheroes who had true-to-life problems, did little to reflect changing sexual mores. Under the guidelines of the Comic Code Authority, Marvel heroines like Invisible Girl and Marvel Girl were good girls in unisex costumes who saved themselves for marriage, while villainesses like the Enchantress got to wear slinky costumes and show off their sexual side, inevitably linked with an evil nature. The Enchantress was a slinky sexpot, ripe with sensuality—an otherworldly Anita Ekberg in form-fitting green armor who wove her spells and manipulated men to achieve her diabolical goals. "Your will is my will!! I am your master! You must obey the Enchantress!!" she says in classic femme fatale mode, as she transfixes the noble thunder god Thor, making him her sexual slave. Messing with a sexual woman was still a long dark hallway to doom.

A decade after Catwoman's redemption, there was still a feeling that a powerful, sexual woman needed to be reformed. "I answer to no one!" says the lethal Madam Medusa, a villainess the Fantastic Four encounters in 1965. Medusa had unusually aggressive powers for the times—a cascading mane of living hair; yards of red locks that she could control to do her evil bidding. Clad in a purple costume, Medusa was beautiful, ruthless and deadly, manipulating the men around her as easily as she did her magic tresses. Her fate was especially disappointing. Revealed to be a member of a lost race called The Inhumans, Medusa was not really bad at all. She was betrothed to the Inhumans' king Black Bolt, who possessed a powerful, destructive voice that forced him to remain silent all his life. Reunited with her silent lover and no longer a femme fatale, Medusa's role was now to hang on his every non-syllable and communicate his unspoken command to the world. "…he has a destiny to fulfill—and I must wait until it be done!" Medusa says, resigning herself to a life of service. Her master's voice, indeed.

Actress Julie Newmar's portrayal of Catwoman on the 1966 *Batman* TV show catapulted the villainess to new heights of popularity. But when the feline thief was reintroduced to the comic book pages, she was portrayed less as a savage mistress of sexual desire, and more as a love struck woman trying to become Mrs. Batman. In 1967, the feline thief attempts to convince the Caped Crusader that she has reformed in order to win his heart.

"Do I go back to my crime career as Catwoman—or are you going to say the magic words 'Marry me' and make me the happiest girl in the world?" Catwoman asks, now placing Batman in the role of redeemer, savior, and lover. The strict guidelines of the Comic Code Authority ensured that despite her wild criminal ways, Catwoman still needed a ring on her finger before taking a trip to Batman's bedroom. Catwoman's newfound need for validation caused her to give up the power and independence she had tasted twenty years earlier.

The teenaged Legion of Superheroes operated blissfully free of adult supervision in their 30th century headquarters. Most of the girl Legionnaires dated a male teammate, but for the most part these love entanglements were less torrid than the romance comics that DC Comics published every month. Still, readers wondered if these kids were really that chaste, and stories provided glimpses that showed it wasn't all work and no play around the Legion HQ. "We're having the big computer decide who'd have the most fun kissing whom! It's a riot!" chuckles Invisible Kid, as Light Lass and Chameleon Boy lock lips at a 1966 make-out party.

As early as 1968, a Legion of Superheroes reader had written a letter to ask, "Couldn't the heroines' costumes be a little more . . . well . . . a little less?" Artist Dave Cockrum gave the team of super teens a makeover in the '70s. The girls in particular went the way of all flesh, trading their prim miniskirts and capes for sexy, revealing costumes. The heroines still dated their male teammates, but the concept of sex had now clearly entered into the Legion's untainted world; over twenty healthy teenage heroes and scantily-clad nubile heroines living together in a futuristic dorm, sans chaperone, filled the minds of young readers with sexual possibilities. In a 1974 story, Cockrum drew Legionnaire Dream Girl in her bed, with a barely visible lump beside her that canny readers recognized as her beau Star Boy. Reflecting on this in 2000, Cockrum commented, "I realize that it probably seems pretty infantile by today's standards, but it was a VERY risqué thing to do in the early '70s."

But the writers still had to work around the Comic Code Authority, and sex still had to be implied, despite the girl Legionnaires' skimpy costumes. The girls now coyly referred to their boyfriends not as "darling," but "lover." But there was also the question of what hormonal young heroes would do when their goody two shoes girlfriends withheld sexual favors. In a bizarre 1974 story called "Brainiac 5's Secret Weakness," the green-skinned teen genius, unbeknownst even to him, creates an incredibly lifelike sex doll that looks like his prudish girlfriend Supergirl, but is much more physically affectionate. "Driven by loneliness . . . you yearned so much for the real Supergirl . . . your subconscious mind compelled you to use your super-science to build your own Supergirl!" says the mechanical bride, who has sadly fallen in love with her maker. Naturally in the end, the robotic Supergirl suffers the fate of all wantons, and is tragically destroyed.

In 1976, *Doonesbury* creator Garry Trudeau shocked the nation by showing his divorcee heroine Joanie Caucus in bed with a man after a night of unmarried sex. This prompted thirty newspapers to drop the strip, but sent a message that mores were changing. Throughout the 1970s and into the 1980s, writers were able to slip sex under the radar of a Comic Code Authority that was beginning to lose power. Sex was no longer presented as something shameful or repellent, as the sexual revolution removed the moralistic stigma from premarital relations. Marvel's Black Widow led an urbane life of freedom, sipping martinis with famous film directors or jetting off for weekends in Switzerland with playboys. It wasn't a stretch for readers to imagine her taking a lover if she chose. The Justice League's Black Canary and Green Arrow enjoyed one of the more openly sexual relationships among unmarried comic book characters of the time, certainly much steamier than their teammates, old married couple Hawkman and Hawkgirl. Even the X-Men's teen heroine Kitty Pryde felt the stirrings of sexual desire. On a 1983 mission in deep space, where the X-Men faced imminent death, fourteen-year-old Kitty wants to disregard statutory rape laws and give in to her passion for the nineteen-year-old Colossus. When Colossus tells Kitty that she's too young for that kind of fun, her response expresses the philosophy of many adolescents regarding the pitfalls of life. "When you're doomed, what's the point of playing by society's stupid rules?!"

The heroine least likely to turn into a sexual provocateur was the strapping, green skinned She-Hulk. The She-Hulk, like Ms. Marvel and Spider-Woman, was another attempt by Marvel Comics to spin off a female version of one of their popular male heroes. The Hulk was born in 1962, and was literally the stuff of drive-in movies. Scientist Bruce Banner was accidentally caught in an explosion when a gamma bomb was detonated in the New Mexico desert. In the aftermath, the gamma radiation turns the meek physicist into a giant, bestial monster. Banner has no control of the rampaging beast that he transforms into whenever he becomes angry. Throughout the '60s and '70s the Hulk was a misunderstood antihero who had few friends, and was often the victim of his own misguided anger.

By 1980, readers learned that Banner had a younger cousin named Jennifer Walters. Jennifer was a criminal lawyer in Los Angeles who had gotten on the wrong side of a powerful crime boss. The vagabond Banner is visiting his cousin when a hit man guns her down. As Jennifer lies dying in his arms, Banner has no choice but to give her a transfusion of his gamma irradiated blood. When Jennifer awakes in a hospital bed, her cousin is gone, and a band of killers is at her door, ready to finish the job of rubbing her out. But the thugs aren't prepared when the gamma radiation in Jennifer's blood turns her into a muscular, green-skinned virago with a head of big hair. "Now let's see how tough you are—against me!" she bellows, before pulverizing the men. When Jennifer's anger fades, she turns from her "She-Hulk" persona back to that of an ordinary woman.

The male Hulk was described as "Incredible," but the She-Hulk was billed as "Savage." Where Jennifer Walters was levelheaded, her She-Hulk persona was in a perpetual state of PMS. She-Hulk was born out of Jennifer's anger, smashing anything that got in her way. But, unlike her cousin the Incredible Hulk, She-Hulk retained her intelligence. She was just pissed off all the time. Despite being a statuesque seven feet tall, She-Hulk was portrayed as more of a female galoot than a sexbomb. "Wow! This broad's big!" remarks a policeman, after capturing the rampaging female. Like her cousin, She-Hulk didn't go in for an elaborate costume. She was usually depicted in a tattered white dress that showed off her heaving green cleavage.

The Savage She-Hulk was cancelled in 1981. By the end of the series, Jennifer had learned how to control her transformations, and had made a decision to simply remain She-Hulk all of the time. Readers saw a different kind of She-Hulk when she joined The Avengers two years later. Now sporting a conservative pantsuit and heels and, oddly enough, smoking a cigarette, She-Hulk looked less savage, but still brutish. Pixyish team leader Wasp played fairy godmother to her new protégée and whipped up a chic new wardrobe for She-Hulk. When Avengers hothead Hawkeye caught sight of the stylish new She-Hulk, he cackled, "Talk about trying to get silk purses from sow's ears!" Rather than flatten Hawkeye with a punch, She-Hulk instead silenced the archer by picking him up and kissing him. Hawkeye's reaction was repulsion, as if he had been smooched by a transvestite. Later, when the Masters of Evil attacked the Avengers, Wasp forbade She-Hulk from charging into battle wearing a designer original. This left the green skinned heroine no choice but to strip down to lacy bra and panties to join the fray. The sexualization of She-Hulk had begun.

Despite She-Hulk's lingerie battlefield look, she was still more bruiser than bombshell during her time with the Avengers. Her superhero attire usually consisted of 1980s aerobics class favorites like Danskin unitards, sneakers, and leg warmers. Eventually She-Hulk found her Pygmalion in the form of artist/writer John Byrne. In 1981, Byrne had taken over the reins of Marvel's flagship title the Fantastic Four, returning the floundering comic to its former glory. Byrne had the Thing leave the Fantastic Four in 1986, and replaced him with the She-Hulk as the powerhouse of the team. Under Byrne's pen, She-Hulk turned from an angry beast to a big, gorgeous girl who was as smart as she was sexy and strong enough to take on any threat. As a member of the Fantastic Four, She-Hulk was the quintessential 1980s power woman—powerhouse lawyer by day, entirely capable of a man's job; by night, a seven-foot, emerald-hued hard body.

The reinvented She-Hulk wasn't just sexy, she was sexual. She began a relationship with brawny Wyatt Wingfoot, a Native American member of the Fantastic Four's extended family. "I'm She-Hulk almost all of the time because I *want* to be. Because it's *exciting!*" the heroine told her beau, explaining why she didn't change back to her Jennifer Walters persona. In truth, the She-Hulk gave Jennifer more than just a life of adventure, it opened a world of sexual freedom to her. She was big and beautiful, and could be unapologetic about her sexual appetite. In Wyatt, she found a man who wasn't threatened by her size and strength, and only laughed when she picked him up under one arm to carry him off to the bedroom.

Sexual desire has always been a tricky issue to deal with in terms of the female image in American culture. As much as men want a steady supply of sex, an equally enthusiastic interest from a woman was often seen as unseemly. Females like Mae West, Madonna, or Sharon Stone who have projected an image of aggressive sexual desire are often seen as threatening, or somewhat emasculating. This could be because their appetite for sex is shown as being as strong as a man's, and they are not embarrassed to say as much. On the other hand, traditional dumb blonde sex symbols of yore like Marilyn Monroe and Jayne Mansfield were shown as easy prey that men could trick into having sex. The modern version of this archetype is a centerfold/celebrity like Pamela Anderson, whose image is that of the dumb blonde, but now possessing an insatiable sexual appetite.

She-Hulk, as portrayed by Byrne was something else. She was as gutsy and outspoken about her sexual desire as a man would be. But there was another element added—humor. The humorous sexual angle had already been played up in earlier *Fantastic Four* stories, like when a men's magazine photographed She-Hulk as she sunbathed topless on the roof of the team's skyscraper headquarters. But when Byrne relaunched the heroine in a new solo series, *The Sensational She-Hulk*, she became a new kind of sexual dynamo—the funny girl with the big boobs.

The Sensational She-Hulk was more irreverent than most. First off, She-Hulk knew that she was in a comic book. She would break the "fourth wall" by addressing the reader, or lambasting writer Byrne for placing her into ridiculous situations. She-Hulk acknowledged that the world, specifically men, looked at her a certain way because of the way that she was built. She answered one reader's letter about her lack of costume with the comment, "Why do I get the feeling that there are a lot of you who'd be perfectly happy if my book was twenty-two pages of me skipping rope in the nude?" When Byrne featured this athletic display four issues later (albeit with her naughty bits obscured) the heroine commented on what it took for a woman to succeed. "I mean, here I am, a successful lawyer, a member of the Avengers, a reserve member of the Fantastic Four, no less . . . and just because I happened to make a joking remark in the letters page . . . I end up with all the dignity and respect I've worked so hard to gain wiped away in the name of *cheap thrills* and—maybe—higher sales!"

She-Hulk's sexual image was a running joke in the series, as covers featured the heroine in revealing outfits and provocative poses for the sole purpose of selling comics. Making a statement on the fact that male comic book readers traditionally had not supported a title starring a woman, a 1992 issue showed a smiling She-Hulk whipping off her top, announcing, "Okay. I'll admit that this cover has nothing to do with the story this month . . . but I've got to do *something* to sell this book!"

But not all writers were as deft as Byrne in dealing with She-Hulk's healthy approach to her sex life. Over the years, She-Hulk was shown having casual relationships with several men, and as a result, not looking that great. In one notorious episode, she was asked to defend the reformed villain named Juggernaut in her role as a superhero attorney. After getting the massively powerful former felon off the hook, the two wind up in bed together. When She-Hulk later makes a play for the brooding X-Man Wolverine, he tells her he has no interest in hooking up with Juggernaut's "sloppy seconds."

When She-Hulk got a new series in 2005, she was initially portrayed as a promiscuous party-er. When the butler at the Avengers' headquarters comments on She-Hulk's "frequent overnight guests" and asks that she provide a list in advance for security purposes, her response is, ". . . I don't usually know what I'm doing from night to night." She-Hulk has to deal with the implications of her free-spirited lifestyle when she is hired by a high-powered law firm to work in her identity as smart, capable Jennifer Walters. In one case, a rival lawyer proposes that the gamma radiation that has transformed Jennifer into She-Hulk also causes her to be more uninhibited and promiscuous in her superpowered form. She-Hulk is mortified when she then, under oath, has to recite a lengthy list of her past lovers, exhausting the court reporter.

The whole issue of She-Hulk's sexuality brings up the question of the double standard. Like Samantha Jones on the series *Sex and the City*, She-Hulk is a woman who freely engages in sex with the same abandon as a man would, yet is viewed as a tramp. After being seduced into bed by her Avengers teammate Iron Man, She-Hulk asks him how he gets away with sleeping around. "When you do it, everyone calls you a player. When I do it, they call me a skank." As a heroine, She-Hulk is more powerful and often displays a more heroic nature than Iron Man, Wolverine, or Green Arrow. All three of these men have numerous liaisons with women, and are considered charming rogues as a result. But She-Hulk's reputation suffers as a result of her sexual lifestyle, and in the end drags down her image as a hero.

Sex may not have been something that could be shown overtly, but it often manifested itself in other disturbing ways. Comic book covers have traditionally shown heroes in a dangerous situation in order to generate suspense and excitement. But with female superheroes, there is often an undercurrent of sexuality in violent scenes. 1948's notorious *Phantom Lady* #17 shows the busty heroine struggling to free herself from ropes, as she casts a smoldering gaze into the eyes of the reader. Even under the Comic Code's regulations, sex and violence still managed to work their way onto covers. 1971's *Wonder Woman* #196 shows Diana Prince in chains, clad in hot pants and a torn blouse, with the barrel of a rifle trained on the large red target drawn on her naked back. The heroine stares into the eyes of the reader with a mix of fear and defiance.

By the 1980s, the violence was more brutal, and explicit. A 1984 cover shows Legion of Superheroes member Dawnstar bloodied and broken, her thigh and snowy wings studded with arrows. The helpless teen heroine stares plaintively at the viewer, a drop of blood trickling down her large exposed breasts. Other covers had an almost 'snuff movie' quality, glorifying violence inflicted on heroines. One 1985 cover of the *Fantastic Four* featured only the green skinned face of humiliated member She-Hulk as a tremendous boot kicked it. Other covers showed close-ups of anguished heroines gasping for breath as their heads were held under water. Wonder Woman's

A pneumatic Phantom Lady stuggles to free herself from her bonds and still look sexy at the same time, *Phantom Lady* #17, 1948

sexuality was untouchable, so artists compensated by showing the heroine defeated and defenseless, yet still sexy. The 1990s offered a parade of often uncomfortable images of the Amazon princess beaten and bruised, or chained and grimacing as a gun was pointed at her head. One cover was just a close up of her face wincing with a contorted expression that could have been the result of either orgasmic pleasure or excruciating pain.

As the Comic Code's power waned throughout the 1990s, allusion to sex became more frequent. When Marvel Comics dropped the Code entirely and switched to its own rating system that was aligned with the standards of video games, sexual content became more common and explicit. Throughout the 1980s, independent publishers infused the market with more adult material that was not subject to the restrictions of the Comics Code. Writer Alan Moore's *Miracleman* was a postmodern take on a Captain Marvel-type superhero who could transform himself from an average man into a godlike being of limitless power by uttering a magic word. While Miracleman was often uncomfortable in his superhero incarnation, his female companion Miraclewoman embraced her Olympian perfection, and all of the sensations that came with it. In 1989, Miraclewoman takes the lead and introduces the hero to the glories of supersex. As they celebrate their roles as the architects of a new utopia on Earth, the miraculous pair strip off their costumes and consummate their love across the skies of the world, climaxing in an orgasm that lights up the night like a fireworks show. Free from the restrictions of the Comics Code Authority, mainstream publishers reveled in mixing sex with superpowers. The telepathic White Queen began having an affair with married X-Men team leader Cyclops. Rather than check into a motel, they committed psychic adultery, and acted out all of their sexual desires in his mind. The slinky Stacy-X was a prostitute before she joined the X-Men, working at a mutant brothel where her power to stimulate body sensations brought her customers to orgasm. Comic book fans who grew up to be writers could now share their fantasies about the sexual peccadilloes of their favorite superheroes with legions of equally curious readers.

As comic books approached the millenium, they followed the rest of popular media by sexualizing young girls. The cover of the first issue of 1994's *Gen13*, a series about a team of slacker teen heroes, features the group's steadfast and super strong leader Fairchild literally busting out of her clothes, as she transforms from four-eyed geek girl to leggy, big-breasted centerfold. By the early 2000s, the X-Men had a new teenage member with the rather unflattering codename Husk. Husk was Paige Guthrie, an overachieving teenage girl from a poor Kentucky coal mining family, who wanted to make something of her life and be the best heroine she could be. When trouble arose, Husk could transform her body into whatever form the situation called for—stone, metal, glass—simply by peeling off her skin. In her evolved form, Husk was powerful, and, depending on the form, indestructible.

Writer Chuck Austen pointed out the fact that regardless of whether her skin was stone or metal, Husk was actually naked when she went into battle. "It's a childish, guilty thrill," Husk thinks. "My little secret." Husk develops a crush on the handsome, winged and wealthy Angel, one of the original members of the X-Men, and her elder by several years. In the aftermath of one battle, Angel feigns unconsciousness as he watches Husk transform from a steel-skinned titaness to a naked nineteen year-old. Their flirtation goes on for several months, as Angel avoids getting involved with the much younger Husk for fear of hurting her. On a mission to Husk's Kentucky hometown, Husk confronts Angel, forcing him to confess his love for her. The jubilant Angel whisks his teenaged sweetie high in the skies. This time Husk sheds not her skin, but her clothes, so that she and Angel can engage in airborne copulation, in full view of her family and the other amused X-Men. As her daughter's clothes fall to earth, Husk's mother walks off with the comment, "Oh, my. I do *not* want to see this."

Not all superhero sex was as sleazy as Husk's induction into the "mile-high club." Some superheroines' stories had a real-life edge to them. The X-Men's Rogue had the abilitiy to absorb the powers and psyches of anyone she made skin to skin contact with. As a result, she led a life of forced celibacy and isolation. No sex was safe enough for Rogue. Speedy, the female partner of Green Arrow faced different challenges. A runaway and former prostitute, Speedy was HIV positive.

Ironically, it was Mary Marvel, the original teen superheroine, who brought back the concept of sex and evil being intertwined. In 2007, Mary fell under the bad influence of Black Adam, her brother Captain Marvel's nemesis, and was transformed into a vicious superpowered Lolita. Now sporting a sexy little black leather cheerleader outfit, a greatly augmented chest and a nasty attitude, Mary successfully made the leap from virgin to whore. "In the end I just couldn't stand being wholesome and plain and boring one *second* longer." The girl who once represented the flower of wholesome American youth now symbolized the turbulent, sexually rebellious side of a teenage girl's nature, summed up in one simple statement. "I'm Mary Damn Marvel!"

With all of this sexual activity filling the pages of comics, the question might arise as to when non-heterosexual coupling would be acceptable. Since heterosexual males primarily support the comic book industry, it should come as no surprise that there is meager acceptance of the presence of gay males in superhero comics, while lesbians are welcomed with open arms. Even in 1998's kid-friendly *Batgirl Adventures*, which is based on Saturday morning cartoons, Sappho makes her presence known. When Batgirl quizzes crackpot villainess Harley Quinn as to whether she and fellow bad girl Poison Ivy are more than just friends, the felon counters with, "Like what everybody says about you and Supergirl?"

Initially, it seemed as though the introduction of a lesbian Batwoman in 2006 was just an effort to make publisher DC Comics look more progressive. But writer Greg Rucka breathed real life into the character during her 2009 *Detective Comics* series. Ousted from West Point Military Academy under the then current "Don't Ask, Don't Tell" policy, the openly gay Kate Kane uses her training to protect Gotham City as Batwoman. Despite being a poster child for gay superheroes, Batwoman is not portrayed as saintly. Her sexuality is presented honestly, not salaciously. Simply put, Batwoman is shown as a complex character, not a stereotype.

In the allegedly progressive 21st century, some of the stigma of sex has gone away, but often not the adolescent titillation. When Batman protégé Nightwing and the hard-bitten vigilante Huntress have a one-night stand after a night patrolling the streets, he is the one who feels awkward about it afterwards. But displaying a modern attitude towards casual sex, Huntress brushes off Nightwing's assumption that there is now an emotional obligation between them. "There's no 'us', Nightwing. There was just one night when you were feeling lonely and I was feeling lonely. Let's call it an agreeable indiscretion and leave it at that." Huntress' modern views on sex are refreshing in a medium where once only bad women were allowed to have a sexual appetite. Yet, the double standard still exists. The X-Men's Wolverine can and does bed dozens of women, and is seen as a macho stud. Meanwhile Huntress is a modern woman who has a healthy sex drive who is viewed as immoral by many male comic book fans.

In what some might call our overly prurient culture, we can regularly read about the latest sexual escapades of celebrities in the supermarket tabloids or Internet gossip sites. Details about stars' late night "hook-ups" and amateur sex tapes have given the public too much intimate information about celebrities while elevating them to erotic deities. Similar fantasies abound in the heads of comic book fans, especially around the most iconic of superheroes. What would sex be like with Superman, say, or Wonder Woman?

Writer/artist Frank Miller explores this topic in 2002's *Dark*

Knight Strikes Again. Set in the future, the series features an older Superman and Wonder Woman as unmarried lovers, and parents of a super daughter. When the Amazon queen finds the Man of Steel a wounded, broken and defeated shell after a battle with Batman, she stirs him back to life with revitalizing sex. "Where is the hero who threw me to the ground and took me as his rightful prize? Where is the god whose passion shattered a mountaintop?" Wrapped in Superman's red cape, the lovers engage in coitus among the clouds that causes tidal waves and hurricanes on the planet below, and leaves Superman invigorated and powerful once again. "Goodness, Mr. Kent, you could populate a planet. I'm pregnant again." Wonder Woman says, confirming what comic book readers had suspected for decades about Superman's prowess, and the restorative qualities of Wonder Woman's holy of holies.

As is often the case with these things, reality may not live up to fantasy. With his brooding persona, dark nature and swirling leather cape, one might assume Batman would also have a commanding sexual presence. But does he live up to the hype when the lights go down? In 2011's *Catwoman* #1, Batman confronts the feline adventuress after she returns from an evening's exploits. Catwoman kisses Batman, initiating a wild bout of sex that is equal parts fighting and lovemaking. An erotic tussle ensues as the two struggle and grind, masked faces locked in a desperate kiss. When it's over, there is an almost wistful look in Catwoman's eyes as she thinks, "Still . . . it doesn't take long . . . and most of the costumes stay on."

So much for romance . . .

1990s: The Babe Years

Betsy Braddock surveyed her face in the mirror. Fate had wrought incredible changes on it.

Betsy came from an aristocratic English family. She gained fame as a fashion model, referred to in the press as the most beautiful woman in Britain. But Betsy was also a mutant. Her power came not from her body, but from her mind. She could read people's thoughts, communicate telepathically. and attack an opponent's mind, to devastating effect.

As a member of the outlaw mutant heroes, the X-Men, Betsy took the name Psylocke. The physically weakest member of the team, Psylocke always felt inferior to her fellow X-Men in battle. "This is a band of *warriors*! And I wonder—do I truly belong and, if so, why?" Psylocke also felt overshadowed by her fellow female X-Men. Team leader Storm was like a stately and wise warrior queen, a mutant Boadicea in black leather. Rogue was the gorgeous and gutsy southern belle with a lust for life, and Dazzler was a sexy and suntanned beach bunny. To cover her insecurities. Psylocke often acted like an intellectual, superior to her fellow X-Men.

Eventually, Psylocke fell under the power of the ninja assassin cult known as The Hand. Using a blend of magic and technology, The Hand transformed Psylocke into the perfect killing machine, and in doing so, unlocked Betsy's secret desire. The next time the X-Men saw their comrade they barely recognized her. Gone was the lovely English rose; in her place was a statuesque gold skinned Asian beauty. Psylocke's sculpted body was wrapped in a skintight costume that showed off every curve and muscle. Her impossibly long legs were crisscrossed with straps that enhanced her muscular thighs. Psylocke's back arched to present her impressive chest for all to admire. A revealing thong showcased her rock hard buttocks. Her face was a mask of almost inhuman Asian beauty, with grim red lips and unreadable eyes.

The old Caucasian Psylocke had been a formidable telepathic fighter. The new Asian Psylocke was a killer, possessing ninja martial arts skills and a ruthless love of battle. She was able to focus her mental powers into a powerful psychic knife, with which she could destroy an opponent's mind with a single blow.

Psylocke didn't know what to make of herself. She had the memories of Betsy Braddock, but a different face stared back at her from the mirror. Her new body finally gave Betsy the fighting skills and endurance of her dreams. She was the object of both fear and desire. Betsy Braddock may have been a lady, but as Psylocke, she was a babe.

It's 1989. Chinese students erect a statue of the Goddess of Democracy in Tiananmen Square amidst protests that would turn into a massacre. The Berlin Wall falls, leading many to believe the Cold War has reached its end. A new world order seems to be on the horizon.

And Psylocke of the X-Men is transformed into a babe. And the babe is the next big thing.

Comic books in the early 1990s were a strange thing indeed. Most comic book fans would just as soon forget that the decade ever happened. It should have been a time of bounty for readers. There were new publishers entering the comic book market, with a bevy of titles that should have infused the industry with fresh energy. Unfortunately, like many other things in the '90s, the comic book world was consumed by hype and the drive to make a lot of money. In the era that gave us one bombastic summer blockbuster after another, manufactured boy bands with formulaic pop hits, and a new James Dean in the form of Luke Perry, comic books of the '90s were just as forgettable as most of the decade's other forms of entertainment.

In the late 1980s, the mainstream press had latched on to the idea that comic books were "cool" again. *Dark Knight Returns,* Frank Miller's dystopian tale of an aging Batman, and Alan Moore's *Watchmen* were on the forefront of these new cutting edge comics, now referred to as graphic novels. The media also made a big deal about the high prices that collectible comics were demanding. Along with "designer" and "gourmet," the term "collectible" was used loosely, and much too often. Comic book publishers began creating much-hyped "events" that might turn into instant, valuable collectables. In 1993, DC Comics released the widely publicized "Death of Superman" storyline, sparking a buying frenzy among people who weren't necessarily even comic book fans, but wanted to cash in on the collector's gravy train. The comic book world was buzzing about what the next hot book would be.

A new magazine called W*izard* fanned the flames of desire

among comic book fans and speculators alike by touting the latest hot collectible comics and their artificially inflated prices. Founded in 1991, the slick and chatty *Wizard* was called "the guide to comics," and ran monthly lists of the 'top 10' hottest collectables. The comic book industry was investing more effort in inventing new gimmicks to exploit this speculator trend than it was in good, entertaining storytelling. This speculator mentality changed the entire face of comics. By the early 1990s, new comic book stores were sterile environments. Comics were sold in plastic bags to protect them, which meant no customers would be doing any casual browsing. Collecting comics was now a serious investment, and young fans were managing their comic book collections like a stock portfolio. The quest to make a quick buck turned an escapist hobby into work. Where had all the good times gone?

Throughout the 1980s, Marvel's outlaw mutant heroes, the X-Men, took angst and xenophobia to the top of the sales charts. If one X-Men comic sold well, more would reap even bigger profits. So, by 1991, the mutants had become a franchise, with their original title, *Uncanny X-Men*, spawning a number of best selling spin-offs. Many of the storylines were elaborate crossovers interwoven throughout all of the X-Men titles, making it necessary for fans to buy them all in order to follow the adventures. To wring some more cash out of their superstar mutants, Marvel announced the release of a new title simply called *X-Men*. The first issue of *X-Men* featured five different collectable variant covers with the same interior pages, and became the highest selling book in comic book history.

The X-Men were the undisputed stars of their industry, and every other superhero comic tried to duplicate their success by copying their visual style of flashy art, big shoulder pads, giant guns, and combat style costumes replete with straps and pouches. The males were handsome and massively muscled, brimming with snarling, testosterone-fueled machismo. Then there were the women. During the 1980s, the females of the X-Men were leather-clad punks bordering on androgyny, playing up the team's image of being edgy outsiders. By the end of the decade, the women of the X-Men had transcended the traditional comic book illustration style to look less like superheroines, and more like supermodels.

In the past there had been a select group of models like Twiggy, Cheryl Tiegs, and Christie Brinkley who had moved from the rarified harem of fashion magazines into mainstream popularity and recognition, particularly with heterosexual males. But it wasn't until the late 1980s that an elite flock of beauties became household names, fueled by the media's need to find new prey, and the public's unquenchable thirst for celebrity. They were the supermodels, and their glamour and beauty outshone the brightest Hollywood stars. They reigned on magazine covers, fashion runways, music videos, gossip columns. They inspired pop songs. Walking the line between fact and fiction, the supermodels raised the bar of beauty to a level that was unattainable for most women, and gave men a new impossible ideal to strive for in finding a mate. People forgot that these women were genetic anomalies, fantasy come to life, living images of ideal loveliness, the creations of photographers and stylists. They didn't have to be brilliant or witty, they just had to look good. Linda, Christy, Naomi, Cindy, and Claudia were a Justice League of Beauty—The Babe Squad.

By the late 1980s the women of the X-Men were drawn with cover girl faces: cheekbones that could cut glass, lithe gym bodies with big breasts and legs "up to there," thong clad buns of steel. Like the supermodels, these mutant glamour girls thrust out their hips and struck fashion model poses that looked more like they belonged in a Victoria's Secret catalog than in a comic book. They were babes.

The X-Men's Psylocke was the quintessential '90s babe heroine. Betsy Braddock originally came to America to learn how to better use her powers from the X-Men. The battle-hardened outlaw heroes didn't let the pretty English lady get into any dangerous situations, because they didn't think she had the physical skills to protect herself. However, when the homicidal evil mutant Sabretooth attacked the X-Men at their mansion, it was a courageous Betsy who defeated the rampaging beast. This earned her the respect of the X-Men and an invitation to join the team.

Betsy took the name Psylocke, and like the nice member of the British gentry that she was, wore a frilly pink costume with puffy sleeves, festooned with ribbons. But this patrician guise concealed Betsy's deepest desire to be a warrior, and throw herself into the thick of battle. The Caucasian Psylocke's transformation into a sleek Asian killer became the answer to her dreams and allowed her to become the kind of woman she'd always wanted to be—a fierce and indomitable warrior. It was the ultimate instant gratification: wake up and be someone else, with a new body and new talents. This was a perfect metaphor for the decade where celebrities' forays into the plastic surgeon's office were making cosmetic procedures the new objects of desire. Psylocke's transformation from intellectual English lady to sexy ninja seductress represented the basic belief of the 1990s that image was all that mattered.

Despite the X-Men's politically correct theme of tolerance, the team was decidedly Caucasian, with the exception of the African-American Storm. Turning Psylocke into an Asian gave the X-Men some visual racial diversity, although she merely looked Asian on the outside, while her mind was still that of an Occidental. But why fuss over details? Besides giving her fighting skills, Psylocke's new body also defined who she now was in the eyes of the world—the hot chick in the thong. Psylocke's perfect body made men drool, so naturally her persona had to change as well. Her sexualized new image consumed the woman she had been and redefined her, stressing the physical over the mental. The old Psylocke had been strong-willed and imperious, but not particularly sexual. In her new body she was a mysterious vixen, a sexual predator in a skintight *cheongsam* out to steal another woman's man, with the inscrutable nature of a stereotypical "Oriental" femme fatale. Her personality was secondary; the most important thing about Psylocke now was the way that she looked. Psylocke's new body was her ticket to stardom, taking her from being the weak forgettable girl in the funny pink costume to the babe with the killer butt, a favorite with fans. The key to success for women in the '90s was achieving an ideal version of themselves. Externally at least.

Psylocke's sexpot makeover was courtesy of X-Men artist Jim Lee, one of Marvel Comics' hot new talents. A group of young up and coming comic book artists rose to popularity in the late 1980s, largely through their work on the X-Men titles. Although their styles were all different, their trademark was highly stylized, dynamic artwork with a slick, commercial quality. Their heroes were big bulging powerhouses with rippling muscles and metallic limbs that toted lethal futuristic firearms. Their females looked like supermodels. And like the real life supermodels themselves, these artists transcended their jobs as comic book artists and became celebrities within the industry and beyond. X-Force artist Rob Liefeld even starred in his own Levi's TV commercial. Their superstar status made these artists very valuable to Marvel Comics. In order to keep its hot artists happy, Marvel Comics handed over control of its biggest properties to them, even though they had little experience as writers. Compelling storylines were sacrificed for weak plots that went nowhere, but provided a good showcase for lots of bombastic artwork. In a few months, it all blew up. The "hot" artists demanded Marvel give them ownership and creative control of their work. Marvel said no, and the "hot" artists said goodbye. Seven in all of Marvel's brightest talents left, and, in 1992, founded Image Comics, their own publishing company. It was poised to be the next big thing, and the hype machines began to gear up.

Image Comics launched in 1992, in the midst of speculator frenzy in the comic book world. Fans were eager to see what these artists could do when free of the editorial control of the mainstream publishers, while speculators anticipated the prices of Image comics to skyrocket. The company was aptly named Image, because, not surprisingly, the comics focused on what each artist already drew well. None of it was terribly original. Cyberforce and WildC.A.T.S. were much like the X-Men, while Youngblood was like Marvel's X-Force, crossed with DC's Teen Titans. Stormwatch was like Marvel's Avengers, Shadowhawk and Spawn were like Batman. Supreme and Glory were basically Superman and Wonder Woman with different costumes and lax moral codes. The Image Comics superhero teams all had a giant strong member, like the X-Men's Colossus, a savage member with claws, like the X-Men's Wolverine, a militaristic cyborg, like X-Force's Cable, and a hot, mysterious babe, like the X-Men's Psylocke. Stories were often incomprehensible, but that didn't matter, since there didn't seem to be any illusion that these were comics that were meant for entertainment, and not for investment. Like the supermodels, Image Comics were beautiful, but without much depth.

Around the time that Image Comics launched, there was a strange blurring of lines between mainstream entertainment and pornography. 1992 saw Madonna approaching her ten-year anniversary of being the next big thing. The singer, sexual provocateur, and arguably most famous woman in the world, was at the height of her power. Madonna was on a mission—she wanted to change the fearful attitude that America had developed about sex as a result of the AIDS crisis. And so she produced a coffee table photography book of her sexual fantasies. Like the manufactured collectable comics of the day, the book was sold in a sealed silver Mylar envelope. The book was filled with images of a naked Madonna engaged in almost every conceivable sexual kink—an erotic laundry list. Was it art, pornography, or just another marketing blitz to sell merchandise?

While Madonna's *Sex* book may have had a voyeuristic appeal for a reader of *Vanity Fair* magazine, it was a far cry from pornography circa 1992. Madonna had a real body, albeit honed to perfection through rigorous training. Mainstream porn was still a man's world, filled with unreal, surgically-altered and shaved visions of erotic women, performing to suit a male's fantasies, not a woman's. In 1992, Pamela Anderson left her role as the "tool girl" on the popular TV sitcom *Home Improvement* to don a red swimsuit as one of the lifeguards on the cable sensation *Baywatch*. *Baywatch* cemented Anderson's place as a sex symbol for the '90s, and as a next big thing. As the decade progressed, the pretty Canadian girl with the augmented breasts grew increasingly blonder, bustier, more overtly sexual, and less real. Throughout the decade, new female lifeguards would join the cast of *Baywatch*, which became the most watched TV show of all time. The majority of them, like Anderson, had breast implants and were alumni of the *Playboy* magazine school of drama, blurring the line between actress and porn star.

Madonna had been exploiting sexuality since the beginning of her career, but always making it clear that it was on her terms. Things were different now. Heavy metal bands' love of strippers and rap music's glorification of pimps inundated America with images of women whose main purpose was to satisfy the desires of men. When the Internet was introduced, it provided a new, anonymous way for pornography to enter people's lives and homes. 1995's *Showgirls* exposed the world of strip clubs and lap dancers to America with its salacious tale of joyless eroticism in Las Vegas. The objectified image of a woman working in the sex industry became less taboo; it was now considered cool.

Supermodel and porn star were two of the only jobs where a woman made more money than a man. Instead of being harlots sequestered in their little corner, female porn stars began to enjoy the blurring of the celebrity lines, and became legitimate personalities. The fake, surgically enhanced stripper look started to work its way into the mainstream world.

The decade had kicked off with *Pretty Woman*, considered to be a romantic classic by many women, but basically a rescue fantasy about a lovable prostitute and the high-powered man who saves her from a life of squalor. The highest paid female star in Hollywood was Demi Moore, who in 1996 paraded her self-consciously fake breasts in the movie *Striptease*, proving how far up the ladder artifice could take a woman. For those who didn't want to go under the knife to release their inner vixen, there was the breakthrough invention of the '90s, the Wonderbra. Let your cleavage do the talking, and you'd be fine.

Things were much the same with the women of Image comics. Women in comics had always provided the eye candy for male readers, but Image took it a step further. WildC.A.T.S. member Voodoo sported tattoos and worked as a pole dancer. When her android teammate Spartan scanned Voodoo with his x-ray vision, he was mystified by her breast implants. Likewise Vogue, the fashion model cum deadly assassin member of Youngblood was described as the "babe with the silicone chest." Vogue's teammate Riptide capitalized on her fame as a crime fighter by posing nude for a magazine called *Pussycat*. Freak Force member Rapture could generate electrical charges, and sported huge breasts squeezed into a tiny costume. She was a foulmouthed African American, and a former hooker. Unlike heroines of the past, many of Image's heroines were non-white. But their trashy personas gave this diversity a slightly racist tone.

Wizard magazine regularly ran spotlights on the hottest babes in comics. A regular feature entitled "Casting Call" showed the star choices of fantasy movie adaptations of favorite comic book characters. In *Wizard's* versions, celebrity babes like supermodels Cindy Crawford, Anna Nicole Smith, or Elle Macpherson, former underage porn star Traci Lords or sexbomb Pamela Anderson always played the superheroines.

By the mid 1990s, the babe factor was rampant in comics. Established superheroines like Invisible Woman had to tart it up to stay current. By the time the Fantastic Four celebrated its 30th year of publishing in 1991, Invisible Woman was the doyenne of Marvel Comics' first family. Over the years she had been heroine, wife, mother, and even served as team leader for a stint. Standing confidently in a wide-legged stance on the cover of issue #375, Invisible Woman looks fearlessly towards the future, ready to take out any menace with the gigantic gun that she cradles in her arms. Invisible Woman wears an update on her old costume that shows she can still give the younger superheroines a run for their money. The "4" emblem on her chest is still there, but now it is a cutout that showcases Invisible Woman's cleavage. Likewise, the midriff of her costume is a cutaway that reveals the heroine's six-pack abs. Invisible Woman's costume is no longer a jumpsuit, but is now a backless swimsuit with a high cut leg that shows off most of her shapely derriere. The thigh-high white boots with black straps give the whole look a kinky finishing touch. Perhaps most incongruous is her 'soccer mom' hairdo. Is this the price for a comic book heroine to be in charge? To look like Meg Ryan dressed as a stripper?

New publishers were entering the comic book market, which still seemed like a goldmine. In an industry where female characters had never been able to sell comics, suddenly there was an avalanche of heroines. But unlike superheroines of the past who played second fiddle to a man, the new women on the comic book racks were lovely yet lethal. Comics of the 1990s were rife with violent, unshaven antiheroes who straddled the line between good and evil. The new wave of heroines had more in common with these desperate males than they did with the proper, cape-wearing kinswomen who had preceded them. A cross between a stripper and a homicidal killer, the new women on the comic book racks were called the Bad Girls.

At the top of the Bad Girls food chain was a group of women who went beyond the usual mask-wearing crime fighter. They represented goddesses of the most primal female power, presented in an overtly erotic manner. First and foremost was Lady Death. Her trademarks were chalk white skin, a massive head of silver hair, and empty emotionless eyes. Oh, and giant breasts, held up by bikini tops made out of skeletal hands. If the Venus of Willendorf posed for the *Sports Illustrated* swimsuit issue, she'd look like Lady Death. Lady Death was the ultimate anti-heroine, the girl you don't want to meet in a dark alley. The offspring of an evil father and a saintly mother, Lady Death started off as Hope, a young girl from medieval times who made a deal with a demon in order to escape a horrific death. Transported to Hell, Hope was corrupted by the evil of the underworld. Renaming herself Lady Death, Hope overthrew Lucifer. Lady Death was the end of the road, and she loved her job. "Yessss, let the bloodlust wash over me! Just give in to what I truly am—the final embrace—Death!" Lady Death was drawn as a pinup that only Casper the Friendly Ghost could get excited by, often seen lolling in pools of blood. Her rival for the job of ruling Hell was an equally busty vampire named Purgatori. On the side of the angels was Avengelyne, a fallen member of God's war host who walked the earth dressed like a leather-clad hooker. And then there was the Magdalena, the modern day descendant of Mary Magdalene, and wielder of the legendary Spear of Destiny. Although she wore a nun's habit, the Magdalena had a centerfold's body displayed in a revealing costume that would not have been sanctioned by the Vatican.

"I'm not bad . . . I'm just drawn that way," lamented the curvaceous cartoon siren Jessica Rabbit in the 1988 movie *Who Framed Roger Rabbit*. This was the case for many of the Bad Girls, who, while actually strong characters, were illustrated like porn stars. They all had postmodern names like Taboo, Siren, Razor, Fatale, Risqué, Hellina, and Ballistic. Sara Pezzini was a dedicated New York City police detective who just happened to be built like a supermodel. She came into possession of an ancient mystical gauntlet called the Witchblade, which gave her immense power and aided Sara in her crusade to fight crime. The Witchblade also formed bony armor that covered just the most vital parts of Sara's usually naked body. There's nothing like a skeletal thong to make a girl feel like taking on the world. Ghost was a spirit with blazing guns and D-cup breasts spilling out of a tiny bustier, who searched the mortal world for her killer. "I'm concentrating to support this costume" Ghost muses, as if the character herself realizes what a ridiculous situation she is in. The toughest of the lot was Barb Wire, a hardcore female bounty hunter and whose trademark line was "Don't call me babe!" The whole Bad Girls trend came full circle when Barb Wire was brought to life in a movie, starring Pamela Anderson. Anderson's lightweight portrayal of the hard-bitten Barb was perhaps the sign that these ladies had worn out their welcome.

At the height of the Bad Girl craze, even comic book legend Wonder Woman had to stoop to wearing a thong to sell some comics. It did the trick. The irony of the whole situation was that finally there were more titles than ever starring women, but they were so highly sexualized that it seemed to cancel out any of their power. "Yes, sometimes the women are idealized, but they aren't demeaned. It's the '90s. It's not threatening to imagine a heroic woman in control. Frankly it's refreshing. How many more superheroes with constipated looks on their faces can we take?" wrote Lady Death creator Brian Pulido in a 1996 *Bad Girls Special* published by *Wizard* magazine. Good rationale, bad execution. Lady Death's breasts were the size of her head, which went a bit beyond "idealized." The Bad Girls were just as ruthless as the nihilistic men who roamed the pages of comic books. They just looked a lot better.

The line between comics and "entertainment for men" continued to diminish throughout the decade. Marvel Comics began publishing special swimsuit issues featuring all of their heroines in scanty beach attire. In its defense, Marvel did show their males in scanty trunks as well. Image countered with "lingerie specials" featuring Wonder Woman knockoff Glory and other heroines. By the time a *Glory and Friends Bikini Fest* hit the stands, Image wasn't even having artists draw pictures anymore, they were just photographing unknown models in swimsuits, and selling it as comics. As more and more Bad Girls titles were launched, the quality of the art got worse, the legs longer and more giraffe-like, the breasts larger, the faces sleazier. The whole effect was less beguiling, and more grotesque.

As progressive as the 1990s were meant to be, with TV sitcom star Murphy Brown becoming a single mother, the image of women remained very restrictive. For the first time since Eleanor Roosevelt, the nation had a first lady who was interested in more than what kind of decorations should be on the White House Christmas tree. Yet Hillary Clinton was demonized for not being feminine enough, and for driving her husband into the arms of a more sensual woman. Disney had returned to fairy tales for source material, and garnered Oscar nods for *The Little Mermaid* and *Beauty and the Beast*, both lessons for a new generation of girls that a female must make sacrifices to get her man and live a happy life.

In the end, it wasn't morality or decency that was the death knell for the bad girls; it was the most American of motivations—profit. The speculator market for comics bottomed out in the late 1990s. A number of new publishers went under. Image Comics was rent by infighting among its founders, many leaving to pursue other ventures. Deadline issues and late arrivals of comic books cooled enthusiasm among comic book fans. By 1997, Marvel Comics had overextended itself, and declared bankruptcy. The 1990s comic book boom was over, and the quarter bins at comic book stores across the nation would be filled to capacity with the hype-fueled creations that had sprung to life during this decade.

And like survivors of a drunken orgy waking up in a rubble strewn hotel room, the superheroines of the comic book world surveyed the world around them in the aftermath of the revelry. There were fewer women around now, but the ones who still stood were made of sterner stuff than the latecomers to the party. These women picked themselves up, and set out for a new day. The first order of business—get some panties that didn't show off all of their butt cheeks. Once that was done, these ladies set out to do what they did best—kick someone else's butt.

Heroine Chic

In May 2008, New York's Metropolitan Museum of Art staged an exhibit entitled *Superheroes: Fashion and Fantasy.* The retrospective, curated by the museum's Costume Institute, took a look at the comic book superhero aesthetic and its influence on contemporary fashion. The exhibition's catalog described it as "radical fashions in which designers go beyond iconography to explore issues of identity, sexuality, and patriotism." The overall theme of the exhibit was the search for the ideal body, and the idea that fashion can create a secret identity for the wearer. Alongside the legendary heroes of the comic book world stood bodies transformed into aerodynamic human airplanes, chrome bikini clad Amazons, scaled creatures of the deep, and cubist, armored warriors.

True to the nature of comic books, most of the exhibits focused around male superheroes. Two exhibits spotlighted the most famous women in comics. They also proved how integral the costume is to the superheroine's legend. A display of patriotic iconography featured as its centerpiece the Wonder Woman costume worn by Lynda Carter in the 1970s TV show. Even with its colors slightly dimmed from the passage of thirty years, the

Wonder Woman costume drew sighs from the museum's visitors. A 40-ish male schoolteacher beamed as he gazed lovingly at the costume and told his class that *this* was the Wonder Woman that he remembered from his youth. Young women gasped excitedly at the sight of the costume, as though viewing the relics of a feminist patron saint. The costume radiated the sense of power and majesty of the most famous heroine in comic books, along with a sense of American optimism from a bygone era.

The other display, garnering a great deal of attention from visitors, focused on the fetishistic aspect of superheroine costumes, specifically as it related to one of the other grande dame of comics, Catwoman. The black vinyl Catwoman costume worn by actress Michelle Pfeiffer in 1992's *Batman Returns*, tattered and stitched together like a bizarre rag doll, transfixed the crowd. Women in particular were drawn to this display, as though inspired by the darker power of the Catwoman suit. The movie version of Catwoman was a luckless woman with no special powers who created a costume that transformed her into something more than human—a lethal creature of the night. Wonder Woman was blessed with mighty abilities from the Olympian gods, but Catwoman's transformation through wardrobe served as a role model for more attainable power.

To coincide with the Met's exhibit, *Vogue* magazine, that venerable bible of all that is chic and stylish, featured stories on comic book inspired fashion in its May 2008 issue. While polar opposites in the publishing world, fashion magazines like *Vogue* and comic books offer different versions of the same opinion that clothes can transform a woman and give her power. *Vogue* presents its reader with the latest styles that can reinvent her as a corporate dynamo, a delicate blossom, or a smoldering vixen. The female superhero's relationship with costumes is much the same.

Clad in a filmy, low-cut blouse and dainty skirt, Spider Queen prepares to vanquish evil, *The Eagle* #4, 1942

For decades, comic book fans have read about bespectacled wallflowers and girls next door who don a mask and costume to transform themselves into crime fighting marvels. The costume gives an ordinary woman the chance to step out of the box that society may have placed her into in her everyday life. She can present the world with an amplified version of herself—a warrior, an angel, a goddess.

Many women complain about the inequity in our society that says a man can wear sensible shoes and a suit to look appropriate for the professional world, while a woman is expected to wear a skirt and high heels. There is an implication that a woman must not only dress appropriately, she must also go the extra length to make herself "attractive" by society's standards. This is much the same in comic books. Superman, Batman, and scores of other heroes wear variations of a circus performer's outfit—a leotard with trunks worn over the top. It is their "business suit," and it covers their whole body. Wonder Woman, Sheena, Storm, and the majority of other comic book heroines wear some variation of a swimsuit, meant to make them look dynamic, but also attractive to a mostly male audience. Like the business executive in her pencil skirt and

high heels, the superheroine must do her job, but still present herself in an often hyper-feminized way. She has to play by the rules of the game.

If the power distribution was more equal in the comic book world, this would be fine. If all superheroines were as indestructible as Superman, leaping across rooftops, smashing through windows, and flying through flames in a skimpy swimsuit wouldn't be such a problem. However, male heroes are usually presented as being unquestionably more powerful than women. Yet, they wear costumes that cover and protect most of their bodies. Women on the other hand, are written as weaker, and presumably less able to protect themselves. Yet they charge into battle with most of

Wildfire, one of many heroines to face danger in a skimpy costume, *Smash Comics* #27, 1941 their bodies exposed. Take Marvel Comic's Avengers, for instance, circa 1973. Captain America wore a chain mail shirt and carried an indestructible shield. Iron Man wore a suit of armor, and the Norse thunder god Thor wore a helmet and carried a magic hammer. Their fellow Avenger Mantis had a flimsy costume with a neckline cut to her waist, a ribbon like skirt that exposed her thighs, and went barefoot, with only her Kung Fu skills to protect her. Not exactly equal treatment for women.

The reason for this superhero fashion double standard is that comic books have always been primarily targeted to a heterosexual male reader. As a result, female superheroes must look attractive to these readers. And in the world of male fantasy, attractive = sexy. So, revealing costumes are fitted onto idealized bodies with large breasts, tiny waists and impossibly long legs. Men need to look powerful and virile, but can't display bulging genitalia showing through their spandex, as it would be too threatening for most straight male readers. Wonder Woman attends a Justice League meeting spilling over the top of her metal brassiere, with much of her butt peeking out from her star spangled panties. Meanwhile her strapping male comrades Flash and Green Lantern are drawn with nary a bulge in their tight briefs.

Looking like a centerfold would all be fine and good except that female superheroes must also look strong and powerful to do their jobs. But not *too* powerful, lest they look manly, and thus unappealing to male readers. A 1943 Wonder Woman story explained how the Amazon princess channeled mental force through her muscles to give her great strength. "Measure my arm and leg muscles—you'll find them no bigger than a normal girl's should be!" she explained, to assure readers that she was still feminine looking, and not a hulking brute. In more modern times, heroines like Power Girl or She-Hulk are drawn with the bulging muscles of a female body builder. This look is usually restricted to heroines whose strong personalities already push them out of the category of being "conventionally attractive" to most men. A female member of the teenage Legion of Superheroes was strong, brave, loyal, and possessed a heart of gold. She was also rather burly muscular, green-skinned, and had brutish, simian features. As a result, she bore the unflattering title of Monstress.

This conflict between being attractive, yet still powerful raises another question. Is power pretty? Females in comic books have historically been given weaker powers. This is presumably meant to be a reflection of the status quo between the sexes in the real world, and a hierarchy that male readers will be comfortable with. Female superheroes are also granted powers that make them look good. The 1960s teen heroine Insect Queen wielded fantastic powers, and wore a pretty striped costume, and a bow in her hair. But when she transformed herself into a gaint fly with six legs, grew powerful beetle jaws, or spun cocoons with her caterpillar body, she coundn't exactly be classified as "cute." Wonder Woman or She-Hulk may not always look like movie stars when lifting a tank, or stopping a runaway train. Their hair will get mussed, their faces will strain with the effort, they may break a sweat.

But a heroine will look like a supermodel if she possesses what is known as "strike a pose and point" powers. For as mighty as the

X-Men's Storm is, she strikes a pose, extends a hand, unleashes a lightning bolt, and looks great. Just like posing for a picture in *Vogue*. Women who don't have to get physical in order to use their powers can keep their looks intact in the heat of battle. There are a lot of sorceresses in comic books. And psychics. And illusion casters. And sonic powered sirens. Gorgeous women who can stand back, cast their spells, invade someone's mind, scream their heads off, and still look fabulous doing it.

There are a multitude of fleet-footed men in comic books— Flash, Kid Flash, Whizzer, Quicksilver, Max Mercury, Johnny Quick, Silver Streak, Speed. Very few women have this power. Spitfire, Jesse Quick, Doc Rocket, and XS to name a very few. Women apparently look better standing still than running.

Then there are the actual costumes that heroines wear. Let's review—these women are crime *fighters*. They may be drawn like beauty pageant contestants, but they are meant to lead lives of action and danger pursuing a quest for justice. But we've already established that dressing like a police officer with a bulletproof vest wouldn't look sexy enough to sell comics. So let's look at wearing the right clothes for the job.

In February of 2000, the eyes of the world were on dancer, actress, singer, and future mogul Jennifer Lopez. On this night, Lopez attended the Grammy Awards in a revealing green Versace gown that was essentially like two large scarves held together by a brooch. The gown's neckline plunged well past Lopez' navel, laying bare vast amounts of the star's caramel colored skin. Lopez made headlines the following day with this daring frock, and the world was abuzz with questions. How did her dress stay on? Were her breasts taped into it? How did she move without falling out of it? If people were amazed that Jennifer Lopez could do something as simple as walk down a red carpet in such a low cut dress, imagine if she had to run in it. Or fly? Or fight a thirty-foot giant in front of a crowd of startled onlookers? Or save a school bus full of kids going over a cliff? Would any woman be able to perform these feats in a neckline as low as La Lopez' without showing the entire world her womanly assets? Because if she was Fire or Vixen of the Justice League, or Starfire of the Teen Titans, to name a few, this would be an everyday occurrence. For your average superheroine, J.Lo's dress was actually quite modest.

Let's move south. In 1992's *Basic Instinct*, actress Sharon Stone earned her place in Hollywood history with the famous leg-crossing scene that showed the audience that she was not wearing underwear under her white dress. But what if you were a powerful superheroine fighting the forces of evil, and you had to constantly worry about flashing the world? Because essentially you're wearing a bikini bottom. In the 1960s, Wonder Woman's starry bloomers went to the length of Bermuda shorts, but by the 1980s, she sported a buttocks baring high cut leg. By the 1990s she wore a thong. It's not so easy to come swinging down from a rope or to deliver a high kick to a villain's jaw if you're thinking about when you had your last bikini waxing done. In the '40s and '50s, proper young heroines like Mary Marvel and Supergirl wore pretty little ladylike skirts. The Doom Patrol's Elasti-Girl wore a striking red and white minidress that was in line with DC Comics' demure style for superheroine attire of the 1960s. However, it was inadvertently more revealing than a leotard would have been. As the fifty-foot Elasti-Girl strode across a great metropolitan landscape, she must have given onlookers below a chance to see whether her panties matched her uniform. Whether you're a giantess straddling a busy intersection, or a nubile teenage girl hovering high in the sky, if you're wearing a skirt, in the words of *Absolutely Fabulous'* Patsy Stone, "... the world is your gynecologist."

If a short skirt seems impractical, consider the alternative. Blonde Phantom battled crime in the 1940s in a floor length evening gown and heels. Really easy to maneuver, dressed that way, when you're fighting crooks while balancing on a window ledge. The vigilante who called herself the Iron Lady also wore a long evening gown. She took her name from the deadly machine-operated iron gloves that she wore—gloves so powerful they enabled the Iron Lady to crush anything. In order to catch her criminal prey unawares, Iron Lady concealed her lethal gloves in a delicate white fur muff. While it's important for a heroine to be dressed for action, were these elegant crimefighters *overdressed* for action?

Iron Lady, *Airboy Comics* v.4 #1, 1947

Then there is the other extreme—minimalism. In the world of superheroine fashion, no one had a more minimalist costume than Cloud. A member of the superhero team The Defenders, Cloud went into battle nude with only wispy bits of vapor to cover herself (incidentally also keeping the Comics Code seal of approval on the comic's cover). And there was Girl One, a member of the superpowered police force in Alan Moore's *Top 10*. Her fellow officers thought that she wore a uniform covered with constantly changing graphic patterns. They weren't aware that the bio-engineered policewoman was actually using her powers to control the pigments in her skin to appear clothed, while in reality she was naked at all times.

Vogue regularly advises women to dress in a style that suits their age and lifestyle. This advice would be helpful in the comic book world, because many heroines are drawn with costumes that don't fit their personalities. Saturn Girl, the sober telepathic leader of the 30th century Legion of Superheroes ruled with an iron will and efficient manner. Yet in 1970, as the sexual revolution beckoned, she switched out of her militaristic red and white costume to a hot pink bikini with thigh high boots. The sexy look was incongruous with the rigid authoritarian persona of Saturn Girl, of whom fellow Legionnaire Timber Wolf once said, "There are times... when I don't think there's a tender bone in your body!" In her peek-a-boo ensemble, Saturn Girl looked like the straitlaced class valedictorian who wore a dress that was too racy to the prom.

What should a woman wear when she really wants to go out and battle crime? Lady Luck was one of the hardiest of the Debutante

Lady Luck's style was both delicate and deadly, *Lady Luck* #88, 1950

heroines of the 1940s. Armed with only her fists and a pistol, she cracked the heads of crooks with the best of the male crime fighters of the day. And what did this tough girl wear? A dress, cape, high heels, and a big flat brimmed hat. To disguise herself, Lady Luck wore a veil over her face like a denizen of an eastern harem. Not exactly intimidating, or easy to pull off in a fight. Consider The Thorn, a sworn enemy of organized crime who first appeared in 1970. Rose Forrest was the daughter of a slain policeman. At night, Rose's split personality would take over, transforming her into the vengeful Thorn who relentlessly hunts down her father's killers. Thorn was as tough as they came, but dressed in a green leather halter-top and micro miniskirt with thigh high boots, she looked more like the entertainer at a bachelor party than the terror of the underworld. Neither of these hardcore crime fighting women used their looks to entice their foes into submission, yet they were drawn as enchantresses.

There are a few rare heroines like Spider Widow, who was a lovely young woman who actually made herself look like a hideous old hag to fight crime. But most women in comic books were, and are, drawn as naturally beautiful and youthful, with bombshell bodies. Men, on the other hand, only need to look strong and intimidating. They can even be unattractive. The Incredible Hulk or the Thing don't have movie star looks, but are still popular. And men can age gracefully, with heroes like Mr. Fantastic and Dr. Strange looking distinguished with touches of gray in their hair. Heroines never age. Or if they do, they just fade away and aren't seen anymore.

Heroism in comic books has a redemptive quality that makes women more beautiful, effortlessly, since readers like their heroines to be drawn pretty. Even women that start out plain eventually metamorphose into stunners. Songbird, a member of the Thunderbolts, was originally modeled after thin, waifish British supermodel Kate Moss, but over time, her body blossomed into that of a traditional shapely comic book heroine. In 1996, Marvel tried to make longtime Avengers member Wasp more formidable by mutating her body into a freakish insect form. Fans hated this transformation, and a couple of years later Wasp was cute and human again. Marrow was a mutant terrorist who could grow bones out of her skin that she could use as knives. When she was inducted into the X-Men in 1997, she was a dreadful creature with horns and freakish features. Two years later she was pretty and sexy.

Of course, comic books exist in the realm of fantasy where superheroes are idealized champions that are perfect in every way, including their bodies. But some critics complain that the image of women portrayed in comics is too limited. They feel that the buxom and often highly sexualized heroines featured in comic books present a negative image of women, particularly to younger female readers. Likewise, a magazine like *Vogue* can draw fire for the images of the young, ultra thin fashion models featured within its pages, which many feel present women with unattainable, unhealthy body images. In order to dispel unrealistic female body images, Internet blogs regularly analyze the amount of Photoshopping done by fashion magazines to make models look thinner and more perfect. Similarly, comic book blogs will critique the latest artwork portraying superheroines to assess not only their salacious costumes, but also the overblown physiques and impossible poses the women are drawn in. As there is a call for greater diversity in the types of women shown both in comic books and fashion magazines, the entire subject ends up becoming politicized, and ultimately polarizing. Fashion magazines would say that a woman's ability to transform herself through dress is one of the weapons that she has in her arsenal to deal with the world, a source of her power. There are those who feel this rule applies to superheroines as well. They would say that a superheroine dressed to appeal to men while at the same time beating them into submission is a reclamation of an aspect of female power.

Along with demands for greater diversity in storylines, the 21st century has also seen a greater demand for comic books that are female-friendly, making costumes a hot topic. In 2012 Carol Danvers changed her superhero moniker from Ms. Marvel to Captain Marvel. Along with the change in rank came a new look. Carol bid adieu to her black swimsuit and thigh high boots, switching to a full body costume that looked more like a uniform, complete with helmet. Captain Marvel's new look was unique in that it was fairly gender neutral, and could easily have been worn by a man. A new heroine took over the Ms. Marvel title in 2014, and sported a costume that was both practical and symbolic. The new Ms. Marvel was Kamala Khan, a Pakistani American teenager from New Jersey. Her costume is based on a *burqini*, the swimsuit that Muslim women wear that allows for freedom of movement but still covers the body, in order to comply with the

Quran. Ms.Marvel's fighting gear is completed with a *dupatta*, the long scarf worn by many women in the Islamic world. 2014 also saw redesigns for veteran heroines Batgirl and Spider-Woman that traded spandex and sex appeal for leather and functionality, presenting a more modern, streamlined vision of a superheroine.

When a designer sends a new collection down the runway and it's met with an unfavorable response, the fashion press can rip it to shreds. In the Internet age, the same thing can happen when fans aren't happy with the revamp of a superheroine's costume. In 2010, DC Comics gave Wonder Woman a new costume meant to "toughen her up, and give her a modern sensibility." The new look consisted of leather jacket, long pants, and overly complex armbands. It looked like it came from a shopping mall Halloween costume shop, and drew immediate criticism from fans of the Amazon princess . The same thing happened the following year, when DC redesigned Power Girl's outfit to remove the trademark cleavage-baring cutout that fans refer to as the "boob window." In both cases, the heroines were back in variations of their more familiar swimsuit costumes within a year.

Styles change; hemlines rise and fall. What is popular one season can become passé the next. Like the fashion industry, comic books are a business. Publishers may try to appease female readers with functional superheroine costumes one year. But if the comics don't sell, you can expect publishers to bring sexy looks back fast. We may never see a heroine fight crime in an evening gown again, but a medium that was built on a foundation of swimsuits and high heels won't be retiring that style forever.

2000 and Beyond: Mother Love?

Kate Spencer needed a cigarette. It was the end of a terrible night, after a series of bad days. Could her life really have changed so dramatically in such a short amount of time?

It was only a few days ago that Kate gave her final arguments in the Copperhead trial. As the prosecutor in the case, Kate had urged the jury to find the cannibalistic, reptilian mass murderer guilty. And more, Kate felt the only way to prevent more innocent victims from falling prey to this bloodthirsty killer was a death sentence.

Kate's worst fears were realized twice that afternoon. First, the jury came back with a verdict of "not guilty," on the grounds that Copperhead was the product of genetics gone awry, and couldn't be held accountable for his actions. Kate was sure Copperhead would kill again. She was having yet another argument on the phone with her ex-husband, when she got the second bit of bad news that day. Copperhead had escaped.

Stealing an access badge, Kate unlocked the high security vault where the artifacts of super criminals were stored. "This has to be done." Kate thought. She found a high tech battle suit that looked like it would do the job, and a pair of gloves with sharp claws that seemed about right. And there was a staff that let off an electrical charge that seemed easy to handle. With her new outfit complete, Kate surveyed the Los Angeles skyline. "Ok, Copperhead. Enjoy your freedom because it's about to end. Permanently."

By the time Kate had tracked down Copperhead, he had already claimed new victims. "OK, Kate—let's do this!" she said, as she sprang from a rooftop to confront the monster. She wasn't prepared for Copperhead's first attack, as his claws slashed across her chest. Kate also hadn't predicted the level of power that she wielded in the staff. Its blast sent Copperhead scuttling down into the sewer. "No, you don't . . ." Kate said, as she followed the creature down into the dark depths below.

When the police detectives investigated the sewers early the next morning, they were shocked at the sight before them. There was the dead body of Copperhead, covered in blood. And scrawled across the wall above him was scorched a name—"MANHUNTER."

Kate's first foray as Manhunter left her relatively unharmed. But her seven year-old son Ramsey wasn't as lucky. Ramsey came across the Manhunter staff, and before Kate could reach the boy, it had exploded in his hands. From atop the roof where she stood, Kate could see into Ramsey's hospital room. His father sat at Ramsey's bedside, but where was she, his mother? She had been out in her Manhunter guise again tonight, trying to capture the escaped killer named the Shadow Thief. Their disastrous battle over the rooftops of Los Angeles had left Shadow Thief still on the loose, and Manhunter with her armored suit damaged and her weapon trashed. "Some superhero I make," Kate thought.

It's 2004. The world waits in fear for the next terrorist attack to hit. In California, Scott Peterson is sentenced to death for the murder of his wife and unborn child. And elsewhere in California, Manhunter is meting out her own brand of capital punishment. She's Kate Spencer, prosecutor, working mother, and superhero.

This new life of hers is making it real hard to quit smoking.

Despite the train wreck that the comic book industry seemed to be in the 1990s, there were some bright spots. It wasn't all nihilistic and naughty women with thongs and breast implants cutting a bloody path through the crime world. As the 21st century beckoned and the comic book prepared to turn sixty, some heroines looked to the future by considering their roles in the world. Did a female superhero always have to think like a man and use force in order to make a difference in the world? Couldn't she perhaps have more impact by acting like . . . a woman?

It's always been difficult enough for the comic book industry to find an audience for a title starring a female superhero, much less two. But in 1996, writer Chuck Dixon and DC Comics began an experiment with *Birds of Prey* that produced something unique in the world of superhero comic books—the female buddy series. *Birds of Prey* started out with a down-on-her-luck Black Canary receiving a call from the mysterious information broker known as Oracle. Black Canary's fortunes had slipped after her breakup with Green Arrow, and his subsequent death.

"I hope I'm not out of line if I say your life lacks direction right now," the female voice on the other end of the line says to Black Canary, as she offered the former Justice League member an assignment with all expenses paid, and a stylish but practical new costume. "I thought it was time to get you out of the fishnets and hot pants. Your profile needs work as well as your life." Oracle also gives Black Canary an earring through which the lady boss will communicate with her operative, as she monitors her progress throughout her mission. While Oracle plays Lady Bountiful by rescuing Black Canary from her shattered life, she demands total obedience. "If you want to go on rolling through life without a clue then do it without me! But if we're going to work together then I am *the word!* Oracle out!"

Birds of Prey was, in '90s terminology, a *Thelma and Louise* of the comic book world. Here were two women who didn't fit in with the mainstream world of superheroes. Black Canary had been a member of the prestigious Justice League, but was now burned out on the whole superhero scene. Oracle had suppressed her emotions and compassion to become a cold and efficient agent of justice in cyberspace. Oracle knew virtually everything about Black Canary, while the blonde heroine never knew who her mysterious benefactress and taskmaster really was. "I . . . don't get out that much these days," Oracle tells Black Canary, never revealing that she had once been the heroine Batgirl, but now spends her life confined to a wheelchair.

The core of *Birds of Prey* was the relationship between these two women; the adventures were secondary. Black Canary becomes Oracle's second body, enabling her to escape the solitude of her lonely headquarters and fight injustice vicariously. Oracle beomes a mother/big sister/life coach for Black Canary, helping the heroine to regain her confidence and get her act together. Black Canary's idealistic nature softens Oracle's cold pragmatism, and over time humanizes her. Working together, the two women are able to move past their personal tragedies, rebuild their lives, and find their way in the world. Oracle seeks out the evil that most of the high-flying superheroes may have overlooked, sending Black Canary on missions to take down cruel dictators and sadistic crime lords. Over time the women develop a genuine friendship, confiding in one another about the ups and downs of their personal lives, even though they have never met in person. It is only when Oracle's base is invaded, and Black Canary rescues her paralyzed boss, that the two women finally come face to face. By this time, a long distance bond has developed between the two that would have made them lay down their lives for each other.

When writer Gail Simone took over *Birds of Prey* in 2003, she accomplished the seemingly impossible—she created an all-female superhero team. The duo of Oracle and Black Canary became a quartet with the addition of the volatile female vigilante Huntress and the long forgotten 1950s heroine Lady Blackhawk. The combination of intellectual boss lady Oracle, best girlfriend Black Canary, hard-bitten but needy Huntress, and lusty, fiercely loyal Lady Blackhawk was like a superheroine *Sex and the City*. This foursome formed a nucleus around which Oracle would pull in various other female crime fighters from around the world, all of them somewhat castoffs of the superhero community. Working together, these heroines helped each other grow into the women they were meant to be.

Simone's run on *Birds of Prey* ended with a passage for original members Black Canary and Oracle, as they consider their lives not only as heroines, but as women. "I have a chance here, Babs. To be something I thought I never could be. Something . . . a little bit like a mother," Black Canary tells Oracle, as she resigns from the team. The heroine had rescued a young Asian girl some months earlier, and decided that being a full time mother was more important than being a crime fighter. And Oracle's stern authoritarian nature also gives way to maternal feelings when she takes the troubled, teenage runaway heroine known as Misfit under her wing, becoming a mentor for the next generation of female crime fighters. As Batgirl, and later as Oracle, Barbara Gordon had worked side by side with Batman, the ultimate, cold masculine hunter of evil. In the end, she finds her true role in life may have been less about crime and punishment, and more about mercy . . . "I'm Oracle. I help people who have no one. People in need."

"But there had to be someone left to save the world. And someone left to change it." These are the words, and the philosophy, of Jenny Sparks, the leader of The Authority. She is a foul-mouthed drinker and chain smoker, a promiscuous bisexual, and she doesn't much care what people think about her. But while the pretty young blonde looks to the outside world like a grizzled, sardonic misanthrope, deep within she has the unquenchable soul of an optimist. Jenny Sparks perhaps best represents the concept of the superhero as fearsome arbiter of order: the judge, jury and executioner who holds the power to inflict her will on the citizens of the world, regardless of the cost.

Jenny had seen a lot in her life, and it had left her cynical. Born in London on January 1, 1900, she was the "Spirit of the 20th Century," and as such represented the best and worst of those hundred years. Jenny stopped aging at twenty, and physically remained that age for the rest of her long life. She had a checkered past throughout the 20th century, where she mixed with aliens and mystery men, and was at various times a spy, a detective, a superhero herself, and an alcoholic burnout. She possesses incredible control over electrical energy, including the power to transform herself into electricity. By the late 1990s, Jenny decides that the world needs to be changed, no matter what the cost. She assembles a team of super beings, some less than heroic, and sets out to fix the world. On their terms, period. Eschewing the traditional superhero garb, Jenny sports her standard uniform of a man's white suit, a Union Jack t-shirt, and cigarette.

Superheroes had always been morally upright, hesitant to impose their vision of world order on the less powerful. Jenny Sparks is the opposite. "We are The Authority. Behave." is the message she telepathically sent out to the world. The Authority monitors the globe from a gigantic alien ship called the Carrier, which exists in the Bleed, the space between parallel universes. When hostile forces threaten the world, Jenny and her team arrive to set things right. "Don't piss us off," Jenny Sparks warns her enemies. To achieve their precise vision of utopia, nothing is beneath The Authority. "We gave up a lot of closely held beliefs when we joined The Authority. I have killed, and I will kill again," says winged Tibetan team member Swift of Jenny Sparks' uncompromising code of conduct. Jenny explodes the idea that a woman can't be as fierce and unforgiving as a man, as the Authority cuts a bloody path through any who would threaten the Earth.

But as harsh as Jenny appeared, her iron-willed crusade is driven by strangely maternal feelings. Wonder Woman wanted to make the world a better place by teaching its people to embrace peace. Jenny Sparks says the Earth is under her protection, and she'll stop at nothing to fulfill her duty. Jenny also knows that she only has a limited time to get her job done. In 1999, the world was gripped with fears about technology crashing due to the "millennium bug." Jenny had her own deadline—as the "Spirit of the 20th century," her life would end when the year 2000 rolled around. For her swan song, unlikely Earth mother Jenny leads the Authority against the biggest foe of all—God. God, or that entity that had created the Earth, is coming back, and plans to purge humanity from the globe. Jenny, however has other plans. "I'm here to save the Earth. I'm here to get us through this century. You might think the planet behind us is yours to use, but here's the news: Earth is under new management. This world is mine," Jenny tells God, as she uses her electrical powers to destroy the entity's brain. With her world safe and a new day dawning, Jenny expires, bequeathing the responsibility of protecting the world to a new generation.

Both Oracle and Jenny Sparks, in their ways, become unexpected mother figures, looking after the needy and unprotected of the world. While married superheroines like Invisible Woman had been shown as more traditional mothers in the past, heroines of the 21st century found their maternal instincts leading them in unexpected directions. Jessica Jones, the star of 2001's *Alias* comic book series, is an embittered private investigator who had once been a superhero, but stopped using her powers after a tragic event in her past. Jessica's booze-soaked nights lead to an on and off sexual relationship with African American superhero Luke Cage, which in turn leads to an unplanned pregnancy. Her baby's birth restores Jessica's faith in the world, and inspires her to once more use her fantastic powers to help mankind.

Manhunter, on the other hand, is already a mother when she becomes an unlikely crime fighter. Prosecutor Kate Spencer feels the need to employ extreme measures to deal with some of the criminals that have slipped through the legal system. Cobbling together a costume out of items that she steals from a police evidence storeroom, Kate becomes Manhunter, dispensing her fatal judgment to the deserving criminals of Los Angeles. Like Jenny Sparks, Manhunter has few qualms about killing, if a villain's death means that no more innocent victims will suffer. And like Jenny, the cynical Kate possesses a droll sense of humor. "How does Black Canary do this in fishnets and heels?" Kate thinks, as she contemplates her new double life. Manhunter made her debut in 2004, the same year America voted to reelect George W. Bush. While the inclusion of gay characters and the presence of strong women gave the *Manhunter* series a decidedly Democratic air, the heroine's preemptive approach towards fighting crime echoed the Bush's methods of removing "evil" from the world.

There were many factors that made Manhunter unique in the modern superhero world. First off, she had a real job. Most heroines in the 21st Century were full time crime fighters, with undisclosed sources of income. Unlike some of the heroines of the past, Kate's hard as nails personality in and out of costume was essentially the same—she was a ball buster in the courtroom as a high profile prosecutor, and a deadly vigilante on the streets as Manhunter. Citing his influences for Kate's character in the classic dames of '30s and '40s movies, writer Marc Andreyko described her as "a woman who ain't afraid to be a 'broad' and doesn't lose her femininity because of it." As Manhunter, Kate often fumbles her way through the bizarre world crime of fighting, while always presenting the face of a ruthless and confident avenger of evil to the public. When a villain crouches at Manhunter's feet and begs for mercy, she finds herself amused by her success. "Looks like my reputation precedes me. I have a reputation. Cool." The combination of Kate's legal career and her night job as Manhunter assured that she would see justice done one way or another.

Except for the Fantastic Four's Invisible Woman, there were few heroines who had to split their duties between fighting crime and child rearing. And unlike the impeccable chatelaine of the Fantastic Four, divorcee and single parent Kate has different challenges, in balancing killers and her kid. In the oddly maternal role of Manhunter, Kate can throw a protective arm around the citizens of Los Angeles by ridding the city of human vermin. But as a mother to her own son, Kate often comes up a little short. "I'm still only a C+ on most days . . ." Kate says, of her parenting skills. Ruthless avenger is a role more suited to Kate's nature than nurturing mom, and it turns out that fighting crime was truly in her blood. In time, Kate learns that she was the granddaughter of Sandra Knight, the original Phantom Lady of the 1940s. Two common themes in comic books of the 21st century are women helping each other to grow, and the passage of knowledge from one generation of females to another. With Sandra as her mentor, Kate's life gains the stability that can come from family, helping her to make her way as both mother and foe of evil.

Some heroines had even more of a challenge balancing motherhood and crimefighting. Technically Catwoman was considered an antiheroine, since she scratched out a decades-long reputation as, depending on the day, a thief, villainess, bounty hunter, and either foe or ally/love interest of Batman. By 2002 Catwoman was at a crossroads. Tired of her reckless life of thievery and plunder, she was looking for a new purpose. Finding herself back in Gotham City's troubled East End, an area teeming with crime and police corruption, Catwoman appoints herself the protector of the people there, a job she knows she is better suited for than the pragmatic Batman. As she contemplates her new role, she thinks, " . . . my world is all just shades of grey, Batman. That's why you'll never really understand me. It's about good people being forced into bad situations. That's my territory . . . in between right and wrong."

Catwoman spent a few years playing mother hen to the

hookers, street kids, and other hard luck cases of the East End. But by 2006 she found herself in a new situation—pregnant as the result of a fling with a police officer who had become her partner in vigilantism. The father was killed before the baby was born, leaving Catwoman to raise a newborn daughter on her own. She attempts to lead a normal life and provide a stable home for her baby, but eventually Catwoman is plagued with nightmares that her dangerous lifestyle will put her daughter at risk. "These lives of ours, they're very ...complicated. I want my daughter out of mine," Catwoman tells Batman, as she asks him to use his vast wealth and resources to find her baby a new home. Afterwards, the feline adventuress is wracked with doubts as to whether she made the right choice. Catwoman lashes out in anger when Batman points out that in reality she never actually wanted to be a mother. But then she realizes that he's right, and comes to an understanding about her true nature. "Under all this . . . under the costume and the claws and the mask and the goggles . . . I'm Catwoman. This is who I am." She then proceeds to steal the Batmobile from under the Caped Crusader's nose, and roars off into the night

Female heroes in comics are often compared to their male counterparts, and at times the medium still questions whether these women are as qualified or committed to fighting evil as men. But motherhood is certainly an experience that is unique to superheroines, and one where their abilities won't be measured against those of their male comrades. In a 2016 series, a very pregnant Spider-Woman finds herself in a dilemma. She's at a doctor's appointment on a high tech, intergalactic space station that's been invaded by aliens. It's at that moment that Spider-Woman's water breaks, and she goes into labor. Spider-Woman delivers a healthy baby boy, after which she hops off the delivery table, grabs some big guns and goes out to single-handedly fend off the vicious horde. In the words heard in the opening of the original *Star Trek* TV series, Spider-Woman, and all superheroines who become mothers, had gone "where no man has gone before."

Carol Danvers had a moment of clarity in 2006. In the almost thirty years since she made her debut as Ms. Marvel, she has run into many obstacles that prevented her from reaching her potential— rape, amnesia, sexism, alcoholism, and worst of all, bad comic book writing. But now Carol decided to rededicate herself to being the best hero she could be. "I can be the person other people strive to be. I can be better than good. I can be the best," she tells her BFF Spider-Woman. Throughout her career Carol had changed her name from Ms. Marvel to Binary to Warbird and back to Ms. Marvel in her journey to find her place in the world of superheroes. But now she was determined to face her future. " . . . I'm not going to run away from anything," she vows. The following year Iron Man asked Carol to lead a team of Avengers, a job he felt she had earned. And in 2012, Captain America urged Carol to change her name one more time, to one she deserved—Captain Marvel.

The new *Captain Marvel* series of 2012 was written by Kelly Sue DeConnick, whose vision of the heroine was "Carol Danvers as Chuck Yeager." Now sporting a full-body uniform that paid homage to Carol's military background, the new Captain Marvel and her high-flying adventures struck a chord with female readers. This gave rise to the Carol Corps, a community of fans who embraced Captain Marvel as their superhero, and attended conventions dressed as her. The Carol Corps unofficial motto was "We will be the stars we were meant to be . . . ," a line taken from the first issue of Captain Marvel's 2012 series. It seems that Captain Marvel had become the star she was meant to be, finally stepping into the role she was created for—Marvel Comics' foremost female hero. It only took her thirty-five years to get there.

Captain Marvel's newfound stardom can hardly be seen as an overnight success. And this is true for superheroines in general. If you peruse the racks of new releases at a comic book shop, you're likely to see more female heroes headlining their own titles. But this was the case in the postwar 1940s and the "Bad Girl" era of the 1990s, and most of those comics didn't have long lifespans. The difference in the 21st century is that publishers seem to be trying to produce comics about women heroes that will appeal to female readers. That goes beyond the way the characters are drawn or the costumes they wear. Powerful women in many comics aren't simply being written as men with breasts anymore. Many of these series are telling stories that aren't just endless slugfests, but instead focus on the characters and their friendships, with healthy doses of humor. It may come as no surprise that many of the more innovative superheroine titles are written or drawn by women.

In order to reach the same heights of popularity as Batman

and Captain America, superheroines need recognition beyond the walls of comic book shops. A few years ago if you had asked an average person to name a female superhero, the response would most likely have been Wonder Woman, or maybe Catwoman. But now as a result of their appearances in the blockbuster movies of the Marvel Cinematic Universe, that list might include Black Widow, Scarlet Witch, or even Gamora, the deadly green-skinned assassin in *Guardians of the Galaxy*. The *Supergirl* TV series and Netflix's *Jessica Jones*, based on Marvel's *Alias*, offer viewers two vastly different visions of superheroines—one hearkens back to a more optimistic era in comics while the other is a dark, adult psychological drama. These movies and TV series bring female heroes to a wider audience, and remind new generations that women can also be powerful.

No matter how many comic books are published or movies are made, the view of heroic women will not evolve unless the stories themselves change. But there are signs of progress in unlikely places. Amidst the bombastic, testosterone-fueled battles that comprised most of 2016's *Batman v. Superman: Dawn of Justice*, there is a moment that changes the course of the movie. Batman is trapped and at the mercy of the rampaging monster Doomsday. But then Wonder Woman suddenly appears to save the fallen male hero from certain death. When Superman arrives on the scene, he and Batman take a back seat to Wonder Woman, as she steps forward to lead the men into battle, like an armor-clad spirit of victory. Readers can only hope this big screen moment will also be a step forward into the future for more female heroes.

Acknowledgments

Thank you to my family and friends, epecially Marlene Braga, Alan Disparte, Kristy Guevara-Flanagan, Will Harris, Michelle Jeffers, Frank McGinn, Trina Robbins, Bettina Sapien, Lou Schubert, Rico Schwartzberg, Sarah Seipel, and Carol A. Strickland.

Thanks to Bill Finn and Barry Finn for use of Miss Fury images created by Tarpé Mills.

A big thank you to the Digital Comic Museum, Don Markstein's Toonepedia, and Grand Comic Database.

A huge thank you to librarians everywhere.

Thanks to all of the men and women who have created the comic books that have entertained and inspired me over the years.

Thanks to Bob Irwin for being a good sport.

Of course, thanks to my editor and partner in crime Tod Davies.

In memory of my friend Michael Lash, who loved comic books.

Art Credits

PAGE 4: George Mandel. PAGE 5: Fletcher Hanks. PAGES 7, 8: Frank M. Borth. PAGE 9: Tarpé Mills. PAGE 11: Klaus Nordling. PAGE 16: Marc Swayze. PAGE 20: Al Gabriele. PAGE 21: Barbara Hall. PAGE 23: John Cassone. PAGES 25, 267: Matt Baker. PAGES 37, 39: Mort Meskin. PAGE 42: John Cellardo. PAGE 44, 53: Robert Webb. PAGES 47, 49: artist unknown. PAGE 251: Fred Kida. PAGE 295: Pierce Rice. PAGE 296: Jim Mooney. PAGE 301: Dan Zolnerowich. PAGE 303: Gill Fox

Index

Index

Index

Index

MIKE MADRID is a San Francisco native and lifelong fan of comic books and popular culture. His other books are the Golden Age comics collections *Divas, Dames & Daredevils* and *Vixens, Vamps & Vipers*. He appears in the documentary *Wonder Women! The Untold Story of American Superheroines.*

For more information please visit *heaven4heroes.com*